P9-CQY-325

101 ROAD TALES

Clement Salvadori

Whitehorse Press
Center Conway, New Hampshire

Appreciation

Writer Salvadori and Artist Brown dedicate this book to the long-suffering Susan Salvadori, without whose considerable efforts the work would never have been completed.

Illustrations and cover art by Gary Brown.

Whitehorse Press books are also available at discounts in bulk quantity for sales and promotional use. For details about special sales or for a catalog of motorcycling books and videos, write to the publisher:

Whitehorse Press
107 East Conway Road
Center Conway, New Hampshire 03813-4012
Phone: 603-356-6556 or 800-531-1133
E-mail: CustomerService@WhitehorsePress.com
Internet: www.WhitehorsePress.com

ISBN: 978-1-884313-73-8

5 4 3 2

Printed in the United States of America

Contents

Introduction

I've been writing a monthly column for *Rider* magazine for nigh on 20 years, since October of 1988. Some were good, some not so good. These were/are meant mostly as entertainments, rather than informative, though at times I tried to combine the two. Since I have been riding for more than 50 years (I began at an early age), and a million saddle miles went by a long time ago, I have had a reasonable amount of experience in the world of motorcycling.

I don't race bikes, I don't restore bikes, and I only fix them when there is nobody more competent around to do the job. I just ride them. I'm a traveling man. I took two big trips without a motorcycle, crossing the Sahara Desert in my sister's VW bus, and hitch-hiking around South America for three months in 1969. But all my other major trips have been on a motorcycle.

I can't really remember how many times I have ridden across this country, beginning with a new 1965 500cc Velocette Venom—not a good machine for the task. I suppose if I really sat down and thought about it I could come up with a number—but why bother? I have ridden in all 50 states, all 31 Mexican states, and much of Canada—which is a very, very big country.

I've been to Europe many, many times, and bought my first motorcycle, a 250cc NSU Max, at age 16 when I lived in Rome—my professor father was on sabbatical from the Massachusetts college where he taught. Since then I have ridden all over that continent, from Nord Kapp beyond the Arctic Circle to Sicily, from Ireland's County Galway to the Dneiper River in the Ukraine—and in the rest of the world as well. I took the old Hippie Highway from Istanbul to Kathmandu, rode from Kenya to Cape Town in South Africa, and spent three months in Australia.

Much of this was on my own nickel, some of it compliments of Uncle Sam. While in the army in Germany I bought a Triumph Bonneville, and when working for the State Department in Saigon I used a Vespa 150 as my official vehicle. The work on the magazines has also helped, with trips to Japan (too expensive for this lowly scribe to do on his own) and Morocco and Peru and many other idyllic (Tibet?) riding venues.

I've ridden in roughly 70 countries on precisely six continents—I'll leave motoring on the seventh, Antarctica, to those hardier than I.

To what end? I've done it because I like to do it. I love to travel, and I love to ride motorcycles. Combining those two has led me to a thoroughly satisfactory life. As one colleague said, I have managed to overcome my education; college and grad school all pointed me towards a life of public service, which is pretty dull fare in comparison to what I have been doing for the past 30 years. Just lucky, I guess.

In this book I have collected 101 of my favorite columns, out of some 225, beginning with the very first, which in retrospect I did not like all that much, and going on to February 2007. A long-time friend, an artist who was flooded out of New Orleans by Katrina and currently lives in Texas, has done the illustrations—which help to break up all those boring words.

This is not a read-all-at-once book. You should pick it up, read a column or two, put it down, and think about what you read. And if it inspires even one of you to get on your motorcycle and take that long-dreamed-of trip, then all the work has been worthwhile.

One? We'll have none of that false modesty. I want to hear that at least a thousand of you got on the road.

Clement Salvadori
Atascadero, California

Advocating Adventure

October 1988

A bit of introduction is required here. After all, you want to know whether this will be worth reading. What is this column about, and who am I to give advice to anybody about touring? On my last trip I left the toothpaste at home; not a bright thing to do, but remediable. In my own small way I have littered the world with lost and left-behind items. I am organized enough to survive, too disorganized to ever expect a trip to go completely smoothly.

Touring is an imprecise art. You never know quite what adventure awaits around the next curve in the road. And it is precisely that lack of precision, that possibility for adventure, which makes traveling, especially traveling by motorcycle, so appealing to so many.

This monthly column will be imprecise as well. The one constant is that it will always deal with the manifold mysteries of motorcycling, especially touring. I will spew forth in a semi-coherent fashion concerning my views on the subject, but we are even more interested in what you, the faithful (or faithless) reader, has to say. You can offer suggestions, criticisms, advice, warnings, questions, and we will deal with as many as we can in the space allotted.

That is the purpose of the column. And who is the columnist? Some Johnny-come-lately, still wet-behind-the-ears fellow who once took a Sunday ride to grandmother's house and thinks he knows it all? Sort of. My first overnight trip *was* to see Grandmama who lived 175 miles away.

I've been riding motorcycles for more than 30 years. Maybe that gives me a certain credibility. It has been a constant in my life ever since I convinced the parents that I was a reliable, dependable, sensible 16-year-old (which is an oxymoron, and before you rush to the dictionary, that means a contradiction in terms).

I love motorcycles. To me a car is like a refrigerator—if the light goes on when I open the door, and it works, that is all I care about. But a motorcycle . . . ah, flowers in the springtime are nothing to the beauty of a motorcycle. To ride a rolling road through a rippling field of ripening wheat approaches a level of pleasure unknown to mere mortals. Enough of this paean and back to the subject of touring.

I've traveled a bit, having been to some 70 countries on six continents. Most of that has been on a motorcycle, although I remember well one time when I actually sold my motorcycle to get the money to go wandering through Central and South America for five months. For me, the most preferable means of transportation is a motorcycle. For several reasons.

First, I love riding a motorcycle. It beats the heck out of an automobile, bus, train, or airplane. I might get cold and wet, but those are minor inconveniences when contemplating the raptures I derive from the experience. Motorcycling is not for everyone, but it is a passion for some of us.

Second, a motorcycle can go just about anywhere. A regular street motorcycle is far better than any four-wheel-drive vehicle. A bridge is out, find a boat to carry the bike across the river. The road goes from two ruts to a footpath, a motorcycle can continue. A bike can get on a train or a ferryboat without prior reservations. It can get hoisted onto an ocean liner like a big suitcase, or loaded into the belly of a DC3. Try that with your Coupe de Ville or Cherokee.

Third, and this may be the most important, it is the friendliest way to travel. You pull up in front of Parton's Grocery & Dry Goods, where three good ole boys are sitting on the porch bench, chawing and whittling, and chances are you will soon be engaged in a conversation. If a sedan or motorhome arrives, this trio might get wondering if there aren't a bunch of extraterrestrials with ray guns hiding in there somewhere, waiting to pop out and zap everybody. With a motorcycle nothing is hidden, everything is out in the open. No Martians in the trunk, no machine guns under the seat. A motorcycle creates a very different atmosphere as you come in contact with strangers, and it is a nice one. The motorcyclist displays a certain vulnerability which is appreciated by those he meets along the way.

My first real trip was at the age of 17, when a friend and I spent the summer tearing around Europe on a pair of used 250s—I had an NSU Max, he had a BMW R26. That was definitely a low-bucks excursion. We began in Italy and the only commitment we had was to meet a ship in England two months down the road. Youth hostels, camping, and restaurant food once a week would see us through.

The number of mistakes we made were beyond count. We left all our tent-pegs behind at our second campsite, and that was in the days when you needed at least 20 good pegs to keep a tent up. I took my Bing carburetor apart outside of a hostel in Austria, for reasons I don't quite remember, and could not get it back together; it was a long push to the nearest bike shop. My father's friend was a doctor, who gave us a first-aid kit that would have done a MASH unit proud; we never needed it, though I attribute that more to luck than intelligence and skill.

We got tired, we got wet because of inadequate rain gear, we fell down harmlessly a couple of times—but it was a great trip. We did not know enough to be worried or concerned or scared; we just took off. When it was over, we pushed the bikes off the ship onto the docks at New York City and rode home to Massachusetts.

The most important tip that anybody could give to would-be traveling types is simply to go. Air in the tires, gas in the tank, money in the wallet; don't worry about anything else. If you're traveling cheap, you camp; if you have bucks, you have the choice of camping or staying at the Hilton. The more money you have, the more opportunities you have, but money does not make for a good time . . . it just eases the bad times.

What holds most people back from touring on a motorcycle is a vague, undefinable feeling of fear. You start imagining all the things that could go wrong. You do that too much and you will end up spending your vacation in bed with the covers pulled over your head. Ride safely, make sure the bike is properly serviced. Don't worry about the weather; take along some raingear and an extra sweater, just to be sure.

I know touring riders who pack the kitchen sink to go off for a weekend, and others who just fill up a tankbag, strap a tent and sleeping bag to the rear seat, and are gone for three months. But they go. That's the point. They are out there, traveling around Maine, Minnesota, Montana; North America, Europe, Australia. To the local state park or around the world. The longest journey begins with a single revolution of your wheels. It does not matter where you are going, it matters only that you are on the road. You're off to have a small adventure. Or a big one, maybe.

The world is really a very nice place, with a lot more to see than can be fit into any normal life span. And I imagine you are reading this because you like the idea of going places on a motorcycle. With this column we are going to have an entertaining and occasionally instructive time, with gripes, groans, and perhaps a flash of minor brilliance appearing on these pages. And when you see that rider coming over that far-off mountain pass, wave when he goes by, because he is one of us.

A Good Wrench . . .

August 1989

It used to be, back when people lived in detached homes on tree-shaded streets, with a swinging couch on the porch and a roast on Sunday, that every family had a doctor who made house calls, a lawyer who drew up wills, a clergyman who dispensed advice, and down on the corner a service station where you and the owner/mechanic were on a first-name basis.

Well, them days have gone the way of nickel cigars and the $2,000 Ford. Now you are apt to go to some anonymous medical center where you have never seen the doctor before and never will again; a lawyer is the fellow who starts the counting beans when you meet him on the

street and say hello; psychologists have replaced reverends at $90 an hour; and when your car is out of warranty you think about trading it in.

So what about your motorcycle? It is a treasured possession and it does occasionally require servicing. Few of us are competent, or willing, enough to do more than check the tire pressures and maybe change the oil. Trying to measure 16 valve clearances will take the mechanical stuffing out of most riders. You can buy all sorts of manuals, but unless you have a certain dexterity with nuts and bolts it is best to leave the job to someone more competent, someone who does the same work day in and day out and gets real good at it.

So we take our loved one to a motorcycle shop and entrust it to perfect strangers. For the privilege of receiving $25 to $45 an hour, they replace our shims and grease our bearings and make sure the steering head is torqued correctly. At least we hope they do.

We trust these people. We have to. These men and women, these workers behind the scenes at any motorcycle dealership, who have our lives in their hands.

How do you know what you're getting? Ah, there's the rub. Most of us go to the shop that sold us the new motorcycle, where the mechanics are supposed to be factory-trained, fully qualified to take care of the machine you just bought. True. . . . sometimes. Word-of-mouth reputation and personal contact with the shop are the best ways of evaluating a service department.

Shops have reputations. Ask around, see what other riders have to say. Benny's Bargain Bikes may have great prices on new models and may sell a lot of motorcycles that way, but maybe the service department is the absolute pits.

A good dealer is one that will not only sell you a motorcycle, but maintain it for you as well. If he has been around a long time and has a lot of faithful customers, take note. I promise you, it is better to spend the extra dollars and be on the good side of a good dealer than to save a few bucks with a cut-rate push-'em-out-the-door fellow, and then have to shop around for good service. Every good dealer knows where you got your machine and his own customers get priority on the service list.

The best shops go out of their way to make the customer feel confident about the quality of the service. At Valley Motorsports in Northampton, Massachusetts, the shop's owner has a waiting area with a big plate-glass window so the customer can look into the operating room. There should not be any secrets back there. A service area cannot really have customers walking around, both for practical and insurance reasons, but letting them see what happens goes a long way toward dispelling any notions that the bike is not getting the attention it needs.

On-the-road repairs are always a bit chancy. Some shops make a real effort to deal with the touring rider. Lakewood Honda in Lakewood, Colorado, is one; the owner understands that the couple on a three-week vacation trip does not want to spend unnecessary time waiting for a bike to be fixed. So he schedules them in right away and tries very hard to get them back on the road in the shortest time possible.

Should trouble strike far from home, one thing you can do is to use the Yellow Pages. Call up, talk to the service manager, find out if the shop is willing to get to work on your problem right away or if you should try another shop. If you find yourself with a problem in some far-off land and you see what appears to be a local motorcyclist, ask him for advice.

All motorcycles should be treated equally, irrespective of the owner, but whether you are at home or on the road, it never hurts to be a pleasant customer. Some people are downright abusive, storming into a shop demanding this and that; this does not help the situation. Nobody has to deal with you; if you come in with a bad attitude you might get the same attitude in return, and then you have to look some more. We, the motorcyclists and the service people, are all in this together, and we need each other. Being nice is a lot better way to get things done than being obnoxious.

You usually deal with the service manager. You have to understand his position. He has a shop full of bikes which have to be pushed in and out every morning, and he tries to maintain a modicum of efficiency. If you want a service done, call up beforehand. Just like your dentist: schedule an appointment. Bring your cycle in after work, pick it up the next evening. You want to be without it as little as possible, and the shop wants to have it around for the shortest time.

When you go in, be clear. You want the 15,000-mile service and a new tire on the back. Specify the tire. The manager writes down the order, gives an estimate, asks you to sign, and if anything startling comes up, he will give you a call.

And then you are out in the unknown. You lie in bed that night, convinced that some drug-crazed sociopath is screwing up the job completely. The tappets will be so tight they'll burn the valves, the steering head so loose the front wheel will shudder when you brake. The new tire will go flat within a week. The drain plug won't be properly torqued and 300 miles from home it will fall out, oil will get all over the rear tire . . . . How could you be so foolish?

The dreaded night and day are over. You go to pick up the bike. Everything seems right. Someone even gave it a quick shine. The mechanic who did the work comes over and tells you he put 38 pounds in the tire, but if you'd like a different pressure, he'd be happy to oblige. He checked the wear on the brake pads, and they should easily last for the life of the tire.

The biggest thrill is when you get the bill and you feel that the service has been worth the cost. Value this dealer. Treasure this service manager. Honor this mechanic.

Mapping It

January 1989

(Note: This was written well before the popularity of the Global Positioning Systems and e-mail.)

The Gallup people did a poll last fall, trying to determine how much geography Americans actually knew. Given a map of the world, 14 percent could not find the U. S. of A. Fifty percent could not locate New York state. For somebody like myself, who loves geography, maps, and traveling, that was quite a shock. These people do not know what they are missing.

I have a house full of maps. There are hundreds of regional, state, county, and city maps for the United States. Plus another whole box of maps of national forests and national parks and state historic sites, et cetera. And a drawer full of maps of various countries and cities around the world, from Afghanistan to Zimbabwe . . . except that last was still called Southern Rhodesia when I motored through there in 1974. And another box full of "undefinables", maps that came out of *National Geographic* magazines, local chambers of commerce, and the map to Captain Kidd's treasure that somebody sold me on Cape Hatteras.

Maps do age. Always check the date of any map you are using, which is usually found on the cover, and sometimes in the legend. If you see 11-85 that means the information on the map was accurate as of November, 1985, but roads can, and do, change. If you are ever at a garage sale or a used-book store and an old road atlas is for sale, buy it. Just to sit down and compare the roads of 1950 Colorado to those of today can amuse me for hours. If you find a little road that was there long ago, and is not to be found on the new map, and you are headed thataway with a dual-purpose bike, keep that old road in mind.

I have a lot of maps of places I will probably never get to, but I love imagining that I will be there. There was a time when gas stations gave away maps; now you have to buy them, or join an automobile club (which usually does precious little for motorcyclists other than to provide maps). Or send a postcard to any number of tourist offices, be it Indiana or India, and you will get back a fat envelope full of disposable hotel brochures . . . and a map.

Some people go to bed with the latest Judith Krantz or Robert Ludlum novel; I take maps. I don't have to be going anywhere, not plotting a route, but I can read a map like a thriller set in an exotic location, like a good travel book, like an adventure in a faraway place.

Maps have scales. Some maps write the scale as 1:500,000, while others will say that one inch equals eight miles; those two are roughly the same. My rule of thumb says that for good, concentrated traveling, a map should have a maximum scale of 1:250,000. That will show all the roads, rivers, ferries, wilderness, and civilization, and show you how to avoid traffic and find a good place to pitch a tent.

The *Big Road Atlas of Britain* has 75 pages of maps at a basic four miles to the inch, or 1:250,000. I have road maps of Venezuela, Kenya and New Zealand. A piece in the newspaper the other day said that there have been no accurate maps of Russia since the 1930s, except for those put out by the CIA—not commercially available, to my knowledge. Intourist, the Soviet tourist agency, does provide rudimentary maps of roads approved for foreigners to travel on, which are few in number.

If I want to look at the big picture I drag out *The Times Atlas of the*

World; at close to ten pounds it is not quite what one takes on a trip. The tattered old *National Geographic* world atlas is nearly as good, and costs a lot less money in the softcover edition. The American Map Corporation's *Great World Atlas* is a trifle abbreviated, but a great deal better than nothing. A thin paperback from Rand McNally called the *Quick Reference World Atlas* sits under my dictionary.

Maps are full of lines and colors and symbols, all carefully explained by the legend. A practiced eye can read a map the way a linguist can read a foreign language. All these lines mean something: good roads, bad roads, railroads. These markings were carefully, precisely drawn in order to instruct, edify, and elucidate. As do the colors, showing state forests, or altitude, or lakes. All manner of maps are made for all manner of purposes.

I'm on an imaginary trip, going north along the Pacific Ocean on California Highway 1. I see it leaves the coast to join with U.S. Highway 101 at Leggett; that means traffic, motorhomes, and semis. Would not look forward to that. But look—what does this thin blue line portend? I put on my glasses and read the very small four-point print: "Usal Road." It goes north along the coast through the Sinkyone Wilderness State Park and on to the King Range National Conservation area. The legend interprets the blue line as "surface not indicated;" presume poorly maintained dirt. Good thing I'm on a dual-purpose bike. Follow that line through the Lost Coast and slip back a century, as around each bend I expect to meet a stagecoach and find travelers riding horseback.

And cities. Going into a city without a map is to plunge into the ancient Cretan labyrinth at Minos. You can stop and ask directions from every gas station attendant, taxi driver and policeman, but it is so much simpler to sit with a map for a few moments.

Take Boston, a miserable city to get around in; even Beantowners get confused. A map of greater Boston shows you how to get to the House of the Seven Gables in Salem, and to the Minute Man National Historic Park. The city map will take you to the *USS Constitution* and the Old North Church. The downtown close-up shows you Faneuil Hall and the New England Aquarium.

The atlas is the real dream-book, where your imagination can run wonderfully wild about the trips you would really like to take. *The Times* has 200,000 place names in its index, 122 two-page plates, and enough definition to allow you to almost see the mountains and plains. The plates show sand dunes, mangrove swamps, seasonal watercourses, gorges, demilitarized zones, ancient walls, oil wells, historic sites, and more.

If I were offered the trip of my dreams the road I would love to travel the most, turn to Plate 24. Head north out of Pakistan, through Gilgit and the Hunza Valley, cross into China at the Kunjerab Pass and come out on the western end of the Tibetan plateau. Jog east to Mazar on what is defined as a "track," then pick up the main road across the center of the plateau to Amdo, drop south to Lhasa, and then exit via Nyalam into Nepal. Most of that will be traveling over 12,000 feet, with no Howard Johnson's, no motorcycle shops. But if the map shows a road, a road means vehicles, vehicles need gas, and people have to eat. The only hitch in my plan is politics, and I can't see any time in the next few years when the Chinese would allow me to take this trip.

But as long as I have my maps, I can dream.

Fools' Rules

March 1989

In my opinion, anybody who rides a motorcycle without first putting on a helmet is a darn fool.

Anybody who wants to solve the problems of the world by passing laws is a darn fool, too.

What's the difference between telling people something is a good idea and making sure they take your advice? A whole lot! It has to do with instilling a sense of responsibility in our citizens.

First of all, why do we have laws? Anytime you get two or more people together, you have the potential for problems. A family has unwritten rules of behavior. A community puts all the rules in writing, so when two people disagree they can go and check up on who is right and who is wrong.

The purpose of these laws is to keep the society, be it ten or tens of millions of people, organized to a degree. We've all heard of good laws, as well as stupid laws, bad laws, unenforceable laws, and laws which courts declare unconstitutional. We need the good laws. We don't need the rest. We do need a country where people do what is right because it is right, not because they are ordered to do so. Good laws are designed to protect one person from another. I have the right to swing my fist; that right stops where your nose begins.

Smoking is a big issue these days. You smoke. I don't. I don't want to smell your cigarettes. You want to enjoy your habit. It's a difficult topic. But nobody is recommending that smoking be outlawed, like Congress tried to do with booze in 1919, passing the 18th amendment to the Constitution, prohibiting the sale of liquor. All that did was create a huge black market in alcoholic beverages.

Helmets are a big issue . . . to motorcyclists. I want to wear a helmet. You don't. I think you're a darned fool. You like the breeze in your hair. Should I have the right to order you to wear a helmet? No.

The law says you have to have a driver's license. That is different. Issuing a license is a way of determining whether or not you are capable of driving a car or riding a motorcycle. If you're an incompetent driver (and we will not deal with licensing procedures here), you could end up smacking into me as I ride along the road. Your having a license is going to protect me. I'll support that law.

Your wearing a helmet is not going to protect me. It will protect you, but do we really want laws that do nothing but protect us from ourselves?

Think about it. A lot of us like to do so-called foolish things. How about skydiving? Or white-water kayaking? Or eating a steady diet of Twinkies? We like to do stuff like that, and maybe it is potentially hazardous to our health, but so what? Can't we lead our lives as we see fit, and not as others think we should lead them? Sure, as long as we don't abuse the children or scare the horses.

Let's use mountain climbing as an example. Sometimes people die while scaling this peak or that. Sometimes rescuers die while trying to save other climbers in trouble. There might be people somewhere who would like to ban mountain climbing.

Not me. Not mountain climbing. I don't climb mountains, but I think I understand people who do. Climbers try to regulate themselves. They rate the ascents according to difficulty and hope that the fellow going up has a good idea of his own level of ability. If he does get into trouble, other climbers will be willing to risk their own lives to get him off the mountain. But leave the laws out of it, thank you very much.

Some of the latest rationalizers on the helmet-law front are saying that people who don't wear helmets can cost the taxpayers money. Yes, it is possible. An unhelmeted motorcyclist falls down, bangs his head, doesn't have medical insurance, and gets a whopping hospital bill. That does happen. But not frequently. I write it off as the cost of doing business in a free society. Let's look at this in relative numbers: How much does a B-1B bomber cost? Or the annual government subsidies to the tobacco industry? Probably more money than all unhelmeted bikers everywhere will ever cost us.

I love the tobacco analogy. Figures don't lie, but liars can figure, and this liar is going to guesstimate that the cost to the public (us, the taxpayers) to take care of the medical expenses of uninsured or underinsured smokers who develop smoking-related illnesses like lung cancer and emphysema will exceed the costs of all uninsured, unhelmeted bikers who bang their heads by at least a thousand fold.

California provides an excellent case in point. A state assemblyman tried to get a helmet law passed last year by maintaining that uninsured motorcyclists suffering head injuries consumed $65 million of the taxpayers' dollars. Nobody on either side of the debate could figure out how the politico arrived at this sum, and it was generally considered to be grossly inflated by a factor of at least 10. A few months later (after the governor sensibly shot down the helmet bill) the California Department of Health and Human Services issued a study on the effects of smoking, which concluded that tobacco-related health problems cost the state of California more than $7 billion annually.

Put that in your pipe and smoke it. I don't buy the "cost to the taxpayer" line at all. As I said, that is the price of doing business in a country such as ours.

I also have another problem with helmet laws. Most people who advocate them don't know a thing about motorcycles. They are politicians who know that the word "motorcycle" is guaranteed to get some press, and they want their names in print (please spell it right).

So they tout the helmet laws, and they don't really have our best interests at heart. The legislators all chew on the subject in between naps, the public gets to read about it, the bill is passed, and all non-motorcyclists say, "Well, that takes care of that problem."

Sorry, it won't. By the nature of the automotive beast a lot of motorcyclists will still die every year, helmet law or no helmet law. After a few years the non-motorcycling public will notice that the casualties are still coming in, and they'll figure, "The helmet law did not work, so I guess we'd better pass a law banning motorcycles." To save us from ourselves, so to speak. That's what I'm afraid of.

And we should not forget that most fatalities in automobile accidents are due to head injuries. Should we legislate that all occupants of a car have to wear helmets? The helmet industry would love it, but perhaps not the automobile manufacturers.

Take 10

September 1989

I hurry too much. It's my own darn fault. I seem to choose to rush, rush, rush, even when I don't want to, don't have to. If a pack of wolves were hurtling after me, it would be sensible to keep going. But there are seldom wolves around these days. More often I keep going . . . I don't know why. Silly reasons, I suppose. Gotta get there. Wherever there is.

Some months back I was taking the southern route across these United States, going west. I spent the night in Lordsburg, New Mexico. Rising before dawn I was on the road by first light. A long day in the saddle would see me 650 miles back to my home in Laguna Beach, California.

I like getting home, getting back to loved ones and a familiar bed. What I was doing was cutting myself a chunk of miles that did not allow for much dallying. I had programmed myself to cover that distance, and anybody who messes around with computers knows how hard it is to alter a program.

Barely an hour after getting in the saddle I was coming up on Bowie, Arizona, one of those little motel towns on the old highway that make a living pumping gas and selling hamburgers to the travelers who turn off Interstate 10. The signs indicate it is the closest town to Fort Bowie National Historic Site.

Fort Bowie. Though I had seen the signs many times I had never been there, never made the effort to go, never stopped in my travels long enough. I had been all over that southeast corner of Arizona, through Tombstone and Bisbee, in the Coronado National Forest and the Chiricahua National Monument, but never to Fort Bowie.

I like going to these places which the government has set aside as national preserves. I find them interesting, edifying, often beautiful. But I also like getting home. I was rushing. I knew I was rushing. And it did not matter a whit if I got home early in the evening or late at night. Or even the next day.

Then my great-aunt Agatha's advice came to remind me, "The time to take the tarts is in the passing." Take advantage of the opportunity. Somebody rather more forcefully said, "There comes that moment once, and God help those who pass that moment by."

This may sound like a curious problem I have, not to be able to stop, but I have it. It was a struggle to break that directional inertia, that destination fixation that I had. It was a beautiful morning and all I had to look forward to were hundreds of miles of super-slab. Not an overly pleasurable ride, but if I kept going the sooner it would be over.

There was the exit. At the last moment I put on my directional signals and headed down the off-ramp into Bowie. Not much there. A few hundred people, a limited array of eateries, rent-a-beds, gas pumps, and the Southern Pacific Railroad.

Fort Bowie was ten miles up a good dirt road, then a mile and a half hike. It is quite amusing how a dirt road, let alone a short walk, will keep the crowds away. I much prefer that to a place where the motorhomes are cheek to jowl. I parked the bike; I wasn't worried a bit about the baggage I was leaving on it. The place did not look like a high-crime neighborhood, and I had not seen anyone since leaving Bowie.

The stroll to Fort Bowie seemed very promising. A little box offered me the borrowed use of a trail guide, and if I kept it I was honor bound to deposit 50 cents. I began to walk through the scrub oak and pinon. A fairly fearless coyote looked at me for a moment before loping off into the brush. The silence was nearly complete, except for the occasional bird breaking into song.

Reading the guide I found that the iron horse was the original impetus for Fort Bowie's existence. In 1854 the US Army sent out an engineering party to survey a route for the future Pacific Railroad. After a 55-mile trek from Lordsburg, with no water along the way, they came through the Dos Cabezas Mountains, over Apache Pass, and found what would come to be called Apache Spring, with fresh water and good grass for the horses.

The railroad eventually went ten miles north, through present-day Bowie, but that was not completed until 1881. Prior to that the mail still had to get through from St. Louis to Los Angeles, so in 1857 the Butterfield Stageline set up a route that covered 2800 miles, which the stagecoach would do in 25 days—impressive by any standards. The route came over Apache Pass and a stage station was set up by the spring. The ruins are there today.

In 1862, during the Civil War, a detachment of California Volunteers was marching to join Union forces in New Mexico and had a fight with the Indians at Apache Spring. After that little battle the US government decided to build a fort there to protect the water source. Peace with the Apache chief Cochise came in 1872, then Geronimo surrendered in 1886, and in 1894 Fort Bowie was officially closed down.

The government sold what was saleable and the rest was left to slowly crumble as wind, rain, and sun came year after year. In 1964 Fort Bowie became part of our national park system. I spent some time looking at the ruins and then hiked out to Overlook Ridge. At the top of this ridge I sat down on a bench and looked down on this piece of American history. I thought about the lives of soldiers a century ago . . . and of the Indians. It was immensely peaceful and I was glad I had come. I had slowed down and stopped to smell the roses.

By the time I got back to Bowie I had spent about three hours on this little detour. Well-spent hours, I might add. Thoughts of Fort Bowie entertained me all the way to Laguna Beach. I arrived home at 1 a.m.

Years ago a friend told me he was cutting way back on his reading. This was a man who consumed half a dozen books in a week. And not necessarily light books, but middling and heavyweight tomes as well. He said, "I miss too much. I've read all these books, thousands of them, and I remember very little of them. Now I spend two weeks reading one book, and I remember it well. I like that better."

That's my problem. I travel a lot, and too often I see very little. I really do want to see more, but the amount of discipline it requires to make me stop, or even slow down, is considerable—though I am getting better at it.

If you should be standing admiring some absolutely stupendous vista, a place that all mortals should give their eyeteeth to behold, a sight which draws the breath right out of your body, and you see me rushing by at a tremendous rate of speed, do me a favor and yell, "Stop, you fool! You're missing something wonderful!"

Yell loudly. I just may hear you.

Nasty Roads

June 1990

It is not good to be too complacent; it is good to challenge oneself. Like on the roads we ride. We love smooth asphalt. If I get on my bike at Point X, with home 2,000 miles away, and I choose to take the interstates all the way, I know that I will have a pleasant ride and be home for dinner on the third day.

However, unless I have to be back in a hurry, I will probably leave those broad black rivers and find some white-water roads to travel. What I am really looking for is a road that leaves behind the bright lights of town and village, that makes me concentrate on my riding skill, that gives me a small challenge, that has me extolling the correctness of my decision to abandon the manicured highway and explore the untended byway.

As a teenager I investigated all the roads in the Berkshire Hills of Massachusetts. While the paved country roads were generally frost-heaved, potholed and adventurous in their own right, it was the dirt roads that attracted me . . . on my admittedly street-oriented NSU 250. Up in Chesterfield I found one, only a couple of miles long, which according to an old man who had been cutting wood and scything hay since before the turn of the 20th century, was the old stage road between Albany and Boston. The local farmers and occasional traveling salesmen now used the much newer State Route 143, constructed during the Depression, and the old road was not much of a road at all, not having seen a dollar's worth of maintenance in more than 20 years, but there were great big oak trees, stone walls, fields of tall grass, and lots of woods. On a bright sunny day it was a perfect destination. I still go back, and have the same wonderful sensation as Alice must have had going through the looking glass.

A little farther along was the Savoy Mountain State Forest, which has a whole network of dirt roads running between the moderately famous Mohawk Trail (State Route 2) and State Route 116. It wasn't really a forest primeval, since nearly all of it was second growth, but 10 miles on those roads could take me half a day. It was not that the going was tough, it was just that there was so much to see, poking along and stopping every 10 minutes. James Fenimore Cooper's *The Last of the Mohicans* might have been set here. The granite remains of an old, old mill hulked beside a frothing stream, the water brown with tannic acid. I had this place to myself, and under the tall trees the roads were dark, and a sense of mystery was everywhere. Wilderness is relative, and for a town-bred boy this was exciting stuff.

Such excitement is all around . . . roads which give you a feeling that civilization and all its benefits are fast receding. I'm not talking about traipsing across the Sahara Desert on a BMW Paris-Dakar, or cutting through the Andes on a Kawasaki KLR. No, these are byways you can ride on any street bike, albeit slowly. Take a Honda Gold Wing over the gravel road east from Marysville, Idaho, through the Targhee National Forest to the south entrance to Yellowstone National Park. Run the Yamaha Venture from Clayton, Georgia along Warwoman Creek in the Chattahoochee National Forest. Nearly every state affords these opportunities.

A while back I wanted to get a closeup view of Shiprock Peak in northwestern New Mexico. It is on the Navajo Indian Reservation, and the closest pavement is Indian Route 13 going by a couple of miles to the south. The road continues on to Red Rock, Arizona, where it turns to dirt as it climbs over the Chuska Mountains. I was on a Kawasaki Concours, which might not be the best dual-purpose bike around, but all I had to do was go slowly.

Washboard and chuckholes wouldn't break the suspension, and a good grip on the bars make the front wheel go where pointed. After a bit Indian Route 13 goes straight over Lukachukai Pass, and Indian Route 68 goes off to the left, around Roof Butte. I went left, climbing up through pine forest, arriving at a spring by the side of the road, running into a trough. Good, cold fresh water, preferable in my mind to both tap water and the bottled stuff.

We, the bike and I, came over the top and started a slow descent along the Tsaile Creek, where a carpet of yellow and blue flowers did not have to withstand the picking compulsion of the urban masses. Sheep were grazing in the little valley, and a sheepherder sat on the step of his little wooden caravan, puffing on a pipe while his black and white border collies kept the woollies in line. It was not quite a set piece out of the past, since a much-used trail bike leaned up against the caravan, the transportation to the nearest trading post.

The way continued, never smooth, always beautiful. Marmots sunned on rocks, a wary eye open for the hungry hawk. Rabbits bounded, and a fox streaked from cover to cover, bushy tail held straight out behind him. The road flattened out, running ruttedly through a stretch of scrub oak and tall firs before ending at the asphalt of Indian Route 12.

The whole stretch of dirt from pavement to pavement was a little more than 20 miles. It took me two hours. I saw two pickup trucks on the way, and a bit of this country that had not given in to real estate developers and franchise stores. I had sharpened my appreciation for nature's beauty, and exercised my riding skills as well.

Eighty years ago, when a bad road was considered good because at least there was a road, the Harley rider would have looked at a long stretch of pavement and probably offered up a prayer of thanks. Now we have the reverse, and should give thanks that a little bit of bad road does exist.

I'm not waxing nostalgic for the Bad Old Days, but the stretch of old road does serve to make me appreciate progress, as well as to remind me of the alternatives to neon lights. All I have to do is forsake the easy road for a short time.

Motorcycle Nerd

July 1990

I don't really understand how it happened, but any information that smacks of motorcycling seems to stick to me, whether I want it to or not. Of distinctly passing interest is the fact that both Yankee S.H. Roper and Frenchman L.G. Pereaux had steam-powered bicycles in 1869.

This is not practical knowledge, nothing that will earn me a living, but it has taken over a large portion of the files of my mind. I do not really need to know that a certain Colonel Holden, late of the Royal Engineers, developed a motorcycle with an opposed four-cylinder engine in 1896, or that the Harley 125 of 1947 was based on the DKW RT125 as part of war reparations. But once I hear these essentially irrelevant facts, they are seared into my brain cells.

Did you know that in 1903 Charles Binks of Nottingham, England, developed a four-in-line engine that could be mounted transversely or longitudinally? Or that the British engineer A.T. Clarke put a transverse-mounted four-cylinder engine in a Clamil in 1922? Or that Gilera had a water-cooled in-line four, transversely mounted, in 1938? Or that in 1962 Val Page designed a 700cc transverse four, with electric starting, for the Ariel company? I cannot get rid of these factoids.

I wasn't raised that way. Not at all. In college I read a great deal of political philosophy, everyone from Plato to Machiavelli, passing exams and writing papers on this admittedly important subject. But none of this really adhered. What I remember most about Professor C. Wright Mills, author of *The Power Elite,* was that he was a very serious and outspoken motorcyclist. And while T.E. Lawrence may have permanently altered the geopolitical status of the Middle East, I think of him as the rider who loved Brough-Superiors.

I do love reading the news and chewing on the editorial pages, finding out what Kissinger and Gorbachev are thinking, what punditry George Will and Ellen Goodman have typed out, but if you asked me to make an intelligent statement on the federal budget I would be at a complete loss; I'm far better at giving the latest quotation on a share of Harley-Davidson stock, or commenting on the list of used bikes in the classified section.

The same has happened with my appreciation of art. My mother, a painter, did her best to instruct me in the finer points of Rembrandt and Renoir, on the differences between impressionism and abstract expressionism. One summer during college, while tearing around Europe on a Triumph Bonneville, I sent her a postcard from the Prado Museum in Madrid. When I got home she allowed as to how she was surprised to receive the card, and delighted that I had gone to soak up a little culture. Never did I have the heart to tell her the only reason I had gone to the museum was because my bike was in for service and I had some hours to waste.

I can still appreciate a museum, and the paintings, but I may not know quite what it is I am looking at. I have what I call the visceral, as opposed to the intellectual, approach to art. I'll take a good landscape artist over Jackson Pollock any day, and I think John Ramos' stunning watercolor rendition of a 1938 EL, titled *Made in the USA*, is comparable to any Winslow Homer.

Be that as it may, what do I do with this motorcycling trivia I've collected? It is certainly not all-inclusive. I'm rather selective and know little about two-strokes . . . except that Alfred Scott did have a very sophisticated 333cc parallel twin back in 1908, with a 180-degree crank, two speeds, and chain-driven primary and secondary. Not enough information to write a thesis, or even a sensible article, but I know it.

Racing is not much in my scope either, though I'm aware that in 1937 Ed Kretz won the first Daytona 200 on an Indian. And that Indian shocked the British Empire by cleaning up on the Isle of Man in 1911, taking the first three places in the Senior TT. Or that the Brooklands racing circuit, opened in 1907 in Surrey, England, was the world's first artificial racetrack for motor vehicles, as opposed to racing on public roads.

Prior to getting my license at the age of 16, that miraculous milestone denoting the arrival of automotive coming-of-age, I knew virtually nothing about motorcycles. I bought a used 1954 NSU Max, a 250cc single, and was not impressed by the fact that it had an overhead camshaft, nor a centrally located single shock, nor by its leading link front suspension. It was what was available, and what I could afford; the technical aspects were tertiary. I do admire engineering progress, but I can be quite happy on a pushrod twin.

I enjoy hearing Ducati lovers rave about the advantages of desmodromic valve actuation, and lauding the virtues of Fabio Taglioni, the man who spent much time and effort perfecting the system back in the 1950s. Perhaps we should not presume that everyone is familiar with the meaning of desmodromic. Etymologically speaking, it is from the Greek *desmo,* or bonding, and *dromous,* running. Technically speaking, it means that the valve is both opened and closed mechanically, rather than closed by a spring action. It was a brilliant idea 40 years ago, when springs were a lot weaker than they are today, but it wasn't new even then. Another Italian, Vincenzo Azzariti, had developed the concept back in the late 1920s. And a quarter-century before that J.A. Prestwich, of JAP engine fame, had built an overhead valve engine with the valves both opening and closing by mechanical means. I have never figured out any use for this arcane trivia other than to irritate *Ducatisti.*

The history of motorcycling remains remarkably vague. Nobody ever bothered to keep good records. A lot of names have disappeared, a lot of different motorcycles have vanished, leaving not a trace. These fragments of motorcycling lore are like having only thousands of pieces of a million-piece puzzle. Maybe all the bits and facts are out there, but nobody has been able to collate them properly. We should not forget that in 1930, Matchless introduced the Silver Hawk, with a 600cc SOHC 26-degree V-four engine, and integrated brakes.

I know that on May 3, 1914, Erwin G. Baker (a.k.a. Cannonball) took off from San Diego on a 7-horsepower Indian V-twin and arrived in New York City 11½ days later. I also know that 11 years earlier, on May 16, 1903, George A. Wyman left San Francisco on a single-cylinder, 1¼ horsepower motorcycle built by the California Motor Company, heading for New York City. It took him 50 days to make the trip, but his was the very first motorized crossing of the continent. Perhaps I should needle the Smithsonian on that.

None of this benefits me. I can't even win barroom bets, because nobody else even pretends to know this useless stuff. But I'm stuck with it.

Anybody know which bike had the first air-assisted suspension?

Give up? The 1909 ASL (Air Springs Ltd.); it did not work very well.

The Magic Carpet

September 1990

I've never met a motorcycle I didn't like—as long as it runs, of course. The point is, I am less interested in the particular qualifications of a particular motorcycle than in its magic-carpet qualities and the places it can take me to.

I met a man back in 1980 on a ferry in British Columbia who was riding a BMW R75/5 with an odometer that had flipped through its five digits and was working on the second 100,000. The motorcycle looked terrible, but he had been doing some serious traveling—probably covering half the roads between the Yucatan and the Yukon. He did not care that the Windjammer fairing was pop-riveted together, that the gas tank was bashed, that the saddlebags needed to be strapped on, or that one of the mufflers had been patched with a coffee can. He had seen the pyramids at Palenque on a full-moon night, the skyscrapers of Manhattan looming across the Hudson River at 5 a.m. on a June morning, and the midnight sun on the road to Inuvik.

He had been places. He had the traveling bug. Had it bad! And his Beemer was his magic carpet. When the wallet got too thin he would head home to Des Moines, pick up his old job fixing agricultural equipment, get a few hundred bucks ahead, and be gone again. The engine worked perfectly, he reasoned, so why buy a new motorcycle? The money would be better spent on gas and food.

I admit the fellow was a bit of an extremist, but I understood him.

A motorcycle is not a single-faceted object; it is many things to many people. Some riders view it as an extension of personality, others as a way to get around a racetrack, or as a cheap commuter vehicle that can be parked close to the plant entrance. I like a motorcycle for where it can take me, and looks, power, and economy are all secondary.

I must allow to the fact that I have been on some machines that I might not want to take on a long trip. I would not recommend a BSA Bantam for trekking down Interstate 55 from Chicago to New Orleans, for example, but when I was staying for a few weeks on a farm in Kenya one of those little birds showed me how to get around thousands of acres. Uncomplicated in the extreme, all it had was a piston, con rod, crankshaft and three gears to worry about. I could always make it run, and it was light enough to drag out of any ditch I wanted to cross.

Now that I think about it, that particular Beezer might make very sensible 'round the world transportation.

I'm just as impressed as the next fellow with something like a Honda GL1500/6 Gold Wing Special Edition, and for covering 100,000 miles of North American highway it would be an ideal ride. I would probably do the Four Corners, Three Flags, and Cannonball rallies if I could find a sponsor to pay for gas and tires. However, I'm a dawdler, not a boogier, so I will take the back roads from Acadia National Park to Death Valley National Monument.

I don't need a Gold Wing to go to those places. If I have $13,000 to spend that won't cut in on my travel money, fine. But I could buy a good pre-owned bike for a fifth of that, and spend the rest on the road. Offer me a well-used CX500 for traveling, and I'll take it. The suspension might be a bit soft, the tachometer broken, the seat torn, but I can spend a few hours putting her as right as she'll be. Then I am gone to see Cape Hatteras in the stormy spring, gone to Canyon de Chelly as the moon waxes full, and gone to the Olympic Peninsula on a clear fall day.

In Yosemite one summer I noted the number of "cruiser" bikes that were out traveling, with throwover bags across the seat and a duffel bungied to the back. One couple on a 700 Shadow had camping gear tied on all over, and they were having a fine time coming all the way from Atlanta.

I do understand that people buy different motorcycles for different reasons. The guy on the Harley Springer may only want to profile down Main Street on Saturday night, while the woman on the FZR600 zips up and down Racer Road on Sunday morning, leaving the bike in the garage the rest of the week. If that is what you like to do there is no need to travel further than that; it is just that I myself like to go long distances. So the performance specs of the FZR impress me no more than the condition of a good-running Seca 650.

Once I even chose travel over motorcycles. I had just finished graduate school and a friend and I thought it was a good time to see South America. Unfortunately the only way I could finance the trip was to sell my precious Triumph TR6R—which I did. As I see it, my Triumph did get me to Machu Picchu and Rio de Janeiro, from the Darien Gap to the Rio Plata—indirectly. Months later I returned to the United States, got a job, and immediately bought another Triumph.

That was a pretty drastic trip, by VW bus to Panama, then plane, bus, boat, and hitchhiking, and I would have much preferred to have been on a motorcycle, any motorcycle, which could take me just about anywhere.

I have friends who love their sportbikes, but if the destination is more than 200 miles, in the truck it goes. I respect their viewpoint, and their tender butts, and I don't try to change their way of thinking . . . although I do believe they are missing something.

One afternoon I stopped for a break in Cimarron Canyon State Park, out in New Mexico's Sangre de Cristo Mountains. That was when the Suzuki GS-E's, Kawasaki GPz's and Honda Interceptors were becoming the rage, and the road up the Cimarron Canyon (US Highway 64) was perfect sportbike terrain. The only problem was that it was a long way from population centers like Albuquerque, even further from Denver.

The I heard the rasp of three bikes being pushed hard, coming up the canyon. A nice sound, at least to the motorcyclist's ear, of engines and gearboxes spinning freely, exhaust notes echoing off the walls, machines moving with purpose. Three sportbikes appeared, nose to tail, solo riders, tank bags and soft luggage securely attached, heading west. The license plates read Missouri. They waved as they passed. Sport touring was coming of age in this country.

For me, the purpose of all transportation is to carry me to places I have not been before, which is why I can ramble happily on both a Jawa 350 and Ninja 900. The former showed me the coastline of Massachusetts, the latter took me over the Sierra passes. Equally good bikes, I'd say—for my particular purposes.

Which is to go traveling.

Top-End Factor

October 1990

Some of us like to go fast—to watch a mile drop away every 30 seconds, to see the pavement narrow as the speedometer needle climbs, to feel the growing herd of horses as the tach closes in on the red line. We want to find out, "What will she do?" To tie the throttle down on a long, lonely stretch of road and see just how good the bike is, to find out if the magazine reports lied.

It used to be, in the Bad Old Days, that you were damned proud if you could "break the ton"—an Englishism for exceeding 100 mph. Thirty years ago an honest ton-up was considered really fast. My first bike, an NSU 250 Max, managed about 80 mph flat out—about half of what a good liter bike does today.

In my feckless youth I flew to England and picked up a 1960 Triumph Bonneville at the factory. My first reaction was, "I will never, ever be able to use all this power." Several weeks later I was in Italy, rattling down an autostrada at a comfortable 80, when a Ferrari came alongside. We were off, tearing down the sunlit road at outrageous (for 1960) speeds, until I felt an abrupt weakening in the engine, and smoke began pouring out the left-hand exhaust. It was then that I learned of the susceptibility of a Triumph's left piston to meltdown.

I do like the feeling of going fast. I'm not a very fast rider in the sense that I am competent at triple-digit speeds, but it does serve to activate that adrenal release. One of the fastest places I have been was on a Honda test track in Japan, one of those oval banked affairs, more like a Mobius strip than a racetrack. Rip down a straight as fast as you can, then instead of slowing and leaning into a 180-degree turn you find the track curves and banks up 90 degrees and you deal with it just as though you were still going straight. There were five lanes on the banked portion, the lowest being almost flat, the top absolutely vertical.

It was a curious sensation, hurtling down the straightaway at absolutely silly speeds, then being compressed by the centrifugal forces as I got sideways to the ground. Getting onto the wall was easy, but twisting those 90 degrees back onto the next straight was confusing. As long as I just looked down at the track directly in front of the bike I was all right, but if I looked toward the horizon I wanted to straighten up the bike faster than the track was flattening out.

Another track taught me a different lesson about speed. Yamaha had kindly invited some journalists to southern France to ride their nice new motorcycles on the Paul Ricard racetrack, home to the Mistral Straight, one of the longer straights in the world of racing. You came out of a chicane onto this back stretch which covered the better part of a mile, and on an FZR1000 you could work up a humongous speed. The only catch was at the end was a right-hand sweeper, which good riders could enter at an exceedingly brisk rate of speed.

My choice was to brake hard before picking my line. However, I knew no more about braking hard at 150 mph than my cat knows about driving a car. I just did not have the nerve to get on the binders in a responsible fashion, though as I went 'round and 'round I would continually delay my braking—while the other moto-journalists went by like I was sitting still. I do not have, never have had, the proper skills to be a *really* fast rider.

I tell you racetrack stories, but most of my speeding takes place on public roads. *Peccavi*—I have sinned, as a Latin scholar might say. I choose empty roads and hazard only myself. I ride a number of new models every year, and every one gets stretched to its mechanical limit at some point or other. Just to see what she'll do.

Sometimes I run afoul of the law, which seems to be the major risk in exceeding the posted speed limit. One afternoon in Southern California half a dozen of us came bustling down the Banner Grade from Julian to Scissors Crossing, a remote desert intersection far from the maddening crowds. We turned north onto San Diego County Road S2, where three of us stopped to fiddle one of the bikes. The other three could not resist the temptation: not a soul around, 17 miles of smooth, uninterrupted pavement ahead, why not?

About nine minutes later we came to the stop sign at the intersection with CA 79, where we would wait for the others. Then we heard the wavering sound of a siren, and careening around the curve behind us came a Dodge pursuit car dressed in the colors of the California Highway Patrol. Bemused we sat on our bikes and watched as the driver locked up his brakes, tires skidding, car sliding towards the edge of the road, bouncing up on a hummock of sand, coming to rest with steam pouring out from under the hood, wheel wells full of smoking asbestos.

The door was flung open and a paunchy civil servant swung his body around on the seat, planting his feet firmly on the ground, and unleashing his truncheon as he stood up and strode forth. The fellow beside me shuddered, his helmet lowering towards his leathers like a turtle's head; DOT and Snell tests certify for crashability, not for getting beat over the head with a nightstick.

The officer knew motorcycles, or at least the whereabouts of the ignition. He reached down and plucked the keys out of all three machines, then walked back to his car and tossed them on the hood. "You boys get over here!" he said loudly, slapping his billy in the palm of his hand. We dismounted and approached this irate, non-fatherly figure gingerly, meekly.

In a bullhorn voice he announced, "You boys are going to die out here!"

Omigod, I thought, we're dead! Vigilante justice! He's going to shoot us all! Cut us down with three bullets and tell the judge that we attacked him!

Not quite. He lectured us for an hour, wrote us up for "Exceeding 100 mph," and let us go.

I know that this is not considered responsible, that I should never advocate exceeding the speed limit, et cetera. A dozen or more letters will come in to the office recommending that I be disciplined, fired, incarcerated, even burned at the stake.

For the record, I do not endorse speeding on a public road . . . but sometimes my right wrist develops a mind of its own.

Souvenirs

April 1991

We do drag home the most amazing objects from our trips. Souvenirs we call them, remembrances. "Dust collectors," says my great-aunt Agatha. Often they stand on the mantle or the shelf until their very origin is forgotten. Then they get relegated to a cardboard box in the garage. But at one time these were all precious items.

Somewhere in my parents' attic is a little wooden bear in a little wooden cage with YELLOWSTONE NATIONAL PARK branded into the top. I threw one of my all-time tantrums to get that prize when we were doing the requisite family tour of the West. I had to have it, and eventually I got it. The owner of the souvenir shop knows who his customer is.

Souvenirs can be anything. My latest is a piece of the Berlin Wall. It's a bit big, I must admit, weighing about two pounds. I was at the Wall after the fall taking photographs, and some enterprising business type had packaged bits of concrete in plastic bags and was selling them at a good rate to the tourists. He was also renting out hammers and chisels so that the more adventuresome could whack off their own piece of history. He came over to admire the Harley I was riding and I asked him to take a picture of me whacking at the Wall. One good blow and there I was, doing my bit to bring the Wall down . . . and acquiring yet another remembrance.

People collect the oddest things when they go traveling, most of them qualifying in the useless category. Sometimes they are all much of a muchness, like the spoon collectors. The only advantage that these silly spoons have is that they are small, an excellent prerequisite for a motorcyclist. But I know people who are positively pathological in their obsession to collect more spoons. They get spoons from the 50 states, the Canadian provinces, countries abroad, but then the whole notion begins to fall apart when one expands into Disneyworld spoons, national park spoons, Fort Ticonderoga spoons, spoons from Dallas and Des Moines.

The logical extreme is that these spoon collectors will end up making their very own spoons, with the address of the house neatly engraved, which they will present with great ceremony to visitors to the home.

Winnebago types tend to put decals of the states they have visited on the back window; motorcyclists fill in maps on the backs of their vests. The vests themselves have become a good way to display collectibles. Part of rally-going is collecting the souvenir pins. Look in the back of any motorcycle magazine and half a dozen small companies offer their services making pins and other tiny knick-knacks that we love to collect. I have the little frying pan pin from the last official Death Valley Motorcycle Ralley, held in 1967. That should be worth something some day. Maybe.

A friend of mine buys postcards as souvenirs. He must have 5000 of them, all just heaped in a couple of shoeboxes, with no rhyme or reason or cataloguing. He goes somewhere, it does not matter if it is Glacier National Park or East St. Louis, and if he happens to see a postcard of the place he is visiting, he buys it. He never sends them, just buys them, carries them home, puts them in a box, and forgets about them.

I asked him why he goes to the bother. He says he'll get around to putting them in albums when he hangs up his helmet. More likely his great-grandchildren will find this treasure in a trunk in the basement.

A few years ago my wife, before she was my wife, made a trip around Britain and found the perfect souvenir for a motorcycling tourist—at least according to her. Every castle, every museum, every historic site had its own leather bookmark, which was attractive, functional, and portable. I open my bedside book of an evening and I might find Stonehenge, or Peel Castle, or the National Motorcycle Museum holding my place. A useful souvenir, I must admit.

Some people say that photographs or written journals do as

souvenirs, but I disagree. A souvenir must be physically of the place, rather than your view or your impression of the place. It does not need to have been made in the place—since many souvenirs seem to have MADE IN TAIWAN on the bottom—but I feel you must have acquired the souvenir in that place.

I have a doorstop which is a great souvenir, a piece of railroad track about three inches in length, with a flattened five-peso piece glued to the top. I look at it, and I remember this Mexico trip all over again. We were taking the train from Chihuahua down to the coast at Los Mochis, the motorcycles tied down on a flatbed car. The whole trip was something out of an Abbot and Costello movie, with interminable waits on sidings, freezing nights in sleeping bags, the kind of journey you are glad you have done once, but would not do again. While we were parked on a siding waiting for another train to come through I found this little bit of track which had been hack-sawed off to make the rail fit, and when the other train came by I had it flatten the coin. Stuck them together and there I am. I keep on intending to have a little brass plate made denoting place and dates so that the archeologists can ponder it in the 30th century, but I doubt that I will ever get around to it.

Some friends are quite inspired in their pursuit of souvenirs, although the tastes differ. Bill and Margery Stermer have the most breathtaking collection of salt and pepper shakers in the form of animals, with pairs of grinning piggies, hugging ducks, and swooning bovines sitting on the kitchen shelves. At first I was a little taken aback, salting my food with a bright green frog, peppering with a laying hen, until I appreciated that this was an art form in itself, akin to Malcolm Forbes' collection of Faberge eggs—although somewhat less costly. But the real import is that each pair of beasts reminds them of a place.

I don't look for any one thing when I travel. Perhaps I should be a little more consistent in my acquisitions. I put T-shirts beyond the pale, as they proliferate like white mice, take up too much room in the bureau drawers, and make better wipe rags than souvenirs. I like to think of souvenirs as merit badges for the Scouts, medals for the military. You should earn your souvenir, not just buy it.

I've got a rusty, ancient belt buckle I found while fixing a flat somewhere in the desert north of Stein, New Mexico; how did it get there beside that dirt road? There is a BMW boxer tappet cover with a copper patch neatly pinned over a hole that I knocked through it while off-roading in the Kashmiri Himalayas. I've got a Triumph piston with a hole that was melted through while I was trying to keep up with a Ferrari in Italy. There is the helmet that saved my life when I tangled with an 18-wheeler. A chipped, enameled cup I got in the tiny village of Livingstone, New Zealand, where a man with a marriageable daughter offered me a job when I was young and single.

And even a spoon. Not a chromed souvenir spoon, but a metal spoon, bent and scratched but free of rust, that I found while camping beside the Yukon River. Now, that brings back memories.

Which is the point of them all.

Cooking the Goose

July 1991

I have done a lot of stupid things in my life, all of which I can safely say I wish I had not done.

I do not believe I'm alone in this; I like to think everybody has approximately the same number of regressive genes that prompt these momentary lapses of good judgment. In my case, a number of these episodes naturally relate to motorcycles. And some do make for moralistic tales, once they are past and done.

For example, last summer I was looking for a place to pitch my tent. I was off in the low mountains of northwestern Czechoslovakia and thought a little rough camping would be in order, finding my own spot in the woods rather than sharing some overcrowded campground. I was on a newly built road that paralleled the old road, so I turned onto the old. Soon I saw a dirt track going steeply up a wooded hillside, a very narrow logging road. Probably a great campsite up there.

I had a big Harley Glide, and should have thought more about where I was headed. But I didn't; I just popped her into first, gave her the gas and zipped right up the pine-needle-covered path. It certainly had not been used much in recent months, probably not at all. Everything was fine until I got a few hundred yards up the track, and then my way was blocked by fallen trees. So here I was, stopped on a 25-degree slope, with no place to turn around. The bike was at least eight feet long, the track wasn't even five feet wide, with a 45-degree ascent on one side, an equally steep descent on the other.

I figured I would have to back it all the way down. It would be a sweaty, slow business, so I shed my jacket, and the flies started to swarm. Nothing like having 10 trillion flies in my face to remind me of my stupidity. I backed down the first 20 yards, then the rear wheel hit some roots and slipped over to the mountainside, the bike fell over, and I was stuck. Fortunately I could pick her up, get her in gear, and move forward to try again. And get stuck again. There was no way I was going to get this behemoth backed down the mountain. I had cooked the goose.

The first time I cooked the goose I was seven years old and Bill Longley, a family friend, was teaching me to row a boat. We were approaching an old mill pond along a quiet river, with Bill in the stern puffing on a pipe and dangling a hook overboard. I dropped an oar; it made a splash and Bill turned around and watched the current pull the oar away from us, heading for a small dam some 300 yards away. "Son," he said, "you just cooked the goose."

I was ready to burst into tears, but Bill saved the day by sculling along with a single oar until we managed to retrieve the lost one. He made the point that even if the goose were cooked, you could still enjoy eating it if you pulled it out of the fire quickly enough.

I was exploring Guanajuato, Mexico, years ago, following a street which turned into an alley, heading mildly downhill, the alley getting narrower and narrower, and a dozen children running behind me screaming something I did not understand. Eventually the alley ended at the top of a very steep, long set of stone steps, which the bike would not be able to negotiate. The kids had tried warning me of that. The place was too narrow to turn around, so I had to enlist several of the bigger children to push me backwards a hundred yards. The goose cost me a few pesos.

It's not always my goose that gets cooked. A few years ago I was riding down in Baja, California, with my buddy Fireball Stein. This was back in the days when if you went south of San Felipe you had to crawl over the Three Sisters, or the "Three Ugly Sisters" as we called the trio of rocky hills. Since then the government has bulldozed a new road through, but back in those times the road was a real slow-goer. Maybe one vehicle a day went over the route, at four mph.

Fireball was ahead of me on a BMW R80G/S and I had a similar R80ST. We were coming off the first sister and the road was all loose rock, where if you put on the brakes the rocks beneath the wheels slid. It was a tricky bit, and I was following about 40 feet behind when I noticed black splotches on the rocks in front. I honked the horn. Fireball stopped. Sure enough, he had whacked the quasi-useless skid plate on the bike hard enough to put a crack in the sump. We didn't have any extra oil with us, and certainly nothing that could fix the sump. Fireball had cooked the goose.

Nice knowing you, I said, I'll drop a note to your mother. I headed back to the nearest community, a fishing village called Puertocitos, where you were lucky to find gas. And I luckily found an American who lived there and had both a boat and an arc-welder. We took the sump off my bike, loaded it along with four quarts of oil in the boat, headed down the coast, located the stranded Fireball, exchanged sumps and wished him a good night. We saw him the next morning.

It all worked out. No matter how bad it gets, until you see St. Pete and the Pearly Gates, there is hope.

It is very easy to despair, to give up, to figure it's all over, but usually there is a way out. Years ago I wrecked a bike in New Zealand, wrecked it real good, bending the front wheel, the axle, the fork and the frame. And there were no replacement parts in New Zealand for this motorcycle because there wasn't even a BMW dealer in New Zealand.

I was distraught. I'd cooked the goose. To satisfy the law I would have to turn the bike over to New Zealand customs officials, and they would drop it off the end of a pier. However, I was staying with a friend who said, "No worries, mate, she'll be right." We loaded the bike in a van, took it out to his place, and dismantled everything. The frame went one way and the wheel another, while a machinist friend straightened the fork and milled a new axle. In a week the bike was back on the road, good as new.

Blasting down a little-used dirt road in Zambia I was exceptionally stupid and crashed, knocking myself unconscious. I came to after a bit, and my amateur mechanic's skills told me that not only was the battery cracked but there was a dead short in the system. And not much traffic on the road, like about one overcrowded pickup every four hours. A well-meaning native came loping by, stopped, and asked if I had a gun. No, I replied. Too bad, he said, because there are lions here. The goose, the goose, was cooked. But it all worked out.

And how did I ever get the Harley off that mountainside? I wasn't going to be able to back down. I could walk down to the road and try to flag some people to help me; but that would have been distinctly embarrassing. I could see the headlines of the local paper: DUMB AMERICAN MOTORCYCLIST TRAPPED ON LOCAL MOUNTAIN.

What did I do? I backed the bike into the mountainside as best as possible, then flopped it over toward the uphill side on the crashbars, leaving the front wheel dangling off the edge of the path. Scrabbling around I managed to drag the front of the motorcycle downward until the whole thing was eventually pointed in the right direction. This may sound easy to the reader, but I had visions of 800 pounds of Harley sliding down the 45-degree mountainside if anything went wrong.

Then I rode the bike back down, and found a beautiful camping site 10 miles farther along. And had goose cooked to perfection for supper. Moral: Now I make sure every strange road I take has a place to turn around.

The Great Coffee Chase

September 1991

I confess: I am a drug addict. I have to have my drug every day. If I don't, terrible things happen to me and I suffer withdrawal symptoms involving pain, headaches and nausea. Vague thoughts of ending it all enter my user-ravaged mind. I'm not proud of the fact that I am addicted, but that is what has happened.

Fortunately, my drug of choice is not yet on the Attorney General's proscribed list. It's caffeine, plain old simple caffeine, the stuff you find in any decent cup of coffee, or for that matter, tea. By my definition, decaffination is indecent and pointless.

Ever wonder why so many people drink coffee? Most of them are addicted, just as I am addicted. I'm not worth a damn in the morning without a good cup of coffee. And this is one of the problems inherent in traveling . . . how do you find a good cup of coffee?

We motorcyclists drink a lot of coffee when we're on the road. It helps to jump-start the system after a night's sleep. It has a warming effect on a cold day. It provides an excellent excuse to linger over lunch while waiting for the clouds to clear. It is a nice way to end an evening over a campfire. And, when properly brewed, coffee has a very pleasant taste.

There is no guarantee about the quality of the coffee you will receive in any place that serves it. You can walk into the most expensive restaurant and have the most miserable dishwater passed off as coffee, or hoist your buns up onto a stool in the quintessential greasy spoon where Maude pulls a cup out of a huge chromium vat, and it is absolute nectar. Don't ask me what the difference is, but I know there is one. It has to do with the quality of the coffee bean, and the care that is taken in the preparation.

Back in the early Ike days, my dad could get a cuppa for a nickel; times have changed, and 50 cents is now pretty standard. But to justify this 10-fold increase in price, a lot of places offer the endless cup. I think I've handled six or seven in a row, but never more. There comes a time when my whole body is awash in caffeine and, even if it is cold and wet outside, I have to be on my way. People have died of caffeine poisoning, just as with a drug overdose.

Historically, coffee became popular in the soon-to-be United States after the Boston Tea Party. It wasn't considered patriotic then to sip tea, and the country slipped into the "caffe arabico" mode. To go further back, coffee became popular in the Moslem countries about 600 years ago, and for a long time the Western world looked upon the stuff as an infidel's drink. But drugs are insidious, and Europe also became addicted.

Long before people ever made coffee at home, coffee houses flourished. These places were frequented by artists, writers and politicians, as well as crackpots and layabouts, and were often seen by the authorities as centers of sedition. Coffee was considered an evil brew by many, and at times the authorities banned it. But the brew won out, and eventually sipping a cup of java (a slang term taken from the name of an island where coffee is grown) became entirely acceptable. As most touring motorcyclists will swear, it is a necessity when on the road.

Coffee comes as a bean, and the bean is roasted. You won't see a coffee farm in the United States unless you go to Hawaii; I find the Kona variety to be delicious. To grow contentedly, the bush needs a hot, wet climate, and an elevation of less than 6,000 feet. Down in southern Mexico I was wending my way along a dirt road from Oaxaca to Puerto Angel, a really gnarly stretch back in 1975, dropping steeply from the high plateau to the Pacific coast, when a moonless tropical night fell . . . it was very dark. I did not relish going on, and upon seeing a light in the window of a farmhouse, I stopped. It was a single-family coffee farm, and I was invited to pitch my tent in the yard and spend the night.

Breakfast was fresh tortillas, scrambled eggs, and dynamite coffee. I wish I had gone into the kitchen to find out how the senora prepared it, but I imagine that in traditional fashion the roasted, ground beans were briefly boiled in a pan of water on top of the stove. That is the kind of coffee you pay attention to when you are drinking it; most of us knock the stuff back without thinking much about it . . . unless it is extremely good, or absolutely miserable.

Coffee is found worldwide. I've had Turkish coffee in Istanbul, $9-a-cup coffee in Tokyo (where coffee drinking has acquired connoisseur status), Colombian coffee in Colombia, Kenyan coffee in Kenya, and whenever I go home to visit my parents in Northampton, Massachusetts, I have great American coffee at the Miss Florence Diner. I've had cowboy coffee, dripped coffee, steamed coffee, percolated coffee, boiled coffee, pressed coffee. I've woken up in nigh on 70 different countries, and I can't think of one where I couldn't rustle up a cup of coffee somewhere. Maybe good, maybe bad, maybe indifferent, but some sort of coffee was always to be found. The coffee in Russia was on the low end of the desirability scale, whereas in Costa Rica it was at the high end.

Some people require the caffeine, but have no palate; in other words, anything will do. I've got a friend, a reasonably sophisticated artist, who drinks instant coffee made with hot tap water; by my standards, Gary Brown is definitely a caffeine Philistine. All he wants is the rush, and none of the preparation. For the record, the first successful instant coffee was marketed in 1867 by Gail Bordon, of Illinois.

For me, the preparation can be as important as the drinking, and when I'm traveling I often carry my own coffee-making gear with me.

Which can create its own problems. I was headed down the Natchez Trace Parkway, and had arranged to meet Brown, who is from New Orleans, at a campground halfway. All well and good, except that the day we were to meet I ran out of coffee. I like my coffee thick, 90 weight, so I carry a small stove and an espresso pot, and an espresso system requires an extremely fine grind . . . not easily found in up-country Alabama and Mississippi. I went into Tupelo, Mississippi, to pay homage to the King and to find some more coffee. The local supermarket did have whole beans on the shelf, and a machine to grind them. But the only settings were COARSE, MEDIUM, and FINE. Clever fellow, I ran a bag through the FINE setting three times, and was on my way.

I met up with Brown as planned, and after a noble dinner he settled into his warm instant, while I fired up a pot of espresso. A large white owl perched on a limb over our heads, hooted a bit, watched for a while, then flew off.

In the middle of the night I was awakened by a crash and a clatter. Thinking it was bandits or badgers raiding our provisions I rushed outside, starkers, just in time to see the owl disappear into the darkness with the shiny white coffee bag clutched in its talons. Obviously the bright waxy paper had attracted its attention. I hope the bloody wretch died of caffeine poisoning. Brown laughed his fool head off as I drank his miserable powdered stuff at breakfast.

But all was not lost. We pulled into New Orleans at four in the morning the next day, and I went to the Café du Monde in the French Quarter, where I had a truly righteous cup of coffee. Followed by a second and a third. I felt a lot better.

Self-Destruction

October 1991

It's low-grade physics; one moment things work, next moment they don't. Sometimes things end with a whimper, other times with a bang. I've had a few of both.

Recently I heard a whimper in a lovely spot called Poison Canyon. A minor California highway, CA 178, passes through there, going from Ridgecrest to Searles Lake and then on to Death Valley. The road runs slightly downhill, heading for the dry lake and chemical wasteland that is the Kerr-McGee company town of Trona—romantically named after the hydrous acid sodium carbonate that is mined there. I was rumbling along on a new Harley-Davidson FXR Convertible, about 55 per in fifth gear, when things stopped happening. No sound, no warning, no out-of-gas sputter, no noise of anything breaking. Just silence, and a very dead engine, and a slowing as the transmission dragged on the belt and rear sprocket. I pulled in the clutch and rolled to a stop, stranded in this desolate defile, waiting for the rattlesnakes and scorpions.

Every motorcyclist's worst dream: the new bike breaks down far from home and dealer.

They don't do this very often. I remain fascinated by the fact that the modern motorcycle is so reliable. Here we have crankshafts and pistons whirling around at thousands of revolutions per minute, with valve trains and gears spinning along, carburetors doling out fuel, ignition systems sparking, oil pumps lubricating, hundreds of bits and pieces moving precisely as planned and 9,999,999 times out of 10,000,000 everything goes well.

It is that ten millionth time that interests me here. In my years of riding I have had a few bikes fail on me, not through neglect or abuse or old age because I am talking of reasonably new bikes, but just because that is the way of our less-than-perfect world.

One of my trips ended temporarily with a righteous noise. I was on a new 1966 Triumph TR6R headed from Massachusetts to Mexico, about ten miles north of Victoria, Texas, cruising along at the legal limit, hot sun beating down, anticipating a little tequila and roast *cabrito* that evening in some small cantina, when BANG! I heard no further noise, just the whir of a well-oiled chain going around; and no throttle response. I declutched and coasted to the side of the road where even I, with my limited technical expertise, could see what was wrong. A big hole had appeared in the bottom of the crankcase, through which I could see the broken end of a connecting rod. Not exactly something to be repaired with the toolkit that came with the bike.

A time for despair. But before I could get into a proper misery a car came along and towed me into Victoria, where the local dealer ordered a pair of cases and eventually got me back together—under warranty. Those gremlins of destruction can wreak havoc in any new machine, be it a $500,000 B2 bomber or a $5 can opener.

That TR6 experience was quite a while ago. Today I would hardly expect a connecting rod to break, but I never presume that something can't go wrong. A new bike can have teething problems. A friend of mine bought one of the very first Kawasaki Concours and at 2000 miles the oil cooler spit off a hose and his bearings were toasted. He was less than happy, but the bike was fixed and now has more than 60,000 miles on the clock.

No brand is immune to failure. The leading German marque loves to tout its reliability, but I remember well the day in 1973 when I left on a long trip on my R75/5, still under warranty. Three hundred miles from home I was suddenly surrounded by a horde of screaming banshees, a most horrendous wail emanating from somewhere in my machine, the agonizing shriek of tortured metal. I was completely unnerved, but as I stopped the caterwauling ceased.

Find a dealer, get a truck. The upshot was that the gears in the rear hub had stripped out—due to my mechanic's having drained the old oil and forgotten to replace it. Not really BMW's fault. In time I was back on the road, restarting the trip. What man puts together, man can take apart—and fix.

Sometimes I have continued to ride a bike that sounded like it was dying the death of 10,000 cuts. I was on a Yamaha Virago test bike one wet Xmas Eve day, heading for the house of friends several hundred miles away. The trip began well, but soon a tickety-tick developed in the engine. Which soon became tackety-tack. And degenerated into bangity-bang. I pulled off the highway and found a garage that would let me wrench inside out of the rain. I presumed that a lock-nut on a valve-adjuster had loosened, but nothing I could do would help.

To hell with it! I'd ride it 'til it quit and then figure something out. It never did quit, but it was making the most godawful racket by the time I returned it to the owners. Apparently a batch of camshafts had been improperly hardened, and their surfaces had worn away in a thousand miles.

A not so curious aspect of some new machinery is that much of it is virtually impossible to work on in anything less than a specialized environment, like one with tools and computers. Forty years ago just about any motorcycle could be stripped down to the basics with half a dozen wrenches and a couple of screwdrivers. No more. Several years ago while riding a Honda Sabre along a jeep trail (not quite Sabre terrain, to be sure, but I think all motorcycles should have a certain rough-road capability) and I heard a faint "Chuck!" I stopped, looked underneath, and saw that the detachable pot-metal sump had received enough of a blow from a rock to crack it. No oil ran out with the engine stopped, but when running, and pressure built up, oil was seeping out.

I had done this to another motorcycle years before, and had taken the sump off, fixed the hole, and continued on my way. I got the Sabre back to a nearby garage that was fully equipped to change the crankshaft on a Ford, but nobody could figure how to get the sump off this silly engine short of dismantling the entire machine. It was just too darned complicated. I ended up renting a van and trucking the beast home.

Sometimes a failure can merely be a cursed inconvenience. While humming along on a Suzuki Cavalcade, a machine never noted for abundant cornering clearances, I noticed that even under moderate speeds mufflers and stands and such were scraping in the curves. I stopped, punched the suspension leveling button, got pumped up, and continued on my way. In a few miles the bike was scrape, scrape, scraping again. There was a leak in the system and I was reduced to getting home on about 12 degrees of lean.

So goes the world. There are no guarantees you won't have problems in your life. A new motorcycle does have a guarantee, but a lot of good that does you when marooned 30 leagues west of Mudville. However, short of conking out in the middle of the Sahara Desert a breakdown is merely an inconvenience. If it does happen (though chances are very good that it won't), grin and bear it, stick out your thumb, and help will be along.

My Poison Canyon experience? Another motorcyclist came along and pushed me ten long miles into Trona, using his right foot on my left passenger peg. In Trona I found Red's Place, a motorcycle repair shop where Red determined that my battery had gone belly-up. It turned out that it had been one of a bad run, with a plate breaking off, shorting the entire system.

A new battery and I was away. Life can be simple.

Accidents

November 1991

A while back a bumper sticker flourished which stated simply: STUFF HAPPENS . . . or something to that effect. The original wording was in remarkably bad taste, and does not bear repeating here.

Stuff does happen, and that is the essence of an accident. The word comes from the Latin *accidere*, to happen. No matter how much we plan and plot, something can happen that throws everything off.

Not all accidents are negative. By accident he knocked on the wrong door. A woman answered, they fell in love, got married and lived happily ever after.

But should I hear that so-and-so had an accident, I presume the worst. For myself, I've given up on motorcycle accidents. Touch wood. It was part of my wedding vows. As a matter of fact, it was an accident that figured in my relinquishing my hold on the bachelor world. The accident was bad, but the marriage has been good.

I was out one fine morning about five years ago on a Kawasaki Vulcan 1500, puttering down a two-lane country road. The engine sputtered, I switched on the reserve, and decided to make a U-turn and return to a gas station five miles back.

A small white car was behind me, and far behind him an 18-wheeler. I pulled onto the shoulder, the white car went by, and I began the turn. The truck driver must have been half-asleep at the wheel, as when he awoke to see me he locked his brakes, putting the rig into a gigantic broad-side.

I completed my 180-degree U-turn to find this huge gravel hauler sliding toward me sideways, taking up not only both lanes but the shoulders as well. This left me no room for maneuvering, so I continued to complete a 360-degree turn and tried to get the hell out of there. Unfortunately, the sliding truck caught up with me as I completed my double-U, and before I could go for a quarter-mile record, his rounded gas tank tossed me a good hundred feet. The Vulcan was summarily reduced to a pile of scrap.

Proper gear and a good helmet saved my bacon, but I didn't regain consciousness until a few hours later in the hospital. My girlfriend/wife-to-be was sitting beside the bed, and she wasn't happy. She bailed me out of the hospital two days later, and when I was sufficiently recovered told me that if I ever did anything so foolish again, she might enter a nunnery.

The moral of that story is that I was at fault. I can blame the trucker for being dumb enough to get his rig out of control, but it was up to me to prevent putting him in that situation. I should have waited and let the truck go by before making my U-turn. I learned the hard way.

Some dolt came up with this silly saying: "There are two types of motorcyclists; those who have had accidents, and those who are going to have accidents." I will admit that the probability of dropping a bike in the course of a million miles is great, but what actually constitutes "an accident?"

Falling over with a Gold Wing on a muddy dirt road does not, in my mind, constitute an accident. To use Pentagonese, that is merely an unexpected eventuality. You dumped the bike. More of an embarrassment. Most riders will inevitably suffer an embarrassment or two in their careers; the unlucky ones will have accidents.

My lifelong (we were neighbors long before we had Schwinns and Raleighs) riding buddy had the classic accident. He was riding down Watertown Street in Newton, Massachusetts, on a BSA Shooting Star.

Some oncoming doofus made the classic no-signal, left-hand turn, and banged up my friend's leg in a big way. He's long repaired now, and has sworn off having accidents. He's got half a dozen bikes in the barn these days, and the whole family rides. Safely.

How safe can safe be? Good question; some accidents are truly unavoidable. Insurance companies have a nice little clause about "acts of God;" I would amend that to include "acts of man and God." If a branch falls from some high-rise tree while I am waiting for a light to change on the street below, that can be considered in the unavoidable category. The same if a freeway bridge decides to collapse in an earthquake just as you are going over it.

Some things you can flat not control.

My first accident was due to gross incompetence on my part. Since my entire motorcycle training had consisted of half an hour on a friend's Whizzer, there were some subtleties that I had failed to grasp, like the use of the front brake. I presumed its major role was to keep me in place while sitting at a red light on a hill. For stopping purposes I relied on the rear brake alone. About three months into my motorcycle riding career I found myself on a two-lane road, with lots of cars heading back to town on a Sunday evening. I was dutifully staying in my lane, then somebody up ahead slammed on his brakes and everybody's brake lights came on. I locked my rear wheel and slithered into the bumper of the car in front of me.

I'm not sure who was more scared, the family in the car or me as I embraced the asphalt. The fellow driving was terribly upset and very concerned about my well-being, while I was merely shaken and slightly bruised. The only damage to either vehicle was a bent footpeg. It was a rude way to learn about proper braking technique; I recommend the MSF courses instead.

Some time later I sold my ultra-reliable NSU 250, with its very good front brake that I had learned to use, and bought a very used, very flashy Indian Chief, Bonneville model. It was one of the last out of the factory door, in brilliant sunshine yellow with saddlebags and spotlights and all the trimmings of a 1950's machine. Basically my teenage reasoning (an oxymoron?) was seduced by the sheer size and glory of the machine, and did not consider how I would slow those 600 pounds.

The rear wheel had a skinny drum, rod operated, that would lock up under an authoritative foot, and the front wheel had an equally skinny drum which worked poorly, and often the brake cable snapped. Which it did one day, and I didn't fix it immediately. The next afternoon I was riding along Crescent Street on the flanks of Round Hill, the residential street having a low concrete wall on the uphill side, an unbroken line of parked cars on the downhill. My attention wandered; I looked over my shoulder briefly, then forward again to see a high school Driver Education car suddenly appear broadside in front of me. The instructor was teaching the hapless student how to turn around on a narrow street.

With the wall on one side, a row of cars on the other and minimal braking available, I locked up the rear wheel, skidded sideways, and gracelessly tipped over onto the crashbars, sliding all the time toward the vehicular barrier. The bike stopped six inches from the driver's door, with me still attached by virtue of having a foot entwined in some of my chrome fixings. I still remember the student's face, staring not at me but straight forward, mouth agape, with the pallor of an overly dead fish. I wonder if he ever did get his license.

I was unhurt, but saw fit to sell the Chief and buy something that stopped in a more normal fashion, and made sure that the brakes were always functioning properly.

We do learn from accidents. Or at least we should, otherwise there doesn't seem to be much point to having them. (That's a joke!)

I still suffer accidents. Last winter I was chopping wood and adroitly ruined a perfectly good boot and sock. A half-dozen stitches and a month in plaster, and all was well. I have now learned, the hard way, to keep my feet somewhat further apart when wielding an ax.

When my wife accused me of going back on my word, I reminded her that I had only promised not to have any further motorcycle accidents. That's what the small print is all about.

Weather

December 1991

Weather is a constant. Good weather, bad weather, hot weather, cold weather. You can be weathered in, or weather-beaten. You can be a fair-weather rider or cheerfully face foul weather.

One sure fact about weather is that you can't do much about it. I have learned to accept whatever comes. I like warm, clear days, but if I have to be somewhere and the heavens have opened up, I put on a rainsuit. If it's cold, I plug in my electric vest. If there is a hurricane warning, I stay at home.

Weathermen get a lot of grief because sometimes their forecasts are not terribly accurate. The story goes that a television forecaster, rattling on about a bright, blue-sky day was called by a viewer who said, "Look out the window!" It was raining dogs and cats. Don't blame the overpaid meteorologist too much, as he is probably in a windowless room reading off the information that a dozen satellites are feeding him.

I know people who won't ride a mile without checking in with their weather radio. If you have a Harley Ultra, mortgaging the family farm to pay for it also bought you several weather bands right in the radio controls. But knowing that it is going to storm does not change that fact.

I slipped into Quartzite, Arizona, early one evening, heading east, and the sky in front of me was full of lightning flashes with rolls of pitch-black clouds on the horizon. Truckers were talking about an accident they had seen, some little pickup blinded by sheets of water blundering into a semi. Nowhere where I was going was that important, and I found a room for the night.

The worst single stretch of weather I have ever ridden through was in South Dakota one late summer's day. At two o'clock the temperature was more than 100 degrees, and my wife and I were headed west towards a huge dark cloud. Good, she said, anything is better than this heat. Except this "anything" was a dust storm swirling across the plains. Turn around, get outta there!

We managed to skirt the dust storm and kept on towards Pierre. To run into hail, big hail, hard hail. Hurting hail. And not a bit of cover to be seen. I was thinking of huddling in a ditch when we came over a rise and saw a barn down in the hollow. Pulled right into the lee side of that baby and waited things out. The hail stopped and we pushed on, right into an exceedingly black and wet cloud, with violent wind and rain. I had an open-face helmet with a snap-on visor and the wind ripped two of the snaps off, knocking the visor down in front of my face. Just as I was going to pull over and lie down beside the road we emerged from under the cloud. A blue sky lit the horizon and we motored on happily to our night's destination.

Weather can happen fast. Or slow. Taking a ferry back from a little trip to North Africa I landed in Sicily on a cold day, having to ride up to Germany and catch a plane home. It got colder; I figured the Russkies had mounted some big fans up in Siberia and were sending all this misery south. The bike had to get back, I had to get back. I stopped over with some relations in central Italy, and left in the morning with the temperature reading 2 degrees Centigrade (about 35 F.) and it never warmed up. Five hours later I was going over the Brenner Pass at 30 F., and two hours after that I was in Munich at 28 F. It was a cold one. Heated grips helped a lot, as did the electric hand-dryers in the bathrooms of the service stations.

One late winter day I was headed into Tornado Alley, down by Del Rio, Texas. In Brackettville I came out of a café after eating breakfast and a gent sitting in a motorhome got out and told me not to go west, where I was headed. Tornadoes were tearing everything up, babies ripped from their mothers' bosoms, Dorothy getting blown back from the land of Oz, et cetera. He had heard it all on the radio. Not feeling like spending a day in Mr. Brackett's town, I pushed on. Saw a few funnels to the south, one to the north, and that was it. A lot of wind, but nothing that was going to blow me off to Emerald City.

On a spring ride I checked into a motel in Richwood, West Virginia. Bogart was starring in the late movie, and then the newsman said that a front was moving in. He did not specify whether this was a cold front or a communist front, so I went to sleep. And there was a foot of snow on my saddle when I awoke. I spent an extra day in Richwood. Gotta roll with the punches.

One product of the weather that I really do not like to mess with is lightning. I know of riders who have been blasted while in the saddle. Don't kid yourself that your rubber tires will keep you safe; the bolt may not necessarily kill you, but you will be wishing you had stayed home to watch a rerun of the *Doris Day Show.* If I see lightning on the road ahead I find a place to wait it out, definitely *not* under a tree or a tall TV antenna.

There is no need to arm-wrestle the weather gods. You qualify as a dumb guy if you try to front a blizzard. You are not smart if you try to ride when you are too cold to think properly, the onset of hypothermia. I've done both, together. In my long-ago college days I was trying to get back to school from my home, a hundred miles distant, one late autumn evening. The radio had said that a storm was moving in, and I was trying to beat it, but about 50 miles out it caught me . . . but good. I was on the Massachusetts Turnpike with only enough money in my pocket to pay the toll.

The toll-taker could hardly believe his eyes when this snow-covered Triumph rider pulled up, trying to get at his wallet with frozen fingers. He looked at me, shaking his head, and said, "You're #@*&% crazy!" He was right. I rode on into Cambridge and when I got off the bike I realized my knees did not work . . . frozen solid. I could barely get up the stairs.

My roommates looked at me as I stumbled in, shook their heads, and watched me fall stiff on the couch. One went to draw a bath, the other two pried the clothes off me, and then all three dropped me in the hot water.

If I had had the money for a motel I would have stopped. I didn't, so I didn't. I'm not much wiser now, but I have a little more money and know the difference between reasonable and unreasonable weather. I promise you, I prefer to ride on a sunny day, 75 degrees, wind at my back. However, if that is not what the weatherman has ordained, I'll ride anyway.

Maybe.

The Generation Gap

March 1992

Dear Charlie,

Good to hear from you. It's been awhile. No excuses on my part, just downright laziness.

So, young Andy is being insolent. No respect for his elders. You can always threaten him with a whupping, but since he's 25 years younger and three inches taller, I'm afraid I'd put my money on him.

Was he really giving you grief about you keeping your old Honda 750? Nothing new to that. I remember when you were giving your own father grief about keeping that miserable wreck of an Indian. I hope he still has it. It will pay his way into a fancy retirement home, should the time ever come.

Funny how we are about the past. When we're young, we scoff at it. When we're older, we value it. Same with motorcycles. And cars. Remember your dad's DeSoto hardtop? Lots of fins and lights. We both thought it was ultra-slick at the time. And I can still remember my parents' bullet-nosed Studebaker from when I was still in short pants. Gone, all gone. If only we had a barn and stuffed all those relics inside. Be rich today.

I will agree with Andy that perhaps a '72 CB750 is not quite the bike on which to do a cross-country trip. Sure, sure, it can be done. Lord knows we both did such foolishness, back then. But I would take his Katana 1100 any time. Less chance of it breaking. Less chance of me breaking.

Time is not quite as destructive of metal as it is of the human body, but it takes its toll.

Give them what you will, today's motorcycles are a whole lot safer, more reliable, and more comfortable than the bone-shakers we teethed on. Maybe that's why we can do so well these days. When I think of the quality of tires and brakes 30 years ago, I'm surprised I didn't crash more often. You had to have an extra 100-yard reaction-time cushion back then, just to give the brakes a chance to work.

And every improvement has taken place step by step. I rode Squariels and Vincents back when they were just old bikes rather than collectibles, and wasn't impressed. Beezas and Trumpets and Harleys were the standards, along with those funny-looking Honda Dreams. Then came the BSA triple, and I thought the entire concept of motorcycling had been rethought.

We've gone through a bunch of bikes, you and I. Andy will, too. The last time I saw you I remember he was already grousing about how your old single-cam was such a dog-slow beast, and why would anybody have bothered to keep one. I think he was smitten by the first Ninja 600 at that time.

Can you remember when the first CB750 arrived at the shops? Everybody, and I mean everybody, went down to have a look. Four cylinders. Overhead cam. Disc brake. Electric starting. What was the world coming to? Even my infatuation with Triumph waned drastically. The Japanese had taken our antiquated world and booted it forcibly into the second half of the 20th century.

Your only regret was that you couldn't find anybody to buy your beat-up Norton Atlas so you could make a down payment on the Honda. I think the Atlas is one of the few bikes which has not appreciated much in value. Lord, that baby shook bad!

Now our bikes have the same four cylinders, but with two overhead cams. And liquid-cooled. And triple discs. And single-shock rear suspension. Even that's old hat now.

I suppose my low-tech attitude has facilitated my passage through several generations of motorcycles. I've never been able to appreciate the more subtle nuances of such refinements as rising-rate rear suspensions, valve overlap, shim-stack damping and flat-slide carburetion. I have great respect for a racer who can run a bike around a track and come back and tell the head wrench that this, that and the other needs work. Not in my competence.

I do appreciate all these miracles of engineering and design, because even if I can't understand them when they are at the cutting edge of technology, to use that overly used phrase, they will eventually become state of the art (another overly used phrase) and improve my more pedestrian approach to cycling.

You remember my first Triumph, that T120R? With magneto ignition (which liked to toast the left piston), Girling shock absorbers with three spring-preload positions, and a rather basic fork. The carburetors were the latest Amal Monoblocs, and valve adjustment was measured by . . . forget the feeler gauge . . . a gentle click for the intakes, a louder click for the exhausts. I fell down a few times, due mostly to tires that didn't adhere well in the corners or brakes that were remarkably insensitive to road slickness. And probably my youthful over-exuberance.

It is undoubtedly in the tires and brakes that I have come to fully savor the advances in technology. They work a whole lot better than anything we were familiar with in our youth. Horsepower is another matter. I am amazed that a motorcycle can turn 100 or more horses loose on the rear axle, but I know that it is just as easy to come to a grievous end with only 50, or even 25 ponies.

Andy's Katana has well over twice the horsepower my Bonneville had, three times the handling and four times the braking. And he can run it 50,000 miles and never think about anything but minor tune-ups and changing the tires. I never remember worrying about tire wear, since the rubber seemed to be mixed with iron dust, but expected to replace a valve or piston every ten thousand miles. I suppose by contemporary standards my youthful pride and joy was a piece of junk.

But it wasn't. Andy is himself in the midst of the wild exuberance of youth, and growing old will not occur to him for a few years yet. I couldn't imagine anything better than my Bonnie, which could stand off a Harley CH at a stoplight drag. I'm sure your father felt that way about his Indian, side valves, tank shift and all; if he could blow away an EL, or maybe even an FL Harley, his day was made.

Imagine 20 years from now, when Andy starts bragging about his wonderful Katana in front of a bunch of squids riding the latest fuel-injected, super-charged two-strokes, running tires that cling like tree frogs and suspensions that are comfortably on the super-slab, then a simple twist of a lever makes them ready for a mountain road.

They'll look at him real strange-like, and when he's left they'll talk about that old codger who doesn't understand what good is. And if he still has that Katana, he'll take it home, polish it up, and think that those kids don't appreciate that without this machine, they wouldn't have theirs.

It's all evolutionary.

Best,
Clement

PS: Tell Andy this: Getting old isn't inevitable, but consider the alternative.

The Chronic Travel Syndrome

April 1992

Loving motorcycles is a passion, but traveling is a disease. A passion can be indulged and sated, but a disease just has to run its course.

I know many people who love their motorcycles, who can be just as happy polishing them, talking about them, or looking at them as riding them. I must admit I envy those friends with two or three primo machines cluttering up a carless garage, a workbench with a goodly array of Snap-On and Craftsman hardware, a stack of moto-mags, an old fridge with a couple of six-packs cooling. I'd much sooner spend an evening in a place like that than stuck in front of a television set. Common interests, good talk, good friends.

But I also know other riders who have that 300-yard stare, always looking down the long road, focusing somewhere in the far distance. These are the ones suffering from the chronic travel syndrome . . . but they wouldn't have it any other way. They have to travel, have to move, have to see what's around the next curve. They've got it bad.

I've got it bad, too. I didn't ask for it; it just happened. Life would be much easier if I could just sit in one place and be happy, but that's not the way it is. Never has been.

There's nothing right or wrong in any of this. Some people have blue eyes, others have brown. Some people are short, others are tall. While some people like to travel, others don't. And some people have to travel. It could be in the genes. Or in the water. It doesn't matter.

I've got the sickness. I first hit the road on my own when I was a sweet 16 and have been going ever since. Not consistently, not endlessly, but a few days here, a couple of months there, maybe a year when I can get it all together.

The purest form of travel is having nowhere to go, no place to be, just wake up in the morning and toss a coin. A sleeping bag, a coffee pot and a fine-running motorcycle.

You need perspective to travel properly, an appreciation for how small you are and how big the world is. Anybody with $350 can get from New York to Los Angeles in five hours and can see the good old U.S. of A. from five miles up. Small world, isn't it?

Wrong. Think of how the Indians saw it, on foot, before the Europeans brought horses to America. How the first pioneers saw it, like Daniel Boone leading his group through the Cumberland Gap. Slow going. Or sitting in St. Joe in 1850, looking across the Missouri River, wondering how long it would take to get to the promised land out there in the west. A motorcycle does go a good bit faster than a Conestoga wagon, or even the Butterfield Stage, but if you're a real traveler you'll slow down. Way down.

The way I want to go from New York to Los Angeles will cost me more and take me longer than the red-eye express, but that's my choice. I'll find every wayward road in the Appalachians, the Ozarks, the Rockies. I'll eat grits and drink a quart of coffee in Omar, West Virginia. Find a place to camp along the Eleven Point River in Missouri, maybe throw a line in the water. Hunker down in a cheap motel in Cimarron, New Mexico, while the rain thunders down like the 40 days and nights all over again.

I'll get cold; I'll get wet; I'll be hungry; I'll be tired. And you can bet I'll be happy. But one trip ends, and before long another begins. Occasionally I'll wonder why I'm doing this . . . then I'll wake up in a tent with a view of all that makes this country beautiful, and I'll know why.

But I can't tell you why. If I could, I'd package it up and sell it to travel agents and make a fortune and never have to stop moving. But it doesn't work that way.

Traveling does not appeal to everybody. Thank the good Lord for that. Somebody has to stay home and mind the store, sell the gas, keep this old country rolling along . . . economically speaking. I'm eternally grateful to all those folk who live in Cave In Rock, Illinois; they fed me great catfish, provided me with a clean room when the skies were nothing but thunderheads and lightning bolts, and gave me a fine memory of a hospitable town. Where would I have been if all those good citizens had been out on bikes roaming through Texas or Vermont? Out of luck. I'm glad they didn't have the traveling disease.

Show me a long line of telephone poles disappearing over the horizon, and I gotta go. That thin strip of asphalt has a power over me that cannot be denied, that just sucks me along. I want to get to the end . . . but I know there is no end. That, as they say in the dictionaries, is a conundrum.

There are nearly 4,000,000 miles of roads in the United States, and a lot more in the rest of the world. I've seen my share, but I want to see more. I know that for every road I go down, there's another one parallel, 10, 50, 100 miles away, that I'm not going along.

I avoid the great, wide, many-laned highways. Interstates are for truckers, for motorhomers and for people in a hurry. A traveler can't be in a hurry; it contradicts the very basics of traveling. Tourists are in a hurry because they've got three weeks to see Yellowstone, Yosemite and the Grand Canyon, and then have to be back on the job. A traveler is more interested in what is over the next rise than in anything 1,000 miles away.

Awhile back I was at a friend's house having dinner, along with a bunch of people I didn't know. I had just come off a long trip and was telling folks what the roads were like in Panama and Alaska and places like that, whom I had met, places I'd seen. Maybe I was boring everybody, so after a while I shut up and paid appropriate attention to what was on my plate. A psychiatrist was sitting across from me, and he leaned over and said, in all shrinkish seriousness, "Good way to find yourself."

He missed the point. Missed it entirely. You don't find yourself by this incessant traveling . . . quite the opposite. You lose yourself. There is so much out there, so much to see, so many people to meet and the more you do it, the more you realize what an impossibility it is to try to do it all.

Sure, I would like to stay at $100-a-night motels, eat the best steaks and drink the best wines, be invited to the White House. But I am equally as happy with a can of corned beef, a loaf of sliced bread and a bottle of $3 red, sitting on my sleeping bag way down east on top of Mt. Desert, watching a full moon rise over the Atlantic.

If you see a dusty bike pulled off into the aspens near Carbondale, Colorado, or gassing up in Big Sur, California, that might be mine. I could be the person working on his third cup of coffee at the Café du Monde in New Orleans at 3 a.m., or stoking up on fried fish in Calabash, North Carolina.

Or I could be the fellow in the phone booth, calling my wife to tell her where I am and when I'll be back. In any case, it's a good bet that wherever I am, I'll be happy. And isn't that the reason we travel?

Out of Gas

August 1992

How many times have you run out of gas on your motorcycle? I've forgotten how many times I have. Lots.

Occasionally I have had what I consider to be good reasons for running out of gas. The best excuse is there was no gas station where there should have been one. Forget those silly gas shortages of the 1970's; to my thinking that was all a trumped-up mess so the oil companies could get richer. I'm talking about when you presume there will be a functional gas station with gas, and it is either closed or out of gas. Or burned down.

Like Red Hill, New Mexico, on US Highway 60. Tearing along westward on a Kawasaki KZ750, the bike went on reserve just after passing through Quemado. No problem, Red Hill was just 20 miles further along, marked on my map like a regular town. To my thinking, on a Monday morning a regular town should have a gas station.

Sure enough, it did. Except it hadn't sold any gas or oil, candy bars or soda pop in quite a long time. Closed up tight. As a matter of fact the whole of Red Hill did not have much of anything, including inhabitants. Maybe if I backed off to about 30 mph I could make it the 28 miles to Springerville.

Not a chance. The engine faltered just as I got to the top of the long grade that winds down to the Little Colorado River; I killed it and coasted down to the valley floor, restarted and got about one mile before it quit for good. And three more miles to town. Fortunately I was close to a house where the fellow had a can of gas for his mower and he volunteered a gallon. But he also seemed to think that I was seriously dumb for not knowing that Red Hill had been shut down for years. Everybody knew that.

Except me.

The usual reason for running out of gas is that the rider has suffered an attack of acute dumbness. One way of being dumb is to try to stretch your range. You see a gas station, but think you can make it to the next one. Or you forget to turn your petcock back to ON after going off RES. Sorry, but all you riders who don't have a petcock system with reserve will just have to imagine what that feeling is about.

With most petcocks the ON position is when the little arrow on the little lever points straight down, and reserve is either 90 or 180 degrees away. There you are, out in the middle of beautiful, scenic America, the engine hiccups, you reach down with your left hand to switch over, and the lever is not where it's supposed to be. Guaranteed to bring a very bad feeling to the bottom of your stomach.

Do you leave the bike and baggage and trust to the goodness of mankind? Push it ten miles? Hope for an empty pickup with a loading ramp and tie-downs to come along? Pray that some Very Good Samaritan will stop and then run into town and come back with the necessary? Or, miracle of miracles, wish that a passing vehicle will have a can of gas on board?

It is never fun.

The old Oklahoma credit card is a useful item to have along, about four feet of clear plastic hose, and if a passing motorist wants to help, you can risk getting a mouthful of gas. It gets a little complicated as a car's gas tank is lower than that of a motorcycle, but if there is no suitable roadside container you can sacrifice your water bottle. I usually take along an inexpensive plastic siphon with a built-in pump, to avoid that gaseous taste. Especially when two of us are going on a dual-sport ride with bikes having unequal tank sizes; the siphon serves as an equalizer.

There are a few tricks for getting that extra mile or two. Before your carburetor starts sucking wind slow way down; 30 miles an hour gives you a lot better mileage than 60. Sometimes that does not work. One time I was on a big Harley FLH, with the two-piece tank, when she sputtered to a halt on Interstate 10 with a tall Shell sign just visible in the far distance. Nobody but Mr. Schwarzenegger or Hulk Hogan is going to push a loaded Harley two miles. I off-loaded some of the baggage, carefully lay the bike down on its left side rollbars/crashbars/engine guards/whatever-the-lawyers-want-to-call-them and lifted up the wheels until that last pint of gas had slurped over to the petcock side of the tank. A lot of cars slowed down to see what the heck I was doing, but after righting and reloading the bike I made it to the gas station.

There is one good reason for running out of gas on a bike with a reserve system—you can't access the reserve. I was on an early FJ1100 which Yamaha proudly announced had an electrically operated reserve; instead of taking your hand off the handlebar and reaching down to fumble with the petcock, you could just hit a switch with your thumb. Except the switch did not work when I was riding the bike. Dealing with the frustration of sitting by the side of the road and hearing that extra gallon of gas slosh around, but not being able to get at it, proved to be an exercise in gnashed teeth.

Then there is always the calculated-risk approach to running out of gas. You know the distance between gas stations and calculate if you can make it. It was 230 gasless miles from Ross River to Watson Lake along the Yukon's Campbell Highway. Would a big-tanked BMW R60/5 make it?

Yes, it did.

The sign at the beginning of the road going from Cloncurry to Normanton, in Queensland, Australia, read: NEXT GAS 244 MILES. I took an extra gallon along that time, presuming my tank would need some help in feeding the 750cc motor over that distance.

Zeroing the tripmeter when you fill up serves as a good back-up fuel gauge. Most of us know, or should know, our approximate range on a tank of gas, and an occasional glance at the elapsed mileage gives an indication of how many miles are left in the tank. But the method is far from fail-safe. If you have a five-gallon tank and average 42 miles to the gallon, you start to worry as you approach the 200-mile mark. Unless you happen to be coming across the Great Plains bucking a horrendous headwind that reduces your mileage to 35 mpg and the engine starts sputtering at 175 miles.

"Err on the side of caution," is one of my many mottos. But I often don't do what I say you should do. I was crossing sparsely populated central Texas on a Honda Shadow and thought I could make it to the next town. Nope. I was sitting there admiring the view, the tarantulas and rattlesnakes and hovering vultures, when a pickup came along with two Harleys in the back. I had to take a fair amount of ribbing about my clone as the fellows pulled a hose off a petcock and filled an empty beer can about ten times, but they were happy to be of help to a fellow motorcyclist. And I was happy to be helped.

Of course I did not make mention of the fact that I was riding and they were hauling. It would not have been good manners.

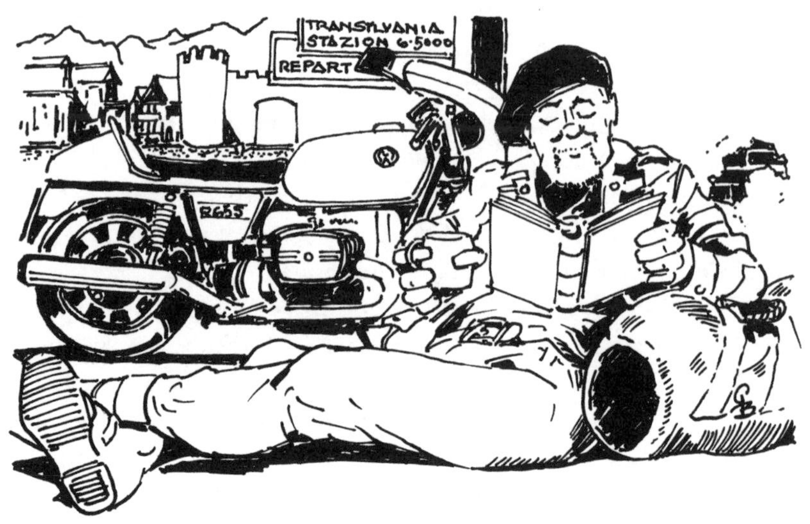

Hard Traveling

September 1992

We all dream of the easy life in which everything goes right, the wind is always at our backs, and there is enough money in the bank to cover the checks and credit card bills. However, the hard truth of it is that we often like ourselves a lot more when we have to struggle a little to overcome obstacles.

I was subjected to a bit of the easy life a while back. I was visiting a friend, and his club was having its monthly meeting; somebody was going to show a home video of his trip through the Rockies. Always up for a travelogue, I came along. I should have stayed at the house and watched *Cheers*.

This couple had taken a three-week vacation, heading out to Rocky Mountain National Park, then up to Yellowstone and Glacier national parks. Nice trip, with great roads, magnificent scenery. Everything went according to plan. Even the weather. They had half a day of light rain, and that was it. The Gold Wing behaved as a Gold Wing should; perfectly. They stayed in a big motel chain and used the chain's reservation system to ensure lodging for the following night. No food poisoning, no speeding tickets, no unpleasantness whatsoever.

They carried the video camera in the trunk, capturing Old Faithful in full glory, sunrise along the Going-to-the-Sun Highway, beauty and perfection all around. Even some good on-the-road shots. And I was bored. I admit, it was my fault, my being bored, but that's the way it went.

Nothing interesting had happened to them. It was a fine trip, yes, but the video showed me nothing I hadn't seen before; I might as well have been at some travel agency browsing through the brochures. Have you ever taken a good look at those brochures? They promise the most wonderful things, but the contents are staggeringly dull.

How could a pamphlet on Key West be dull? Or 16 color pages on New Orleans? Or a fold-out on the joys of Gold Rush Country? Because travel agents specialize in dullness. Their clients do not want anything out of the ordinary, want to be assured of plentiful hot water, clean sheets, and scrambled eggs and bacon every morning.

But we are motorcyclists. The very act of riding a motorcycle moves us away from the ordinary. And when we travel we shouldn't necessarily look for tough times, but we should relish them when they come.

After all, there are several reasons for traveling as we do. One is to give ourselves memories. Memories are the stuff of life, and I find that most of my best memories involve difficult times. Another reason is to give ourselves the very best stories to tell when we are in the company of others. I could bore you with the details of every trip I've ever taken . . . presuming there was something worth the memory. I have hazy memories along thousands of miles of sunny Interstate, one mile, one meal, one mattress much as any other, but 100-percent recall for rainy days in the West Virginia mountains, with a leaky rainsuit and homemade biscuits covered in gravy.

It's a tough one: How do you choose between misery and memory? First of all, you can't aim for misery. It has to just happen. If you beg for a thunderstorm and a bridge washed out and a slide into a ditch overflowing with muddy water, you just may get it and watch as your bike gets swept downstream. That's not hard traveling; that's a disaster.

AVOID DISASTER is my motto, but I don't mind a bad stretch of road at all. Bit of foul weather. It is the spice of a trip. I've been snowed in, rained in, hurricaned in, and while my first reaction has always been, "Oh, this messes up my schedule," my memories have always been good.

I was staying the night with a friend on an old farm along a dirt road near Brownsville, Vermont, and I wanted to be in Boston the next day.

Important business, of course. An overly early blizzard swept in and dumped three feet of snow on the ground; the plow didn't get through for two days. I had a fine time, learned to snowshoe, toboggan and do creative cooking with the contents of the larder. The business? It waited.

Dirt roads are a good example of hard traveling. I got mudded in on a dirt road in the Great Divide Basin, out in Wyoming. Looking for a quiet place to camp, I found a little ranch road running off into the scrub. It was just a bit of dirt, and on this dry evening I followed it for a mile, and set up the tent. About 6 a.m. it began raining hard and stopped after a couple of hours. I broke camp, got on the bike, went five feet and fell down. Picked it up, and fell down again. It was my first real experience with that red, Western soil that turns slicker than snot when it's wet. I wasn't going anywhere.

So I hiked around while nature took her course, and over the ridge found an old cabin down in some trees that might not have been visited by anybody for 30 years. An old iron stove sat unmolested, with rusty utensils, a bed built into the wall, a table and two chairs; the most recent reading material was a 1951 *Colliers* magazine. The place really did look like it was waiting for Randolph Scott or Gary Cooper to come in the door. By the time I finished poking around the sun had come out, dried the road and I was on my way.

One of my secrets of hard traveling is to always carry a book that I want to read, but never got around to. Like Thomas Wolfe's *Look Homeward Angel.* If I do get good and stuck, the book will keep me company. When a little black box went out on my bike in the Balkans some years back, it took me three days to get back on the road, but I got a lot of good reading done.

Last spring I was headed for my cousin's place up in Carbondale, Colorado. I called there the day before I left and she said the temperature was in the 80s. It wasn't even half that by the time I got to Durango. The forecast was ominous, but before I went to bed I looked up at the sky; stars aplenty. No problem; cold or not, I could get over the passes. Next morning the sky was leaden. I packed and headed up toward Coal Bank Hill Pass, which sits at a healthy 10,640 feet. At about 8,500 feet a light dusting of snow began; at 9,000 I passed a snowplow, and the driver must have started wondering. At 9,500 I finally wised up and turned around, appreciating that even if I made it over Coal Bank, I had two higher passes ahead of me.

I was not a happy warrior, as I had promised my cousin that I would be there for dinner . . . and she is one of those well-bred ladies who never lets you forget when you have broken a promise. Back in Durango I learned that the storm was expected to hang about for a couple of days. Okay, if that's the way it is . . . I shot over to Dove Creek on U.S. Highway 666, then north through Naturita on Colorado 141 and found myself on an absolutely marvelous road running through the Dolores River Canyon. It's now on my list of the 100 best.

I was a leather-covered Popsicle by the time I got to Carbondale, in time for a hot bath and a large glass of whiskey before dinner. It had been a hard day, with lots of hard traveling, but it gave me good memories.

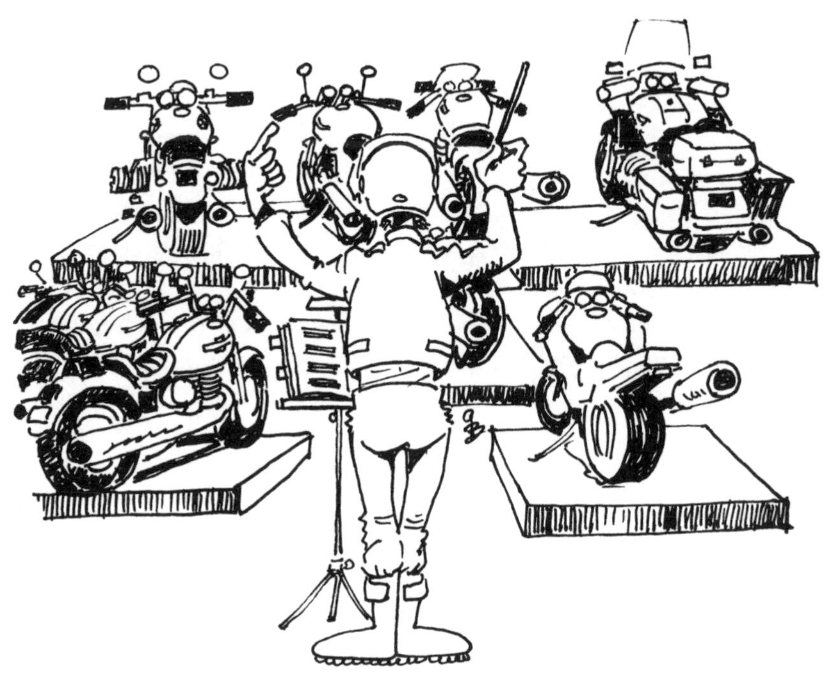

The Music of Motorcycling

January 1993

With spinning countershaft, whirring valve train, and EPA-approved exhaust, all manner of sounds emanate from motorcycles. There is the purr of a flat six, the harsh whisper of an in-line four, the loping cadence of a sporting V-four. Twins and singles have their own very distinctive way of announcing themselves. Pushrods and copious finning require a basso profundo, while double-overhead camshafts and water jackets provide their own soft background.

To those of us who love them, motorcycles are in themselves musical instruments.

So much everyday noise surrounds us in the present world that we often miss the particular subtleties. Take a motel room by a superhighway and the sound of tire whine can drive you bonkers. After a summer years ago on the line at the Noble Manufacturing Corporation, late of Leeds,

Massachusetts, I was impressed at what eight hours of clanking machinery could do to my eardrums. Even sitting at this computer a faint hum intrudes.

Conversely, I relish a lonesome train whistle at a remote campsite. Or standing listening to the relentless wind drone through the open windows of an abandoned farmhouse on the Great Plains. Or falling asleep with the thunder of a waterfall in my ears.

Since I ride a motorcycle every day, and drive a car rarely, some uninformed people think I should be used to noise. I'm not. However, for me the rush of the wind and the meshing of gears and the burble of the exhaust are not noises, but rather my own personal music. There can be too much, of course, but presuming a well-designed motorcycle and a good helmet, the sound will be a Bach toccata and fugue, not a dissonant John Cage extravaganza.

One's taste in music is very personal; I much prefer Bruce Springsteen extolling the virtues of being *Born in the USA* to the discordant sounds (to my ear) of Guns 'n' Roses. I'll take Jimmy Buffett's country rock over any rap or heavy metal.

Maybe heavy metal has its place. I was watching the motorcycle drags one Saturday night, and when they spun the wheel of a monstrous fueler the engine banged and popped erratically. However, with some red-leathered guy hunkering low in front of the huge slick it proceeded to blast down the quarter-mile in record time, taking top honors for the night. It did sound good under full throttle, I must admit, which is perhaps why heavy metal fans always have the volume full on.

In high school I, too, was fascinated with sheer volume, so I put a megaphone on my 250, and as the decibels mounted the horsepower decreased. Older friends I respected told me not to come by again until I had remuffled my beast. Which I did.

As a novice rider, I learned to tell the difference between a Triumph and a BSA twin, the Trumpet having a looser valve train with a slightly rattley tone. Nothing wrong with that, just a bit more clatter to define the difference. A Sportster was markedly different from an FLH, and a BMW sounded like a drum with a velvet skin. The whiffling note of a decelerating Gold Star was absolute magic.

Compared to these, the sounds of a Honda 305 Super Hawk or a Suzuki X-6 Hustler were more like what I heard in my dentist's office. They howled and ripped, an indication of pop music to come.

However, within 10 years I was lost in the low decibels of the air-cooled in-line fours. I approve of good muffling and quiet machines, but the exhaust note of a CB/GS/KZ750 had little personality, little to identify it. A good sound, but anonymous more so in this age of liquid cooling.

There are still sounds that are more particular, like the tickety-tick of a slightly loose tappet on a BMW boxer, the rhythmic cadence of a Moto Guzzi V-twin under easy throttle, the thukka-thukka of an OHC 650 single. I realize that the bureaucrats would like to do away with all this, to reduce the sound of every engine to the same pabulum, but I disagree. If people want vehicles to operate in the same way as refrigerators, fine, but some of us listen for the aural identification of who is coming down the drive. New motorcycles tend to be as unidentifiable as elevator music.

I miss those distinctive sounds. I had a roommate at school who loved classical music (as well as an Ariel Square Four, which he likened to a string quartet), and if the radio was playing a piece that he had never heard before, he could usually identify the composer. I was impressed by his aural astuteness.

A great deal of effort has gone into the exhaust sound of such percussion instruments as the Shadow, the Vulcan, the Intruder and the Virago, but they rarely do anything to stimulate my tympanum. The manufacturers might be better off with 100 percent muffling, and at the tip of the pseudo-exhaust system mount little speakers and an endless tape. Only Harleys sound like Harleys.

Today the EPAcrats want to obliterate any identifying characteristics. The sound of a modern motorcycle is internally and externally suppressed.

I am against noise pollution. I do not want to hear the raucous sound of an open pipe while I'm watching the news, hate the rip of an unmuffled two-stroke on my quiet road. I hate it, and my non-motorcycling neighbors hate it, which is trouble for me. There is a difference between noise and music.

My neighbor makes noise when he sings in the shower, Pavarotti makes music when he sings opera. The child makes noise on his toy drum, the Modern Jazz Quartet makes music. The truck on the highway makes noise, my friend's Low Rider makes music.

For me, the sound that I associate most with motorcycling is one of silence. Perhaps the tinkle-tinkle of a hot engine cooling, but other than that, quiet. That is because motorcycles take me to quiet places, places on hilltops, in valleys, where not a mechanical sound is to be heard. I camped on a wooded hillside not long ago, with a westward view of the setting sun, and a farm across the valley, a mile or more away. I could hear the whack of an ax, chopping wood, coming from the distance. It was a nice sound. Far better than a chainsaw.

My ears respond when I sit in a meadow and hear a nightingale in the evening. And perk again when I hear Craig's Ducati climbing the mountain to join me at my campsite, his Conti exhausts running up and down the tonal scale.

Some people might find the Conti sound objectionable, though to Craig, and to me, it is music. I agree, one man's music can be another man's noise, whether it is a ghetto-blaster on the beach, or a trumpet solo to the ear of a Garth Brooks' fan.

I'll respect your ears if you respect mine. I'll try to keep my sounds subtle, non-intrusive, but particular. Especially on the motorcycles I ride.

The Automotive Century

February 1993

The gas station and grocery store near Elkins, West Virginia, was a down-home sort of place with a pair of old-fashioned pumps out front, the kind on which you have to reset the meter and then start the pump motor. None of this semi-automated, cash register-controlled, PAY BEFORE YOU PUMP stuff.

I topped off the Kawasaki Concours and went in to get a soda, then sat on the bench out front. A pickup rolled in with a youngish man at the wheel, a grizzled graybeard in the passenger seat. The driver got out to pump gas, and the old boy hoisted himself down, cane and all, went over to inspect the motorcycle.

The graybeard lowered himself onto the bench. "That yours?" he asked. Yup. "How many cylinders that thing got?"

Four cylinders, plus liquid cooling and shaft drive.

"Sure is different from those motorsickles I used to have. I ain't rid a bike in mor'n 50 years, but I sure remember ever' one I ever had."

A small piece of history was coming my way.

"I got me an old Flanders when I was 17. It had just one cylinder, but it went like stink; couldn't stop worth a darn, though. Then I had me an Indian, a Scout; good bike, except I loaned her to my cousin, Ralph, and he run her off the side of a mountain. Weren't worth fixing. Ralph never did pay me for her, neither. Then I got a deal on an Ace. Fellow over in Clarksburg had it. It was too much motor for these here mountain roads. You never saw asphalt lessen you went to town, and that old four-banger had more guts than any Model A. She spit off at least three owners before I got her, then she spit me off a few times. I got her cheap, I sold her cheap. Then old Roosevelt got hisself elected, and I never did have another motorsickle. Got married and bought an old Dodge instead. Or maybe it were t'other way around."

I made mention that he remembered all those motorcycle facts well. "You bet," he said, "I can tell you the valve gap on ever' car I ever owned. Out here, ever' man was know'd by what he drove, or what he rode. And you didn't pay no mechanic to keep that engine running, you did it y'rself. You member that stuff."

It's true. I'm a lot better at remembering the motorcycles in my life than I am anything else. My first ride was a Mobylette, a little French-made moped that my classmate, Peter, got when we were 15. It was sometimes faster than a bicycle, and nobody in Northampton, Massachusetts, made a fuss if a kid rode around on such a machine. My second ride was on a Harley 125, complete with rubber-band front suspension.

Neither engine required much more attention than mixing oil with the gas, and carrying a pocketful of spare spark plugs and a plug wrench.

My third ride was on a high-school friend's Whizzer. I wanted to get a motorcycle license, so I gave Alan 10 bucks to teach me to ride and to accompany me to the Registry of Motor Vehicles. Done.

I moved on to my own motorcycle, a used NSU 250 Max complete with overhead camshaft and monoshock rear suspension. None of that made any sense to me; all I knew was that it worked, and that the price was right. I kept that bike for two years, and during that time rode a lot of other motorcycles. Once I had a bike, other people with bikes were willing to let me ride theirs. A Ducati 98, Vespa 125, BMW 250, Horex 350, Triumph 500, Harley 45.

I got seduced by BIG, selling my faithful 250 for a very used Indian Chief that had the 80-inch engine, Bonneville cams, plus saddlebags, spotlights, and a windshield. Big mistake; the second day I blew the engine, sending the pistons crashing through the splashguards at the bottom of the cylinders.

I got a ride on a Triumph Thunderbird with considerable reworked cams and exaggerated compression ratio. Then I rode a Tiger 110 and a TR6C. I was hooked; I had to have a Triumph. The Indian got sold and the pennies saved and eventually I collected a brand-new T120R Bonneville and put 14,000 miles on the odometer the first year.

Thirty years have gone by, 30-odd motorcycles have been owned, and hundreds of other motorcycles have been ridden since then. Each one has left its imprint on my mind. I can't remember all the valve clearances, but I can remember the throttle response, the brakes, the handling, the power.

Compared to my graybeard acquaintance, I was a mere pup. He saw the birth of the Automotive Century, when roads were bad and machinery unreliable. I think I've seen the best of that century, and I know it will never be as good again. Too many people, too many vehicles, too much regulation.

The young man came out, a loaf of Wonder bread in his hand. "Gramps talking bikes to you?" Yup. "He loves that. He's a gearhead from way back. I've got a Wing and a couple of dirt bikes at home, and there's nothing he'd rather do than watch me wrench them."

The graybeard slowly pulled himself to his feet. "Tell you what, boy," he said to his grandson, "you put a sidecar on that big machine of yours, and I'll show you places in these here hills you ne'er knew existed."

And I'll bet he could.

A Motorcycle's Life

March 1993

Flesh and blood age, metal and oil grow older. Many of us do not like to think about the inevitability of aging, but, as my great-aunt Agatha would say, it's a lot better than the alternative.

Human aging is one thing, the aging of a machine is another. Humans can do it quite gracefully, if they bother to keep in reasonable shape. Handsome man, that, referring to Sean Connery; what a good-looking woman, apropos of Doris Day. While an old motorcycle is merely old, paint faded, chrome pitted, case discolored.

The stages in a machine's life are simply: new, used, old, junk. Of course, if the old bike manages to avoid the salvage yard it can pass some invisible barrier and might become a classic, and, with the passage of more time, an antique. If you hang on to just about anything long enough, it will eventually regain value.

You think I'm kidding? That old mayonnaise jar I threw away in pre-recycling days will be a valuable find to some amateur archeologist some 200 years hence. The CB350 my neighbor took to the dump 10 years ago would, in the century ahead, become a collector's item.

I sold a couple of geriatric motorcycles several years back. My life was undergoing some drastic, and positive, changes, and I looked in my garage to see what part of my accumulated encumbrances I could unload. Gathering dust were a '66 Triumph Bonneville and a '66 BMW R69S; the Triumph I had owned for 10 years, the BMW about 15. When I had bought them they were both in rough, albeit quite rideable, shape, and my intention had been to keep and restore them.

Looking at these about-to-become-classic motorcycles I knew that I would never get around to restoring them myself, nor was the money to pay someone else to do it in the cards. I had ridden them both many thousands of miles, and the wear of age was showing in worn steering head bearings, sloppy carburetion, weak brakes, sagged-out suspension.

That was serious aging. Any motorcycle begins to age from the time it is built. You lay the bucks down on your brand new Dream Machine, and even as you ride it away from the showroom the motorcycle has had a minor aging crisis. To you it is still new, pristine, perfect, but to the motorcycle marketplace it is now a used bike.

Then the maintenance begins; it is the motorcycle equivalent of daily calisthenics. The initial break-in check-up can set you back a fair bundle, but it is worth the price.

To slow the aging process, regular check-ups should be attended to, the owner's manual saying how often the oil should be changed, all that. Some riders adhere faithfully to the regimen, others are slack; a slacker's bike ages far more quickly.

By the time the first new tires are needed, the bike is still a youth. At 10,000 miles it can be polished to a perfect shine; it has never been dropped, everything is fine, almost like new.

At 20,000 miles the bike is no longer young. Any thirty-something knows the ease with which a paunch can be developed. You might not want to invest $150 in a major tuneup, and the swingarm feels fine so why get it greased? And so what if the coolant has never been changed?

Some people buy a bike and never do more than put gas in the tank. A fellow I knew used to work on Gold Wings, just Gold Wings; Joe Christian was the best Wing wrench I ever met. I rode up to his shop one day to find a customer sitting on an exceptionally filthy GL, talking to Joe.

The fellow had come in, his Wing running ratty. Could Joe fix it? Having been ridden for five years without so much as an oil change, the whole machine had deteriorated to the point that Joe told the man there was no use trying to do anything. Of course he could make it run right, for a little bit, but then something else would go wrong. Ride it 'til it drops, advised Joe, then put a bullet through its head.

That kind of abuse happens to a lot of bikes.

The odometer hits 30,000, and the owner figures it is not worth investing any money in this middle-aged machine. So he sells it. The new owner is overjoyed; he's got a bike! He pops for a minor tune, maybe a new battery, and advised that new shocks would be in order, buys low-cost aftermarket replacements.

In the next 20,000 miles the second owner keeps the oil level up, puts on fresh tires, and replaces the brake light bulb. Other than that. . . nothing. There is now a rip in the seat, covered with duct tape. The fairing and the right saddlebag took a bit of a crunch on a sand-covered corner. A subtle click can be felt in the steering head and the fuel gauge doesn't work. One day the beast is shined up better than it's been shined in the previous 19,000 miles and an ad appears in the Weekly Swapper: For Sale: Motorcycle. 50k. Cheap.

A young guy buys it; he's low on bucks but high on energy. The bike does need a proper looking at, but with the local shop charging $45 an hour he can't afford that. Riding season is coming, and the far coast is calling. It's not really fair to this old war-horse, but maybe it, too, wants a last sniff of the open road. The summer is a good one, but by the end the alternator is plumb tired out, and the battery doesn't hold a charge too well anymore. It gets parked for a long winter with 60,000 miles on the odometer.

After a while the owner gets tired of the old motorcycle taking up space in the too-small garage; anyway, he's into skydiving this year. Time to get rid of the bike, but the battery is dead. He tries to get it going with jumper cables, but it just won't fire. Not wanting to go through the hassle of selling it through the paper, he borrows a friend's pickup and loads it on. This time it's going to the motorcycle graveyard, the salvage shop. A one-way trip to the glue factory.

He gets a hundred bucks; there is always a market for side-panels, bits and pieces. The bike is dissected, exhaust pipes hung up, wheels put aside, the saddle stuck up with 200 other saddles in the rafters. The fork gets kept, the frame is trashed; no call for that item, ever. The junkmaster writes down in his book what he's salvaged, so when somebody calls with a request for a starter motor, he can thumb through the grease-smudged pages and say, “Yeah, I got it.”

No funeral, no wake, no memorial speeches. A few vital bits may contribute to some other motorcycle’s continuing on for a while. Ashes to ashes, rust to rust.

But it was a good life, a motorcycle’s life.

The Destination

April 1993

You have a free weekend ahead of you. Or a week. A month. Maybe even a year. Get on the bike; it's time to travel. But where do you go? Where are you headed? What is your goal? What is the destination?

No matter how precise or how vague it is, there always has to be some sort of direction in which to point the motorcycle. It can be as simple as heading toward blue skies or taking the road not previously traveled. It can be as specific as Daytona Beach during Bike Week or a visit to Great-aunt Agatha two states away.

My first destination was quite traditional . . . I went off to grandmother's house. I was 16, had just acquired a motorcycle license and a used NSU 250, and we were living about 175 miles from the ancestral homestead. I wanted to take my first long ride, and my objective served to allay my parents' concern over their last-born's negotiating the hazards of the open road . . . if I didn't show up at Gran'mama's for supper they would soon know about it.

I followed the back roads that I had so often seen from the car, but everything was different. The towns and villages looked different, the scenery was different and the road was very, very different. I had no idea that a car's windshield could distort reality so much. And there was no cranking the steering wheel over, just leaning. I was impressed. I was also hooked.

Since then I have chosen a thousand other destinations. I can spend hours looking at maps, making a list of places I want to see. Or thumbing through an address book, figuring which friend from long ago I want to visit. I have chosen a national park as a turn-around for the summer's ride . . . Voyageurs, in Minnesota. I've gone north to Norway to see the midnight sun beyond the Arctic Circle, and south to Panama to see if mangoes grow on bushes or trees.

There is no precise way to come up with a destination; there are probably as many different reasons as there are riders. You could do a historical trip, visiting Civil War battlefields, or a genealogical journey to find your own roots. Maybe you want to see the Rocky Mountains, or the Okefenokee Swamp. It could be Dodge City; it could be Disneyland.

I met a man on Cape Hatteras who came from Nebraska and had set out simply to see The Ocean. A rather broad objective, perhaps, complicated only by the practically infinite number of routes he could take to get there. He was 28 years old, and wanted to stick his toe in salty water; he didn't really need a map, as he could have just followed his Voyager 1300's compass east. Or west, for that matter. He said he had chosen the eastward direction by the flip of a coin.

Years ago I went off to see the ocean, too. Having never seen the Pacific I left my home in Massachusetts and headed more or less west on my Velocette Venom Clubman. It was a very vague sort of trip, as I zigged and zagged across the country to visit friends and places. I learned many things, including that a big single was not the best way to get across the Great Plains, and that Tioga Pass in Yosemite National Park was the best motorcycle road I had ever been on. I traveled cheap, pitching a tent at Swan Lake, near Cairo, Illinois, sleeping in an abandoned barn somewhere near Russell, Kansas, rolling out my sleeping bag on the high desert west of Winnemucca, Nevada.

Eventually I crossed the Bay Bridge and onto Highway 1. Oh, my goodness gracious me! The Pacific, and especially the road bordering it, was far better than I had ever anticipated. It was a most excellent destination.

Any destination should never be too far for the time allowed. I can get on an interstate highway and do 800-mile days, but I prefer to follow the small roads, take my time, enjoy the process of getting there as much as the actual arrival.

One way to choose a destination for a weekend ride is to lay out the map, get a compass, draw a 250-mile circle around your home, and look for some spot on the edge of the circle that you might like to see. Who knows what you will find? From St. Louis, for example, 250 miles reaches to the bucolic byways of the Ozark Mountains, to quiet camping at Iowa's Nine Eagles State Park, the urban pleasures of Chicago or the descent into Kentucky's Mammoth Cave.

And a thousand other places. Remember your math: the circumference of a circle is the diameter (2x250=500) times pi (3.14); that gives you more than 1,500 miles of possible destination. The line you draw will intersect 100 small towns, 1,000 places you haven't seen. Lead Mine, Wisconsin; Ruth, Nebraska; Fort Scott, Kansas; Gold Dust, Tennessee. I've been to none of those places, but their names are appealing.

The longest journey begins with a single step. . . or a mile rolling over on the odometer. If you can go 10 miles, you can go a hundred; if you can go a hundred, you can go a thousand. Without even leaving the continent you can ride north to Alaska, east to Nova Scotia, south to the Darien Gap.

My own horizons expanded when it came to destinations. I was working in Europe one year, finished the job, and decided to go home to Massachusetts the long way. After packing my BMW R75/5 I headed east toward India. I saw Mt. Ararat off on my left, ate roast sheep in a Tehran bazaar, watched a full moon come up over the Himalayas, and caught a boat in Bombay. Not having any timetable, I traveled as I wished, stopped when I wanted, and all I knew was that my destination was ultimately east.

It took me two years to get back to Massachusetts. A very good two years. It was traveling at its best, and always ahead of me was that goal, that place that I would eventually get to. It was a great trip, equally as good as the one to grandmother's house.

Now, about where to go next weekend. . . .

The Riding Ambassador

May 1993

Ever since there have been motorcycles, adventurous people have strapped a sleeping bag and a change of clothes to the luggage rack and gone off to have a look-see at the rest of the world. But not in the numbers that appeared in the 1980s. Forty years ago you could buy a Harley or an Indian with windshield and leather bags, or bolt a Craven rack and pannier bags onto your Triumph or BSA. However, the full-dress Harley Tour Glide and the Honda Interstate moved the whole concept of touring on a motorcycle up about six notches.

Our grandfathers would not have gone farther than the county seat without a kidney belt, 40 pounds of tools and a few extra chain links, while we presume the comfort and reliability of the modern motorcycle. And it is not just the big touring-rig owners who are spinning the odometers, but the sport-touring and cruiser types who are seen in every national park every summer. Bungee a sleeping bag to the back of a 10-year old 400cc twin and you can have the cheapest, happiest summer of your life; pack a change of underwear and a rainsuit into the bags of your Gold Wing or Ultra, and all you need is a credit card to guarantee a great vacation.

And we motorcyclists spend money. Lots of it. We don't pack our homes on our backs like the Winnebago types, with a week's supply of liverwurst sandwiches in the fridge. We eat lots, and we eat well. We usually stay in motels. And we stick our noses and wallets into every museum and souvenir store.

Money, that root of all evil, and a lot of good times, is what greases the wheels of any economy. Enterprises like Bea's Bide-A-Wee Motelette and Wall's Drug Store are out to make a buck, as is Pop's Corner Service Station and Mom's Home Cooking Café. And touring motorcyclists contribute a lot of those bucks that help Bea and Mr. Wall and Pop and Mom earn a living.

We the tourists are out to have a good time. The people running the restaurant, motel, gift shop, tripper trap, whatever, are hard at work trying to make sure we have good time. It's not easy work, and they have to smile all the time, too.

Sometimes, though, we motorcycling tourists are a little nervous about our acceptability. Are we going to be treated nicely? And what do we do if we aren't? Make a scene? Accept the situation? Lay waste to the place? Or try to set a good example?

There are people out in the world who have a bad attitude concerning motorcyclists. Your average drug-dealing, homicidal pimp pulls up to the motel in an expensive car and, of course, there is room at the inn. Your friendly medical doctor on a motorcycle might be turned away; Sorry, full up.

It's an irrational response that some misguided people have, sort of a mechanically based racism: you ride a motorcycle, you're a bad person. The frustration can be considerable, and the temptation to lash out is great.

In my humble opinion, the best approach when such unpleasantness occurs is to turn the other cheek. Don't reach over the counter and grab the scrawny clerk by the shirtfront; instead, ask if he could kindly recommend another motel.

Do appreciate the legitimate problems that motorcyclists can create. When six of you crowd into a little café, rainsuits streaming with water, you have to figure that the waitress will not be overjoyed. Until she gets a nice tip. On a cold day the stack of helmets and riding gear can be a real bother in a crowded restaurant; ask where you can put them.

At the motel you may be paying anywhere between $20 and $200 for a room, but it does not give you the right to abuse the place. Do not . . . and though I've said this before I will say it again . . . use the room towels to clean your bike; it's a guaranteed way to make trouble for the next motorcyclist. Be considerate, and understanding of the businessman. Ask for rags at the desk . . . most motels are brimming with used towels they will gladly part with.

When you are a motorcycling tourist, you are a goodwill ambassador. We are a minority, and that means that we have to be extra good. That's the way our society works. Not fair, perhaps, but who said life is fair?

When I'm out touring around, I'm such a nice guy my neighbors wouldn't believe it. I like touring, and I like to be accepted. I like friendly receptionists and cheerful waiters. I'll put in that extra effort to keep the image of the motorcyclist shiny. And if you are the next biker to come along, perhaps you'll be pleasantly surprised.

And one day I may be the motorcyclist coming along after you. That will be my reward.

Tiltmeters

September 1994

Some years ago I was hired by the state of California to do a little Expert Witness work. A motorcyclist had crashed on a right-hand curve, going wide and center-punching an oncoming car. He, with his deep-pockets lawyer, was suing the state on the grounds that the corner was improperly marked, that the speed advisory should have been a great deal lower.

The state had located the same model and year of motorcycle for my use, and I was soberly charging around the corner to show that the speed advisory was okay.

Just to clarify the point, there are speed limits and speed advisories. A limit is a limit, and you can get popped for exceeding it; these are represented by rectangular white signs with black letters reading SPEED LIMIT and black numbers. An advisory is a square yellow sign with black numbers, and is just that, an advised speed.

The road had a 45-mph limit, the corner had a 25-mph advisory. With the CalTrans fellow taking pictures I hustled around the corner at 25, 30, 40, and 45 mph. For good measure I did a 50 and 55 as well but things began to drag seriously as I tried for 60.

Anyway, the moral of the story is that the motorcycle rider had plenty of ground clearance to get around that corner on his side of the road, at any legal speed.

My theory was that his tiltmeter was set for 33 degrees when it should have been adjusted to 38. Happens to most of us at one time or other.

There are three aspects of lean anytime a motorcycle goes around a corner: one being mechanical, the second involving part of the inner ear, or cochlea, and the third, physical conditioning.

The mechanical aspect is easy to figure out: how far that motorcycle will lean over before something drags. On the low end of the scale is a 1994 Harley-Davidson Softail Custom, which official Harley specs show has SAE-approved lean angles of 29 degrees on the right side, 31 degrees on the left. The standard Sportster 883 has 36 degrees on the right, 40 degrees left. If I get on a Kawasaki ZX 750R, I could probably get up to 50 degrees before anything scrapes.

But that 50 degrees is not going to do me much good, because my cochlear tiltmeter goes off at around 42 degrees. I may know in my heart that the motorcycle and tires are capable of more lean . . . but I am not.

Why not? Because of my own internal sense of balance. That varies from person to person, rider to rider.

It was Jean Foucalt who invented the gyroscope in 1852, which has become the basis for all modern mechanical-guidance systems. Humans have their own rudimentary inner-ear gyroscopes, but they are far from perfect. An airplane pilot suffers this on a very practical level; flying into a cloud can cause him to lose all sense of level flight, which is why planes are equipped with artificial horizons and gyroscopes.

In the cochlea are the utricle and saccule, minuscule organs that are essential for the sense of balance. They are covered by a membrane with minute calcium carbonate crystals called otoliths, or ear stones. These ear stones lean like little magnets to the pull of gravity, like a whole bunch of tiny plumb lines. But just like a gyroscope, the response is progressive, not instantaneous.

I learned that the hard way once. Late one night I pulled into my garage, put my foot down, killed the ignition, and suddenly found myself in complete and utter darkness. I could no longer tell which way was up, and the motorcycle and I ended up in a heap on the floor. No, I could not blame liquor or anything, it was just that my sense of equilibrium was temporarily skewed.

Another disorienting moment I had was at Honda's factory test track, which has a vertical wall at each end. It was easy coming from the flat at 120 mph and bending gently until I was at right angles to the earth, but coming off the wall and trying to adjust my orientation 90 degrees to get back on the flat was confusing. I never did feel comfortable at it.

The third tiltmeter factor has to do with one's physical conditioning and how that affects the skills required to lean into a corner. According to Vincent Fennell, an M.D. and Kawasaki ZX-11 rider, not much research has been done on the subject, but essentially it is a proprioceptive system that keeps a person oriented by using the stimuli in the muscles, tendons and joints, whether riding a motorcycle at speed or getting out of bed in the middle of the night.

Doc Fennell feels that while the inner ear may possibly have some effect on cornering ability, the willingness to get a knee down is more based on athletic prowess, physical coordination, and the seat of the pants. Coordinated muscular effort can give a body a precise feeling of where it is, whether walking into a dark basement or sliding tires on the racetrack.

Dennis Pegelow, who runs the DP Motorcycle Safety Schools, feels the same. He believes the way to improve one's corning ability is to have confidence in the equipment and oneself, to be relaxed, and to practice over and over and over.

Age does not have to be a factor. Look at the Battle of the Legends at Daytona; Roger Rieman and Reg Pridmore are not couch potatoes.

People, riders, have different limits to their tiltmeters. Kevin Schwantz's is vastly more expanded than is mine. And mine varies from side to side. I can get more lean on a left hander than a right-hander. It also can vary from day to day; sometimes I'm slow, sometimes I'm verging on fast.

But I don't try to force it.

A road racer or go-fast rider always seems to have his head angled up a couple of degrees from the lean of the bike, keeping those little ear stones slightly more vertical. He is making sure that he won't get target fixation, won't forget to bring the bike back upright.

A few weeks ago four of us were out for a ride. Three of us had been riding for many years, and had ridden together a lot; the fourth fellow had been at the sport about a year. We three led at a nominal pace, went into an uphill right-hander, then into a sharper left-hander, still with no critical lean, but rider number four blissfully ran off the road on the second turn, flatly refusing to push the bike down another two degrees.

A separated shoulder ensued, but what really perplexed the poor guy was why he hadn't made the corner. We had set an easy pace, he had the bike in front to follow, and he had simply not done what was needed. He could not figure it out.

"Adjust your tiltmeter," I advised.

The Fastest Production Motorcycle Made

October 1994

I sit in the saddle of a Yamaha FZR1000 or a Honda CBR900RR or a Suzuki GSX-R750 or a Kawasaki ZX-11 and I am perfectly at home. These are fast motorcycles, with brakes and handling to match the speed.

I probably would not buy one, but that is strictly my own personal preference. It has nothing to do with my ability to enjoy such a machine; it is just that I have come to prefer slightly less "focused" motorcycles.

Although at one time I had to own "the fastest production motorcycle made," and it did me proud.

I was an impressionable teenager in 1959, reading about Triumph's new twin-carb 650. It was touted as an absolute butt-kicker, with performance that would humble anything on the road, including the Harley-Davidson Sportster.

"The Bonneville Triumphs are the fastest motorcycles made anywhere in the world today," said the ad. I had to have a Bonnie. Sacrifice was in order. My dates paid for themselves, my parents' gas got consumed, I used books from the college library rather than buying my own, and I had a job. In a year I got my money together, bought a ticket to London on Icelandic Airlines, arranged for the pickup of a new 1960 T120 at the factory in Meriden, and was on my way.

Back then, I might add, one saved enough on the factory price to pay for the airplane ticket, and when I was done playing around the speed-limitless roads of Europe, the factory would crate up the bike and ship it back to my local hometown dealer.

I thought that a summer on the lam with such a bike would be in order, especially since a Massachusetts traffic judge had recently advised me that driving was a privilege, not a right.

I took a train from London to Coventry, caught a bus out to the factory, and walked in. Everybody knew I was coming, everybody was happy to see me, and I was given a cup of tea and a guided tour of the premises.

Then we went outside, and there was my blue-and-white dream machine.

"Would you like us to show you how it works?" asked my guide.

"Good God!" I responded. "Here am I, taking delivery of the world's fastest production motorcycle and you think I need a lesson! Why do you even ask?"

A little embarrassed, my guide said, "Well, last year two Yanks came here to pick up a Thunderbird, which was parked right where yours is. One of them kicked it to life, rolled it off the stand, put it in gear, went down the driveway, across the road and into the ditch on the other side. I asked his friend why he had done that. The friend allowed as to how he'd never really ridden a motorcycle much before. The Yank broke his leg. So it is now policy to ask."

We sorted that out, and I went off to break in my new motorcycle; the factory had offered to do that first, essential maintenance for free. The next evening I was back with 500 miles on the odometer. The tuneup was done the following morning, and then I was ready to travel as many roads as I could in 10 weeks.

In this day and age 50 horsepower does not sound like a lot, but in 1960 it did. Especially considering the meager adhesive aspects of the

Dunlop K-70 tires and heat-dispersing qualities of the single-leading-shoe brakes. But I was impressed . . . you bet I was. I had a new Bell helmet, a horsehide jacket from Lewis Leathers, Acme boots, and the world, at least the Western European part, was mine.

In my first week I was sure I would never be able to control all those two score and 10 raging horses. Too much for the likes of me. Scotland, Ireland, Wales, England, France . . . by the time I got to Madrid I had those half-hundred ponies well corralled.

Well, more or less. I crashed in the Scottish Highlands, running off the road to avoid a startled sheep. And I'd put myself in a ditch in Ireland one soft summer evening, on a level, lonely country lane. Temporarily forgetting which side of the road I was supposed to be on, I went over to the right side when I saw an oncoming motorcycle . . . exactly as he did. While I was trying to figure out why this fellow was dead set on hitting me head-on I went onto the grass verge and into the ditch. My presumed antagonist stopped, looked down, and asked, "And now why'd you do such a stupid thing?"

He and his passenger helped me pull the bike out; no harm done.

I was learning. The European roads weren't exactly awash in fast motorcycles or cars, and I was pretty much king of wherever I went. Until I got on an autostrada in Italy, cruising along at a comfortable 90 mph somewhere in the vicinity of Bologna, and a flashy red car went by me. Let it go. Then another.

Spit on me once, shame on thee; spit on me twice, shame on me. I took off after the Ferraris, determined that Britannia's iron would rule the day. After some 10 miles of speeds bordering two miles a minute there was an abrupt decrease in power and wads of smoke began pouring out the left exhaust. I had holed a piston on the Bonnie.

I limped off the highway on one cylinder, found a railroad station, loaded the bike into a baggage car, and trained back to Milan, the nearest Triumph dealer of repute.

After having that little botheration fixed I rode up to Scandinavia, and understood immediately why Swedes were held in awe by puritanical Americans. Then a quick run back to Italy to see how Mediterranean passions compared to Baltic, and the final dash back to Britain.

I was into serious miles that summer, more than 10,000 of them. The big cost was gas, but even that was not too horrendous in those times. I slept at youth hostels, made my own meals, lived frugally. Twice the alternator failed, with temporary cessation of night riding, but Joe Lucas's magneto always kept the plugs sparking.

It was a magnificent summer. I rode like a mad bandit. Hundreds of miles every day. I only suffered one flat tire . . . in the middle of Paris.

My Bonnie was a product of 20 years of refinement, good, solid, state-of-the-art technology, with a cradle frame and Girling shocks and splayed-port head with twin Amal Monobloc carbs. Nothing exotic, but it withstood most of my abuse.

Although by the time I got back to the factory the bottom end was knocking a fair racket. I explained that this motorcycle was advertised as a 120-mph machine, I had gone 120 mph, and now listen to it. The lads said not to worry.

Two months later the Bonnie arrived at my local Triumph shop, the Draper Garage in Northampton, Massachusetts. Woody uncrated and set it up, and showed me the handwritten note warning that the engine had been completely rebuilt. That kind of consideration put me squarely in the Triumph camp for years.

In 1964 I bought another new Bonneville, as considerable changes had been made. This one had a unit-construction engine in a new frame, plugs fired by twin contact breakers, and at 365 pounds dry weighed 40 pounds less than its predecessor. And it put out a claimed 52 horsepower.

Life was less simple then, and I had a lot more competition. All the other British manufacturers now offered big two-carb twins, and I had to look out for BSAs and Nortons and Royal Enfields, as well as the presumptive Sportster CH.

The Bonnie's star was fading, but it had been a good run; owning the fastest motorcycle had been unmitigated fun. Now my inclinations were running more to distance than to speed, and my next new Triumph was a single-carb TR6R. Maybe it lacked a few miles at the very top end, but I didn't have to balance those silly Amals anymore.

Not to say that my delight in going fast has abated; maybe if I could get a deal on that new Kawasaki ZX-9R. . . .

ZPG vs. EPA

December 1994

I'm listening to this guy whining about government regulations screwing up the pleasure he gets out of motorcycles, namely the regulations that the Environmental Protection Agency brings to bear concerning emissions from engines.

Obviously Harry has not been to Mexico City or Athens recently. Or to Denver on a bad smog day.

Harry says that nobody has the right to tell him what he can or cannot do with his possessions. He spends his money, it's his. . . to do with as he chooses. If the feds want to mandate that the factory puts on a catalytic converter, fine; it's his constitutional right to take it off. If he wants to change carbs or camshafts or exhaust system, nobody can tell him not to.

Nice thought; would that life were that simple.

He's sporting a wedding ring, and I ask if he has any children. Four, he says proudly; three boys and a girl. He's already got them all into dirt bikes. He puffs up a bit, happy to be talking about family; he was the youngest of four siblings, too.

Zero Population Growth (ZPG) is not a concept that Harry is familiar with. "Well," I suggest, "perhaps you are the reason behind the government regulations."

Huh?

Too many people. Put one person in a house that is a thousand square feet he'll find it big enough. Put two, they'll make do. Put 10. . . they will have a problem. Same with this planet; Mother Nature could go about cleansing the air when the number of vehicles was X, but when the number got to 2X, even 3X, it was like a septic system getting overloaded. Ma Nature could not catch up.

Hence the government intrusion.

Nobody worried much about air pollution in this country back in 1950 when the population was about 145 million, driving a modest 35 million motorcycles, cars, and trucks. Now we are up to 265 million, and in this affluent era we have almost 200 million vehicles on the road. I ask Harry what other internal combustion engines he has in his possession. He's got a pickup, his wife has a people-mover, the oldest boy goes to a community college and has a car, and his daughter has one, too. Plus there is a motorhome. And his boat, with a 35-horse outboard on the back. He has two dirt bikes and an ATV, plus his dresser. And a little generator for when he's out camping. For his backyard he has a riding mower, and a 20-incher for the tight places. And a leaf-blower.

If he could hook all those crankshafts up in line Harry would be generating enough horsepower to move the *USS Saratoga* along at a good clip. And for every pony, there's pollution.

With the proper equipment and conditions an engineer can precisely measure how much air pollution any individual engine puts out. Size and horsepower have less to do with the equation than the condition of the powerplant. A 1995 Lincoln Town Car will probably emit less poison than a 1965 Norton Atlas, but any piston and spark-plug arrangement puts chemicals in the air that you wouldn't want your baby to breathe.

My little Briggs & Stratton-powered lawn mower generates about 3.5 horsepower, and I have been told by those who study such things that if it is way out of tune it can put out the same amount of hydrocarbons (nasty stuff) in one hour that my neighbor's new Chevrolet will expel in a 350-mile trip.

The problem in this country, and in many cities around the world, is quantity. Nature refreshes Herself . . . if She can. Look at it like a leaky boat; if you have a pump which can take 10 gallons a minute out of the hold, then you can ship nine gallons indefinitely. If you start taking in 11 gallons, you are going to sink.

By that notion, we are sinking this planet, not so much by the engines as by the number of people using them.

For the last two generations Harry's family has been doubling in size. And along with that size has come affluence, and with that affluence the desire to have more vehicles. When Harry was growing up in the Eisenhower era the family had a Plymouth and a push-mower. But he and his brother and sisters all had their own cars before they were 20.

Back in the 1950s few people thought about the harm all this combustion might be doing to the environment. Awareness came in the 1960s, and President Nixon signed the order establishing the Environmental Protection Agency in 1970. And that related directly to the internal combustion engine.

Anybody who has contemplated suicide knows that if you sit long enough in a closed garage with an engine running, you will die. Which should indicate that what comes out of the exhaust pipe isn't good.

The EPA began regulating the amount of hydrocarbons, carbon monoxide, and nitrogen oxides that could be emitted. Car engines are 80-percent cleaner than 25 years ago, says Martha Casey, press officer for the EPA.

Two-wheelers have it relatively easy; rules relating to motorcycles, established in 1977, are a good deal more lax than those for automobiles, and don't even deal with nitrogen oxides. California, with about 12 percent of the country's motor vehicles, has set its own, more stringent, standards, including evaporative emissions from fuel tanks. As California goes, so goes the nation.

The pass/fail test for vehicles is based on an 11-mile urban trip, with lots of stopping and starting, speeds up to 62 mph, and an average of about 20 mph. Put the vehicle on a single-roller dynamometer, run it through those 11 miles, analyze the emissions, and there you have it. The regs are a great deal more complicated, but that in essence is what goes on at the main EPA lab in Ann Arbor, Michigan.

Harry can whine and moan about catalytic converters, sealed carburetors and all the rest, but as long as we keep on increasing the number of people on this planet, we are going to need the regulations of outfits like the EPA. Next year the EPAcrats are going to start regulating the emissions of all those small garden engines that destroy the calm of Sunday morning.

And the rules will continue to, necessarily, become more stringent, unless we decide that Zero Population Growth is the way to go.

The Politically Incorrect Motorcyclist

February 1995

Five vehicles are in front of me, a camper leading. Third in line is a motorcycle. Everybody's freight-training, minding the double yellow, chugging along at about 45 mph.

Not deriving much pleasure out of this modest pace, at the next opening I zip across the two yellow lines, past two cars and the motorcycle, pull in, clear the next curve, get a short straight, and I'm gone. Lots of room, no danger, merely violating the often overly conservative, federally mandated, no-passing regulations.

A few minutes later I pull up to the Pozo Saloon. I'm talking to some friends outside when the overtaken motorcyclist arrives. He parks, takes off helmet and gloves, walks over to me and says, "You shouldn't have overtaken when you did; it gives all motorcyclists a bad name when people see you doing that."

Well, golly gee! I stand reprimanded . . . by one of the p.c. fuddy-duddies.

If any of you readers consider yourselves to be of the "politically correct" nature, I recommend you sharpen your pencil and prepare to start writing irate letters to the editor, or switch on your computer and flame me with some angry mail, demanding that I be fired, tarred and feathered, drawn and quartered.

That last was a quaint medieval custom in which four draft-horses were attached to the politically incorrect person's extremities and sent off in different directions.

Massachusetts, when I grew up there, was known as being a reasonably progressive state. Of late, however, it is suffering regression to an infantile status. Proof of this lies in the fact that the commonwealth has ordered a change in all signs that read: SLOW CHILDREN CROSSING. Some nincompoop bureaucrat and his "politically correct" ilk have determined that this semiotic indication . . . that drivers of motor vehicles should slow down because children may be crossing the street in the vicinity of the sign . . . may be an insult to developmentally disabled children.

I could take it a step further and ask whether these developmentally disabled children are slow of wit or slow of speed because they eat too much junk food and are fat. My response to all this is a Bronx raspberry. I find that the people who bother to waste their time on these p.c. efforts are boring, useless, and should be required to go earn a living.

It is also considered politically incorrect to use words that the reader may not understand, and I would judge that less than half of you could give me a definition for "semiotic." Go look it up in the dictionary; if you don't have a dictionary in your house, go to your local public library. If you don't know where that is, I rest my case.

While you're at it, run up "motorcycle" on the library's computerized filing system, and if there aren't at least 20 books in that category have a chat with the librarian about mechanistic discrimination and the expensive legal problems that might result.

What has all this to do with our dedication to the art of riding motorcycles? I could come up with an array of flippant answers, but instead I will simply say that I find, and you are free to disagree, that the insidious virus known as p.c. activity has infected my favorite sport.

A sharp-penned, politically incorrect editor of a club monthly has been smirking into his dry martinis for years while skewering real (as in: paid) motorcycle magazine editors in his sordid, albeit entertaining, publication. This is a no-win situation for the skewered, as Dr. Mayo (not his real name) has little better to do than needle those who do work for a living; he does it just for fun. I approve.

Occasionally his acerbic monologues get unwarranted attention, such as an opinionated editorial piece he did on the perils of a press introduction. Most motorcycle magazine editors tend to be rather good riders, and it is part of their profession to find out just what the lean angles of a new motorcycle are; Dr. Mayo is somewhat conservative in his riding style, more in line with my great-aunt Agatha than with Miguel DuHamel. The good Dr. Mayo's little piece of fluff and nonsense was fun to read, and prompted an angry response from a defensively p.c. editor, which was equally fun to read. Though I doubt the author meant it that way.

A much briefer reply could have skewered the skewerer: Such as: A second-string football player from Middleville High should not expect to have a good time playing with the Buffalo Bills, although he could learn a lot if he bothered to watch how they did things. Which would have sent Dr. Mayo to the whetstone to sharpen the point on his skewer.

The reality of motorcycling is that many riders ride like Dr. Mayo, while a small percentage go like bats out of hell, but most motorcyclists take a middling road. The bat-out-of-hell types tend to get the press, and the TV specials, and have become the outlaw bikers of the '90s, but I would dare to say that 95 percent of us cross the double yellow on occasion.

It seems one can't say anything even remotely negative about motorcyclists without causing an uproar. Are we motorcyclists losing our sense of humor, bowing to the stuffy, p.c. aspect of any situation? I think *The Wild One, Easy Rider,* and *Wild Angels* are quite entertaining movies. Not a p.c. thing to say, of course, as these movies show motorcyclists involved in drunken brawling, taking drugs, and even blaspheming.

Perhaps the next blockbuster movie will involve a wild bunch of polyestered Gold Wingers meeting for Sunday breakfast and going for a ride. The plot will hinge on an alternator going out. I can hardly wait for the hate mail on that.

Several years ago a TV commercial prompted many motorcyclists to protest. The humorous ad showed a loutish type in the doorway of a nice house, a parked motorcycle seen in the background, and the lout saying to the meek householder that he was here to pick up his daughter; "You don't have a problem with that, do ya?" Obviously my p.c. motorcycling cronies did, as the motorcycle soon disappeared from the picture.

We've become such a touchy lot. I say "Brit bike" a lot, and have yet to have a Brit take umbrage. But if I say Jap bike . . . dear me. I will have created an international incident and a swarm of fuddy-dudding Pacific Rimmers will descend upon and berate me for insensitivity. They will probably threaten me with a Singaporean swatting.

Heard the hoary old joke, the natural resting position of a motorcycle is lying on its side? Here they come again, the fuddy-duddies, trampling my roses and scaring the cats, shaking their fingers in my face and telling me that I shouldn't say such things.

Hey, guys, I do try very hard to keep the rubber side down and the shiny side up . . . but I think I'm going to go for a modestly fast run up Pozo Road this evening. Going like a slowish bat out of hell may be politically incorrect, but it's fun.

The Wave Debate

May 1995

Today I rode 250 miles, just a piffle over to Fresno and back. In accomplishing this minimal feat I passed a number of motorcycles, and I ran a little test.

The results were thus:

At some motorcyclists I waved, and they waved back.

At some motorcyclists I waved, and they did not wave back.

Some motorcyclists waved at me, and I waved back.

Some motorcyclists waved at me, and I did not wave at them.

Some motorcyclists did not wave at me, and I did not wave at them. Or was it vice versa?

Perhaps there is enough material here for a doctoral thesis: The Theory and Practice of the Wave: A Sociological Interpretation.

About a month ago I received an irate phone call. It was Q, demanding to know why I had ignored him as he rode down El Camino Real, the main street of our middling-sized burg. The fact was, I had not noticed him. Granted, he should be easy to notice since not many Triumph Hurricanes prowl the streets of this town of 23,000 inhabitants.

Obviously I had been thinking about something else, something far removed from the idea of exchanging a friendly wave with other motorcyclists. It happens.

I read 40 or more motorcycle publications a month: national magazines, regional magazines, lots of club magazines. And every month there are a couple of letters to the editor about "waving," maybe even an editorial. Apparently these scribblers think that you can make determinations as to the health of our motorcycling society by the percentage of waves returned.

A guy on a Zundapp waved at somebody on a BSA, and the BSA did not return the wave. The downfall of motorcycling as an American pastime is on the horizon.

A fellow on an Indian writes that the Marusho rider did not respond to his gesticulations, which means those darned rice-rocketeers are insidiously destroying The American Dream. These wave-happy folk are serious, really serious. They take it very personally when a wave is not returned.

To paraphrase Rhett Butler's words: Frankly, Harry, I don't give a damn. Maybe the guy on the Harley who did not wave back was me. Or I could have been the guy on the Kawasaki. Or the Honda. Or the Ural. Or anybody. I ride a lot of bikes . . . and I don't always wave. I'm a cheerful, friendly sort of guy. My wife loves me, or so she says. The cats will get on my lap on a chilly evening. We are invited out to dinner by people I am bold enough to call our friends. Just an average dude, that's me.

I ride down a road, see an oncoming motorcycle, and my tendency is to wave. It is a pleasurable thing to do, and merely says, "Hi! I'm having a good time on my bike, and I hope you are, too."

Back when I began riding there were one-tenth as many motorcycles on the road as there are today, and since we were such rarities we did usually wave at each other. Today you can find yourself waving a whole helluva lot. Try riding within a 100-mile radius of Sturgis in August. You won't have time to pull in the clutch and shift gears if you wave at everybody.

Some days I'm going down the road and am immersed in thought, pondering serious questions like: What is the meaning of life? or, What shall I have for lunch? And I am just too distracted to wave.

I certainly do not mean to insult, or affront, or provoke a conflict. I am merely thinking about other things than waving at oncoming motorcyclists. So I don't respond to a wave, or I return it too late for the other guy to see. I have visions of the other rider taking this all quite badly, calling a special meeting of his club in order to discuss this problem of non-waving motorcyclists, and perhaps getting legislation passed that would require motorcyclists to wave to each other.

I am sorry, truly sorry, I promise.

Maybe I got out of bed on the wrong side, which would mean I would have to crawl over my wife, and if it is 5 a.m. she might not be happy at being awakened, and that has set the tone for the day. So I'm grousing along U.S. Highway 101 and I flat do not feel like waving. That's allowable. At least I think it is, or maybe the Behavior Police will take my license away for not being suitably cheery.

Waving is merely an exhibition of friendliness, and, to a degree, good manners. If you like being an unfriendly fellow with bad manners, that is your choice. To each his own.

If I pass a motorcycle stopped on a lonely road, I always inquire as to the welfare of rider and machine. This is a courtesy which motorcyclists should show one another.

Although the number of chowderheads with flat tires and no repair kits can almost make one despair.

If I am in the fast lane of the Daniel Boone Expressway in St. Louis (Interstate 64) during evening rush hour, and at the last moment I see a bike pulled into the breakdown lane, I might not go to the trouble of circling around and coming back to see what is wrong . . . especially if I am due in University City in 20 minutes.

Sorry, but that is the way it is.

If I were crossing the Sahara Desert, I would most certainly wave at any passing rider. As a matter of fact I am sure we would both stop and talk about the road conditions. But I am not so concerned about waving at other motorcyclists during the Love Ride in California.

The wave is an acknowledgment of another rider. It is a nice thing to do, but it certainly is not mandatory.

Back to the main drag in Atascadero, California: Q said he might consider forgiving me my transgression if I came over for some tri-tip barbecue.

Done deal. Make mine rare.

Close Calls

June 1995

I am on my way home, going west on California 58, coming off the Temblor Hills and down to the Carrizo Plain. I could follow the paved highway over the Roller Coaster, but decide to go straight and take the unpaved road that goes by the near-nonexistent community of California Valley. Just to vary the routine.

The gravel road is straight as an arrow's flight, with gentle undulations. I'm beating along at about 50 mph, smelling the spring in the air, figuring to be home for supper. There's nobody out there but me.

Until I come over a rise and find 500 sheep dozing in and alongside the road directly in front of me. No time for anything but a very quick prayer and a sensitive squeeze of the brakes. Slowing down 800 pounds of Harley-Davidson Tour Glide on a dirt road cannot be done in too much of a hurry, because if the discs lock up life will get real exciting real quick. I just want to get this bike going as slowly as possible before the inevitable dilemma occurs when two objects try to occupy the same space at the same time.

Fortunately the sheep were as concerned about becoming mutton as I was about crashing, and began moving quickly out of my way. This sea of wool was parting before me like the Red Sea did for Moses.

And then I was clear, with half a thousand sheep tearing off across the valley, I imagine with shepherd and dogs soon in hot pursuit. My adrenal gland was kicking out hormones like nobody's business.

Close calls happen every now and then. Better on a motorcycle than in an airplane. I was coming into Chicago's O'Hare Airport one fine, cloudless day, crammed into a window seat on a DC10, and while idly staring at the passing landscape I noticed another plane which seemed to be vectoring in on us.

Obviously the pilots and the tower knew what was going on, so I continued to admire rooftops and horizons. But I snuck a look at the other plane, and it was getting closer. I didn't want to appear like a damned fool, so I tried to distract myself by counting cars on a road below. But that plane was continuing to move in on us.

Maybe I was the only one who was seeing this. Just as I worked up the gumption to yell for a stewardess, our plane accelerated and veered off to the left. A moment later the pilot came on the loudspeaker and said that because of congestion on the ground we were having a go-round, which would only delay us 10 minutes. Hah!

Close calls are a fact of life. We all go through lots of them, and cats go through even more.

Keeping a close call from becoming an accident has to do both with luck and with rider atttention. Luck is not negotiable; it's either there or it's not. Rider attention, though, is a skill which should be constantly honed to a fine edge.

What is important is the reaction of the rider to an incipient close call. Racers are primed for the unexpected, street riders are not. A dog runs out, a bend in the road develops a severely decreasing radius, a wooden pallet appears in front of you on a dark night . . . what happens?

Some riders freeze. I've frozen, with an "Oh my God!" on my lips as I skidded into the back of an unexpectedly stopping car . . . my very first accident. Some riders panic and do the wrong thing. I've done that too; ask Fireball Stein, who watched me kiss a cactus down in Mexico.

It all comes down to reaction time. When seconds get split, you don't have time to think about what you should do; you've got to know. As my parachute instructor said at Fort Benning, "If your main chute hasn't deployed at the count of four, pull your reserve. Don't think about it, do it, 'cause I promise you you're falling faster than your stupid brains can work."

A few years ago my wife-to-be was headed up Palomar Mountain on S6, a well-known county road near San Diego, California. It's twisty, getting twistier the higher one goes. She was on a Kawasaki EX500, going around a couple of fast turns, then setting up for a much tighter corner. She knew the road.

Any Palomar rider knows to stay well on his side of the road, but the Winnebago-ist coming down wasn't aware of the rule. Sue was neatly leaned into the left-hander when she saw the motorhome straddling the center line, a wide-eyed, terrified flatlander frozen at the steering wheel. Maybe four feet of pavement were left to her, which isn't much when heeled over.

Hitting the 'Bago was not a viable option. Straightening up and going onto the dirt shoulder would probably put her and bike down the side of the mountain; not a good idea.

So she threaded the needle, helmet practically grazing sheet aluminum, Dunlops scratching at the edge of the asphalt. But all that decision-making had to take place in split-seconds.

Some riders are good at this from day one. Me, I've had to learn it over the years. The more I ride, the better I get . . . I think.

When I was 17, I was tearing through a French village on my NSU 250. I had one helmet on my head, another hanging off the side of the gear on my luggage rack.

I turned onto a cobbled road going out of town, and a big truck was chuffing along at about five mph. Another big truck was overtaking it at about seven mph, with a great big orange arrow sticking out from the cab; that was before blinking turn signals. Heck, I'll just run down the gutter on the left and take them both.

I was up alongside the cab of truck number two when I realized the front wheels were actively turning to the left. He wasn't overtaking, he was making a left turn! And I was in the way!

I didn't want to brake on slick cobblestones, and I couldn't make the turn at my speed. But I headed that way, hit the curb, bounced up onto somebody's lawn, ploughed through a flower bed, and came to a stop. The truck was standing in the road, my extra helmet hanging from his front bumper.

I walked back to pick it up. The driver looked ashen as he took the helmet off the bumper and gave it to me. "*Vous avez de la chance, mon ami,*" he said, "*vous avez de la chance.*" You're lucky, my friend, you're lucky.

I went down the road a mile, parked, and sat there for an hour, shaking. Close call.

One bitterly cold early winter day in Massachusetts I went for a ride. I needed to clear my head, and thought that half an hour out in 20-degree weather would do the job. It hadn't snowed yet, so the roads were clear. I was bustling along, getting colder and colder, wondering why I was being so foolish.

The wind-chill factor at 50 mph on my unfaired BMW R69S was putting the temperature close to zero. I was on a little back road and as I shivered around a curve I saw a b-r-o-a-d stretch of ice in front of me. A small stream that ordinarily went under the road had frozen itself out of its sub-asphalt passage, flowed over the road, and a 30-foot stretch of bumpy ice was right there.

Too late to brake, too late to pray, too late to do anything but ride it out. I'd crashed before on ice, and knew how quickly it takes you down. Neutral throttle, light touch on the bars . . . and I was across and back on pavement. And warm. My adrenal gland had pumped so much epinephrine through my body in those split seconds that I was toasty right down to my fingertips. Amazing stuff, adrenalin; too bad we can't call it up on demand.

I rode into Haydenville feeling quite exhilarated, had four cups of coffee, and went home with a very clear head.

If I were a cat, I would have about two lives left. So I work hard at paying attention when riding, because I never know when the next close call will come along.

Why We Love Motorcycles

July 1995

It was a very nice dinner party . . . a dozen people, lots of plates on the white tablecloth, three glasses at every setting, and while I was trying to figure out which fork to use to eat the salad, my neighbor tried to engage me in conversation.

After all, one of the purposes of these little get-togethers is to natter away amusingly.

"And what do you do?" she asked.

A perfectly reasonable question. She wasn't prying, wasn't doing anything but trying to find some common ground that would allow us to converse in a manner that we would both find entertaining.

"I write for motorcycle magazines," I said.

"How fascinating," she observed, without a hint of sarcasm, tilting her well-coiffed head as she absorbed that nugget of information. I liked that response a lot better than the abrupt "Oh" that I sometimes get, indicating that any further verbal intercourse would be entirely unwelcome. "Tell me something, if you can," my dinner companion continued, "why do people love motorcycles?"

Fair question. I could have always done the stupid thing and said, "Well, lady, if you don't ride one yourself I'm afraid I can't tell you."

But that is a flat-out dumb response, the sort of swift, mindless repartee for which Mrs. Grady would have given me a "D" on in fifth grade. Why do we ride? Why do we love motorcycles?

You can come up with many different superficial answers, but there has to be some aspect that is common to all aficionados of motorcycledom.

We are a disparate lot. We have Grand Prix and Superbike racers making megabucks on world circuits, as well as hundreds of thousands of enthusiastic spectators lining the racetracks. Touring riders rolling their two-wheeled pachyderms along the byways of the planet. Antiquarians seeking to find the right carburetor for a 1921 Bradbury V-twin. Poseurs cruising the length of Hollywood Boulevard. A utilitarian commuting to work on an aging Suzuki GS450E. Collectors trying to get an example of every British vertical twin stuffed into their garage. Dirt bikers hauling their machines out to the desert in the backs of pickups. Sport riders scraping pegs on Appalachian roads.

Not every devotee is a rider. I know mechanics who would rather twiddle wrenches than ride; model makers who spend 40 hours perfecting the Tamiya Bimota Tesi; stamp collectors who admire their Vincent Black Shadows and Indian Chiefs under a magnifying glass; artists who cast them in bronze; painters who put them on canvas.

Now we see motorcycles in the advertising world, more and more. British and Italian machines as fashion statements, Japanese bikes as symbols of grace and speed, and Harleys promoting just about anything.

Some riders say that to ride is exhilarating . . . it makes the blood rush, the mind clear, the adrenaline flow. To a degree that is true, but what is the single factor that affects all those who love motorcycles, including those who ride slowly, or not at all?

Here is one possible response: It is the aesthetic, the beauty of the machines, that is the universal attraction. It doesn't matter who you are or what you do, but it is the physical beauty of the motorcycle that attracts the eye, which can be enhanced by the beauty of the motion.

We'll leave the economy-minded commuter on his unkempt CX500 out of this one—the exception that proves the rule.

The rider, the advertising exec, the collector, the racer, the spectator . . . they are all wrapped up in how a motorcycle looks, whether standing still or leaning into a corner. This aesthetic concept is all philosophical; ever since man has figured out he can think, he has been wondering about the nature of beauty.

I can stand on a corner at a race track and admire the elegance of the mechanized centaur carving the apex perfectly every time. And the riders find beauty in their ability to run a perfect lap, every shift just right, every move precise, spot-on.

I can go to a show and be captivated by a restored Brough SS80, paint and chrome buffed to glory. Or a customized Harley, with elaborate coloring and subtle adjustments to everything from the front fork to rear swinging arm. Or Jay Marino's lithographs of Indian Fours and Chiefs. Steve Posson's *Glory Days* statue in the foyer of the AMA Heritage museum.

I like to watch Dan Kyle wrenching on an Erion Racing Honda and Steve Huntzinger putting together an '08 Thor. To me there is beauty in witnessing the application of human ingenuity on an inanimate object, especially when the object itself is beautiful.

Of course, the purest aesthetic for me is to get astride a motorcycle and ride. Up California's Big Sur coast, for example. It doesn't really matter what I'm riding . . . old, new, sporting, touring, cutting edge or fuddy-duddy. The beauty of the motion is what counts, the response to the throttle, the angle of lean, the sea to my left, the mountains to my right, the ribbon of asphalt before me.

Beauty has many facets: the motorcycle itself, with lines and curves and colors; an artist's interpretation of the machine; the mechanic's fascination with efficiency; the accomplished rider's ability to move the motorcycle along the road, around the track.

All that, of course, went through my head in a split second, and I said to my dinner companion, "We find them beautiful."

She thought for a moment and then replied, "Yes, I suppose they are. I guess that is why my daughter bought one."

The Rain Riders

September 1995

Springtime along the coast of Central California can mean rain. And not your run-of-the-mill East Coast rain that gently falls, with which I am quite familiar, but the Pacific Ocean type of rain. Lots of it, in torrents.

I had to return a test bike to the Rider offices, which lie about 160 U.S. Highway 101 miles south and east of me, and a week's worth of the wet stuff was already in action. Storms were rolling in from the ocean like artillery barrages over the trenches of a World War I battlefield. Thunderheads would come in and pour down for six hours, then the skies would lighten up and patchy blue bits mixed with showers would arrive, until the next regiment of black clouds would come in over the Santa Lucia Mountains and flood out the people in the valley below us.

I loved it.

I suited up in the comfort of my home, which is always a good way to begin a rainy ride. It gives you time to prepare yourself properly to do battle with the elements. Standing under a leaking tree while struggling to pull on rain pants is not nearly as pleasant as sitting on a chair in the kitchen and dashing a splash of talcum powder inside the rubber boots to facilitate their going on. This calm approach is far more to my liking.

Rain boots on, rain pants on, bottoms snapped down over the rain boots. Waterproof jacket on, collar tightened down over an absorbent kerchief made from half an old tea towel, helmet on, then a pair of heavy rubber gloves with liners inside, the gauntlets fitting under the cuffs of the jacket, the cuffs snapped down tight.

I was as water-resistant as I was ever going to be. The neck is always the weak spot on a rainy ride, so the kerchief could soak up the wet and then be replaced by the other half.

Seven o'clock. Engine started, and out from under the carport. Heavy breathing was fogging my shield, but after I was out of the long, water-puddled drive and onto the road, it cleared up.

Five minutes later I was on the highway, heading toward the Cuesta Summit. It's a piffle by Colorado standards, only 1,522 feet above sea level, but "A Big Deal" on the California coast. It was clouded in at the top, and traffic was slowing. I crested the Cuesta and was coming down the south side of the grade when I saw a Honda Gold Wing coming up the hill, passing traffic, sending up a rooster-tail of spray. The rider was rainsuited right up to the chin, and we gave this big wave and bigger smile to each other as we passed. We couldn't see the smiles, of course, but we both knew they were there.

My kind of rider. Heck, if we had been going in the same direction we would probably have pulled over to some café and swapped stories about rain riding for an hour. And discreetly admitted to each other that one side benefit to rain riding is to see the faces of the cagers locked up inside their claustrophobic cocoons as we go swooshing by; such people don't, and probably never will be able to, understand.

I like the men and women who don't hide out when the wet weather comes, who know how to go mano-a-mano with Mother Nature when she's in a bad mood, who can ride 400 miles in a driving rain and love every mile of it. And be reasonably dry when they arrive.

Don't get me wrong, if I had my druthers the sky would always be sunny, the temperature about 75, and the wind be at my back. But into each life a little, or a lot of, rain must fall, and there is no reason you have to sit at home. Fair-weather riding is a good thing, but foul-weather riding can provide its own entertainment.

According to my paternal grandmother's line of thinking, suffering builds character. That is one way to rationalize the vicissitudes of temporal existence, I suppose, but my feeling about rain riding is that it provides a different sort of pleasure, that it can be truly fun. Rain is good; rain is important; we need rain; we should enjoy rain.

To ride happily in the rain, you have to keep in mind the Boy Scout motto: Be prepared. I see some guys riding through a storm in leather jacket and jeans, knowing they are soaked through to the skin. They'll get to where they're going, rip off all the wet stuff and climb into a dry martini, or a can of beer, and tell the assembled multitudes what a bitchin' ride it was.

But that's not being a rain rider; that's being a wet rider. Rather like the person who suffers through a night of camping out, not enjoying it at all, not willing to repeat the experience, but happily boasting about his wilderness prowess.

I've been a wet rider on occasion. Mostly because I looked up at the sky before I left home and said, "Nah, it'll never rain today," leaving the raingear in the shed. And knowing myself, I know I'll do it again some day.

My first rainsuit was a pair of rubberized pants and an old U.S. Army poncho that I would tie around my waist; it didn't work very well. After a year I found myself in soggy old England and went into a London shop called Pride & Clark . . . it had everything that a motorcyclist could dream of wanting, including a heavy, black "Clubman" suit made of some miracle (1950's variety) petrochemical byproduct call PVC . . . polyvinyl chloride. It was thick, clumsy stuff, like the old-fashioned oil-skins that fishermen used to wear, but it was certainly "water, oil, and petrol proof," as the brochure read. The Brits loved that early PVC, but I never took to it. I always wondered what happened to that suit; it just seemed to have vanished. I like to think the material was chemically unstable and after so many years it collapsed into its basic molecular structure.

The Age of Plastics was upon us in the 1960s, and a lot of lightweight raingear came on the market. But it all seemed to have a tendency to rip or crack or otherwise let the water in. I'd pack a suit away, not use it for three months, then bring it out just as a storm approached, only to find the crotch of the pants had disintegrated. Many a rain rider got home in a foul mood and with a wet wallet.

Of course there was the waxed cotton alternative, but I never cottoned to that. The venerable Barbour Company still makes it, but it is too antisocial for my liking, as it develops a stink of its own. No passenger is going to hang tight onto you when you're wearing a freshly waxed jacket.

Today a plethora of good raingear is on the market, much of it using the 1990s version of PVC, infinitely better and lighter. However, to qualify as a dedicated rain rider you have to be willing to put it on and get out and ride in the rain, whether it's a commute or a trip.

The more rain, the better. The first 15 minutes of falling water washes the oily residue of passing cars off the roadway, and then everything is fine. A certain caution is advisable, mostly watching for the motorists who haven't changed their windshield wipers in 10 years and can't see a damn thing.

As the rain pours down it is blown off your curved faceshield by the wind, while droplets whirl around in the peculiar vortexes behind the fairing. The tread pattern on your tires squeegees away the water, and the rubber grips clean asphalt. The ride is good, the passing countryside scrubbed and sparkling bright.

And if you come up on a motorcyclist with CLEMENT written on the back of his helmet, that'll be me. Give me a honk and pull in at the next roadhouse, and we'll talk about the pleasures of the wet day's ride. And hope that it has stopped raining by the time we're done.

The Motorcycle's Graveyard

December 1995

I needed a footpeg for a Seca II and I didn't want to pay the OEM price. It's not that I don't wish to support the manufacturers and distributors of new motorcycles, but I felt that $60 for a simple metal casting was rather excessive. Instead I went down to see Dan at "Bits & Pieces: The Central Coast's Motorcycle Wrecking Yard" . . . my local graveyard.

Not many people have been to a motorcycle cemetery. The English use the expression, "motorcycle breaker," which I like much better than "wrecking yard." Don't know why, as the term "breaker" is equally

destructive as "wrecking." "Salvage yard," on the other hand, has a reasonably good connotation. I could spend lots of time dissembling on these thoughts, deconstructing words and phrases . . . but in order to keep the flow of hate-mail down to an acceptable level, I won't.

Back in politically incorrect days there used to be junk yards, with acres of cars behind raggedy fences, and some vicious Dobie who stood guard all night in return for a bowl of kibbles.

There weren't many motorcycle junk yards, because there weren't many motorcycles. Usually they got ridden until they were plumb wore out, and there wasn't much worth salvaging at all. Often an old bike just got shoved in a corner of the barn and left . . . the forgotten Indian 101 Scout or Excelsior Super X being the dream of many antique buffs today.

Beginning in the late 1960s astute entrepreneurs realized that a lot more motorcycles were out and about, and that meant that you could collect a big pile of junk, or salvageable items, and make a living by selling needed bits and pieces to needy riders.

In the last 25 years the notion of motorcycle salvage yards has grown and blossomed. They're everywhere. A recent magazine ran a list of more than 400 salvage operations, and probably didn't get the half of them. These salvage yards range from the big, computerized operation to the little guy who figures there might be some money to be made if he parts out those 20 bikes he's collected over the years.

Dan's place, my local yard, is a fine example of a small operation. It was started back in 1975, and when Dan was graduating from high school in 1983 it happened to go up for sale. With a little help from dad, there was Dan, CEO, president, treasurer and janitor of his own business.

He was a young man, with a passion for motorcycles, and this seemed to be a natural. Out here in San Luis Obispo county, half way between Los Angeles and San Francisco, he doesn't have much competition, the next salvage op being about 100 miles away.

His is a one-man operation; when he's not at the shop, the shop is closed. He himself, and only he himself, knows where everything is. You want a cylinder head for an '82 GS750, he can go back and haul it out for you; nobody else can. He did attempt a computerized system some time back, but after trying it for a while, Dan figured he was much better at keeping it all in his own little cerebral computer; he was spending too much time keying stuff in.

He gets about five calls a day from people with bikes to sell, whether it's a fellow with a rusted KZ1300 that has been sitting behind the garage for five years, or an insurance agent with a crunched CBR600F2 to unload. Dan's got limited room, and only brings in about 15 bikes a month. He usually strips them down, keeping the high-demand items like undamaged plastic bits and sheet metal, forks, wheels, gas tanks; he also has an assortment of frames, cylinder heads, carburetors, et cetera. Sometimes he ends up junking the motor and other pieces; there's not much call for the well-used bottom end of an XS1100. To make a little money off the unusable, Dan has two bins out back, one for scrap steel, the other for aluminum.

Pricing is really up to the whim of the owner. The rule of thumb is 50 percent of what a dealer would get for new stock, but popular items might go a little higher, and something not much called for might be lower.

Dan did not have a Seca II peg on hand, which is not surprising for an operation his size.

At the other end of the salvage spectrum are the big guys, like Denny at Sport Wheels, some 25 miles southwest of Minneapolis on US 169. Out in the middle of farming country is a large, two-story building bordering the busy highway. Several other buildings in the area also belong to Sport Wheels; with five to eight thousand motorcycles on hand, Denny needs some room.

Sport Wheels has been in business for more than 25 years, and Denny had been wheeling and dealing in pre-owned motorcycles before that. Being a sensible man, his wife, daughter and son-in-law, and a dozen employees, help run the operation, which allows him lots of time to go riding.

When a salvage bike comes in, the info goes on a computer; nobody's head could deal with the quantity of material that Sport Wheels has on hand. First of all, the VIN numbers are checked to make sure it is a legit bike, and not something stolen. Good idea.

There are unscrupulous types out there. Need some plastic for your FZR 1000? Midnight Salvage just happens to have the fairing, without a nick on it. Maybe it was liberated from some unsuspecting owner's garage the week before. It is reasonably easy to tell whether a salvage outfit is reputable or not, if one is at all perspicacious.

After Sport Wheels establishes the bike's bonafides, the salable parts are listed—fenders, seat, swinging arm, regulator, etc. A removal ticket is attached to the bike, and as bits are taken off, they're checked off by hand. Until there is nothing left, ideally, or the remainder gets crunched.

Denny is hooked into the Orion hot-line system; with this high-tech communicator Sport Wheels is in instant touch with 50 or more similar enterprises. A salvage yard in Texas has a call for a CB900C transmission, doesn't have it on hand, keys in the needs, and Denny's back with price-quote and ready to have the tranny shipped out by UPS that afternoon.

Very efficient. And it makes a great deal of sense. There is no point to tossing out the perfectly good motorcycle parts which can happily be recycled; it would be wasteful.

Upwards of half a million motorcycles will be junked this year. Worn out, crashed, or just plain un-loved. Some might fall in a river, or be buried in an avalanche, but most will get to the salvage yards. It might be a 22-year-old Titan with 55,000 miles on the long-broken odometer, or a brand-new Vulcan that got nailed by an errant truck while parked.

Anyway, there I was with the need for a Seca II footpeg. I dialed Sport Wheels. Bingo!

All is fair in love, war, and saving a few bucks.

A Boring Bike

January 1996

During the usual press introduction where a lot of moto-journalists were eating and drinking at someone else's expense, not that it would ever influence our integrity, I was extolling the virtues of my wife's Seca II; one fellow could barely stifle a yawn. It was quite obvious that he felt that the machine did not warrant my plaudits, that the motorcycle in question was on a par with a good refrigerator or the collected words of American philosopher William James.

His world (the moto-scribe's, not James's) is rather circumscribed by high performance; he races, edits a magazine for racers, and has a long and commendable record in the world of fast motorcycles and riders. And if one is focused on one aspect of the sport, be it road-racing or land-yachting, one can sometimes fail to see the pleasures that the other fellow derives from his particular motorcycling niche.

I have never ridden what I consider to be a boring motorcycle, though some have certainly been more exciting than others. And I've been on a lot of bikes. From 49cc mopeds to the 1500cc Vulcan and Gold Wing. From a 98cc Ducati Gran Sport, shades of 1956, to a Bimota SB7. And I had a very good time on all of them.

Even on a BSA Bantam, 150cc version. Years ago I was staying on a ranch in western Kenya, and thought I should do something to help earn my keep. The manager, a long-time friend of my sister's, took me into a barn and showed me the little two-stroke covered with dust and cobwebs.

"Here you go," he said; "you can get this working and be useful." And I did and was. For a month I rambled all around the little town of Kitale, running errands, carrying lunch to the tractor drivers, doing the many little things that John needed done. Six horsepower on a good day, three speeds, and a flywheel magneto/generator which put out just enough juice to the headlight that an oncoming bicyclist could see my glowing bulb at 50 feet, but I could not see a thing. And equatorial nights are dark.

But I had a great time. Wasn't bored a bit.

Some riders think that if they're not on the latest neck-snapping 916 or YZF, it's not worth the effort. That an ATK or CR is the only thing to have off the pavement. That Saturday night on Main Street requires a Low Rider or a Thunderbird. That touring is not touring unless done on a Voyager or K/LT. However, it is the principle of boredom which is at issue here, not the capabilities of any machine.

Boredom is really a product of the Age of Leisure. Many people in this world have no leisure-time at all, and they would not find a little moped boring in the least. It's only rascals like us leading rather comfortable lives who find the time to raise a hand and stifle a yawn when I start talking about a 750 Nighthawk.

The performance parameters of the Nighthawk are certainly different from the VFR750, or RC45, but the entertainment quotient remains constant. Any motorcycle can be fun to ride. And a lot of the fun has to do with where you ride.

Back in 1970 I had a job in Saigon, compliments of my Uncle Sam. Along with the job I had access to limos and helicopters and Air America turboprops, but I needed some round-town wheels. Saigon was a helluva place to drive, with crammed streets and no parking. I went down to the motor pool to see what the offerings were; several Vespas were in a corner. "I want one of those," I said to the guy in charge, a young Vietnamese crisply turned out in pressed black slacks and a spotless white shirt.

"I am sorry, but the scooters are only for couriers; you cannot have one," was the polite reply.

I was reasonably sure that this local-hire knew he had a very good thing going, and was undoubtedly lending, or renting, some of the scooters out to his buddies. Parked next to his office was a very fine specimen of a Vespa, obviously his own choice.

"I'll take this one," I said, walking over to it.

"You cannot have a motorscooter. You must have a Scout. Or a Fairlane." He was getting pretty snotty.

I smilingly told him, "Look, Nguyen, do not forget that you work for me, and nowhere do I remember seeing that the motor pool director is entitled to his own vehicle. You sign that scooter out to me right now, or you'll be looking for work tomorrow."

The hollow threat worked, and ten minutes later I was tootling down Tu Do, to have a celebratory lunch on the river. A 150cc scooter, albeit with four speeds, may not quite be the stuff of dreams, but for Saigon wheels it did me fine. And I was the envy of my colleagues who spent many hours in traffic jams.

Bikes aren't boring, people are boring.

No, scratch that. People aren't boring, not even the ones who say they are bored. Forrest Gump was as close to boring as I've seen in a time, but even he, fictional character that he was, had some redemption. Though what it was escapes me at the moment.

At a recent rallying of motorcyclists a friend of mine, who considers himself a master of fine conversation and swift repartee, said that he found a lot of the other riders to be pretty boring, to have nothing to talk about that he found interesting. I felt that the problem was his, that he lacked the skills, or perhaps patience, to draw people out, to appreciate their real character.

The same with motorcycles. A sport rider can be baffled by the appeal of the cruiser bike, a dual-sport enthusiast mystified by touring rigs—unless he opens his mind to different ideas.

Some adrenalin-inspired riders feel that the only way to avoid the issue of boredom is to ride a motorcycle at the very limit of its capabilities—maybe even a little beyond. Whether it is an over-loaded touring bike or an over-powered sport bike, the thrills can be comparable. Motorcycles have usually been designed with a specific performance envelope in mind, but that does not mean a sport bike can't be taken on a cross-state jaunt, a touring bike down a twisting road.

To tell the truth, I cannot really imagine anyone being bored while on a motorcycle. Just to have the ability and the freedom to ride—it doesn't matter what on—is a marvel in this complicated world.

If you face the same twenty-mile stretch of road morning and evening 500 times a year, don't think of it as boring. Think of what it would be like to walk it, or take a horse and buggy; appreciate what you have. Boredom is really a product of a lack of imagination.

Motorcycles aren't boring. Boredom to me is sitting stalled in a traffic jam in a Dodge Viper when I could be cutting lanes on my aged GS850G.

I think I'll take the Seca II up the Big Sur Highway this evening; we'll see how boring that is.

The Summer of '56

February 1996

How does one's passion for motorcycling and traveling begin? Mine had to do with the traditional American coming of age ceremony—getting a driver's license.

And choosing my first motorcycle had to do with reading magazines.

Hitting 16 was a major event back in the Eisenhower years. It was as though the gates to the garden of sin were opened. Any 16-year-old would know how to lie about his sexual prowess, how to cadge a can of warm beer from an older guy, how to look cool when lighting up a cigarette, and how to talk knowledgeably about the most important thing of all . . . wheels.

My signifying birthday came in the middle of a Massachusetts winter. Dad gave me a couple of lessons in driving the family Ford, but quickly came to a sensible decision and passed me on to a professional. In March I got my permit to operate a four-wheeled motor vehicle, filling in the written test I had been properly prepped on, and then driving a licensing inspector up Main Street and parallel parking in front of the DMV office. A snap; that's what you paid the driving school for.

While my parents were quite generous in loaning me the family car, like any red-blooded American kid I wanted my own wheels. I wanted a motorcycle. The only motorized two-wheelers among my friends were little bitty things, and I wanted a big motorcycle, a real motorcycle, a motorcycle on which I could ride up to the high school, kick down the sidestand, light a cigarette, and have the girls go wild.

All right, agreed my trusting parents, but you will have to earn the money and pay for it yourself. Fair enough.

A job was easy to come by in 1956, as the work ethic was in full force and the pay was minimal. I got summer work at the local college on the building and grounds crew, cleaning the dorms, ripping off old wallpaper, scrubbing kitchens, et cetera. For $1.15 an hour. It was that or work piece-rate in the nearby shade-tobacco fields.

I had a friend teach me to ride his Whizzer and take me down again to the DMV. No written this time, and the inspector merely stood out front and watched me disappear around the corner; if I didn't come back in a reasonable time, I flunked. I circumnavigated the block, returned, did a mandatory figure-8 in the parking lot, and was cleared by the Commonwealth of Massachusetts to ride a motorcycle. Now all I had to do was buy one.

It would have to be a fall purchase, as I needed all summer to save up. I began to research my decision. A couple of motorcycle magazines were available down at Lizotte's, the local newsstand, tobacconist, and (some said) off-track betting joint, but I was always loathe to spend the necessary 35 cents. One of the older guys on my work crew, Ronnie, had a chromed and fox-tailed Harley 45, and he gave me his magazines to read. Naturally he promoted his brand, saying that the English stuff wouldn't stand up.

Sounds familiar.

Interesting information was in those magazines, and some 30 different brands were being touted. Harley was the major advertiser, but the little two-strokes did not interest me, and the 55" KH and the 74" FL were hopelessly out of my range. Indian was promoting its Trailblazers and Tomahawks heavily, but Ronnie counseled against the new range of Redskins. "No good," he said, "they're just selling limey junk under the Indian name."

Many of the British makes had full-page ads which I scrutinized carefully. Reading a road test I first looked at the top speed; that I could understand. Triumph had a Trophybird 650 that did spectacular things in the go-fast department, like 112 mph.

In the big-Brit category BSA had a Road Rocket; Ariel, a Huntmaster twin; Matchless, a Super Clubman; and Norton, the Dominator 99. But these were dream machines; no way was I going to get enough money to buy a used, let alone a new, one of these fire-breathers.

A few minor-league English marques were available, like Velocette, with the new 500cc Venom, and the Panther Model 100. Some shops still had unsold Vincents for sale, that company having gone out of business the year before. Two-strokes like the Dot and James and Francis-Barnett and Excelsior were on the market, but no ring-dings for this kid.

Many continental European bikes were being advertised: Adler, BMW, CZ, DKW, Gilera, Horex, Jawa, Maico, Moto Guzzi, NSU, Parilla, Puch, TWN, Zundapp. Some were too sophisticated, or strange, or piddly, for the likes of me; I wanted mainstream.

In August an NSU 500 went 211 mph at the Bonneville Salt Flats, and an NSU 250 was clocked at near 200 just before it crashed; then a Triumph 650 went 214 mph. These were important facts in an impressionable boy's mind.

Equally important as the hardware write-ups were the other stories in the magazines. Since I knew nothing about a motorcycling life-style, it behooved me to figure out what I could do with my bike after I bought it. I read about the races at Daytona and Catalina and nearby Laconia. I wasn't interested in racing myself, but it certainly seemed like a lot of people just went to have a good time.

I also read the travel stories. A fellow named Cliff Boswell wrote about touring and camping with a motorcycle, with articles on places like the Big Sur's California Highway 1 and Death Valley, and Mexico's Baja California. He certainly made it sound as though you could have a good time for little money, traveling on a motorcycle.

Two college fellows wrote about tripping around Europe on a pair of Triumph Tigers, a 650cc 110 and a 200cc Cub. The story told how the mis-matched pair cheerfully conquered mountain passes, managed rainy roads and sodden campsites, and wanted more.

I read everything in the magazines, including all the ads, the little bitty ones as well as the quarter- and half-pagers. Since the parents had mandated a helmet, even those ads got my attention. Clymer was offering an aptly named St. Christopher model, and Geno an aluminum and leather "touring helmet."

September came, I had only $230 in the kitty, and financial reality forced the purchase of a used NSU 250—with a little help from Dad. I don't remember the make of my first helmet, but after a night left out in the rain it appeared to be made of layers of cardboard glued together; the folks then bought me a Geno. Soon I went traveling on my 250, having taken all the advice I read to heart. Since then I have camped in Death Valley and Baja, seen the races at Laconia and Daytona, and toured Europe. I now live only a few miles from the Big Sur Highway, with some of the best riding in the world all around me.

Those magazines of the summer of '56 did me proud.

Dirt Road Tales

March 1996

I've long been a proponent of dual-purpose motorcycles, and I consider any motorcycle to have the possibility of at least a little bit of dualism. A three-way compromise is required, taking into account the condition of the road, the capabilities of the motorcycle, and one's own skills.

There are good dirt roads and there are bad dirt roads, and the badder they are the more fun they usually are; within reason. And while an FLH or a Voyager are essentially pavement-pounders, they are quite capable off the asphalt. And skill . . . that's just a matter of being willing to learn.

In my feckless youth I intrepidly rode my Indian Chief down an abandoned road deep in the Berkshire woods of western Massachusetts. When I got to a muddy patch I presumed that fast forward motion would see me through to the other side. The 600-pound motorcycle got bogged down to its axles. I was a long, long way from anywhere, and it took me several hours to drag it backwards to firm ground.

The lesson I learned was that motorcycles do get stuck.

My first real appreciation of dual-purposing was on my 1960

Triumph Bonneville, with state-of-the-art Dunlop K70s, and finding the miles and miles of dirt roads in the Quabbin Reservoir watershed in central Mass. After the Quabbin Dam had been constructed in the 1930s several small towns ended up under water, and the old roads that had connected these with other communities were all part of the hundreds of square miles of woods that provided the run-off to keep the reservoir full.

Hardly anybody used them, as they went nowhere, and I could fly along on a fall day, scattering red and yellow leaves in my wake, just me and my motor having a wonderful time. Today, unfortunately, these roads have been declared off-limits to motorized vehicles. Spoil-sports.

Granted, the road-oriented R-series Bonnie was not intended to be a dual-purpose bike, but the only difference between it and the cross-country C-series was that the latter had high pipes, a skid plate, and slightly knobbier tires. In the '60s most British twins and singles could be had with nominal off-road equipment, like the Norton P11 and BSA B44 Victor, but when that industry collapsed, so did the availability of big-bore dual-purpose machines.

So you made do with whatever you rode . . . like my BMW R75/5. The longest stretch of uninterrupted dirt road I've been on was a thousand-mile stretch up through the middle of Australia. My /5 had street tires and short handlebars, which provoked many adrenalin-raising moments when I would hit a long stretch of little tiny stones that the local road crews laid down thickly in an effort to anticipate the annual rain and mud. The front wheel would be ploughing a shallow trough, and I'd have to hang on tight to keep it pointing in the forward direction. I had a grand time, but must admit that after four days I was very glad to see pavement again.

My feeling is that any road is a good road, and the worse the condition of the road, the better the sights will be. Which explains taking a Gold Wing from Seven Lakes up to Chaco Culture National Historical Park in New Mexico.

Chaco is a marvelous place, but back in the early '80s the dirt road was a rutted mess. A Chaco ranger told me she liked it that way, as it kept the number of visitors way down; I agreed with her. A night camping out amongst those Anasazi ruins could make one believe in spirits.

I've been mechanically thwarted on my dirt excursions, too. I tried to ride a V65 Sabre up Echo Canyon Road in Death Valley, the sign at the beginning of the road advising four-wheel-drive and high clearance. About two miles after I left the pavement I was clambering up a rocky ledge and heard the sound of metal striking stone. I stopped, inspected, and, sure enough, I had cracked the sump. Fortunately it was a downhill coast all the way back to Furnace Creek, but I had to haul the bike to Los Angeles in a van. Ignominy.

My first go-round with a Japanese purpose-built dual-purpose bike was on a friend's AT125 two-stroke back in the late '60s. Jane was kind enough to let me try her new toy out, and while I found it a lot of fun, and awfully agile, I was a four-stroker, a big-bore fellow. These tiddlers might have their place, but it wouldn't be in my garage. Jane, a stern advocate of efficiency and cost-effectiveness, now rides an aging XL175, having turned down her husband's recent offer of a new DR because it was pink.

The '70s passed, and late in 1980 BMW came out with its first big dual-purpose machines, the R80G/S. New horizons were opening for me. I could run down to Mexico on the pavement, and then explore the bottom of Copper Canyon. This was great stuff.

The Europeans were taking these motorcycles seriously. Cagiva/Ducati produced the Elephant, and even Moto Guzzi tried the NTX 750; Paris-Dakar styling was all the rage.

The Japanese saw the niche for these sophisticated (i.e. electric starter), biggish, on/off-roaders and leapt into it. Honda sampled the waters with its shaft-driven, top-heavy XLV750; not a good one. Kawasaki came along with the KLR600, later 650, a large single with serious bad-roadability. It was one thing to zap down an old mining road on a thumper, quite another to kickstart the hot engine on a 100-degree day; I wanted the complicated simplicity of a button. Honda upped the ante with the NX650 and the Transalp, both excellent machines which did not sell a damn in this country.

Many Americans did not fully appreciate big dual-purpose bikes. Dirt riders wanted something really dirt-worthy which they would haul out to the forest or the desert in the back of the truck. And most pavement types were not interested in upswept pipes and skid plates. The Europeans, on the other hand, loved the d-p's . . . note the name, Transalp, rather than Transrocky.

I continue to find my pleasure in the unpaved. And to appreciate the advances in dual-sport technology. I'd like to see Yamaha's Super

Tenere and Honda's Africa Twin come into this country . . . but they won't, at least not until the OEMs figure they will sell in sufficient numbers to make the exercise profitable. I think Harley should turn out a dual-purpose Sportster, on the lines of the early CH.

I admit, I am more interested in the road aspect of these machines than in the serious trail riding that is so popular. Both are noble endeavors, but I lean to the street side of the dualism.

I want to try the Triumph Tiger for a blast down Baja and do the 50-mile beach stretch south of San Ignacio. Two thousand miles of pavement, 400 miles of dirt and sand—it would make a fine trip.

A Taste for Motorcycles

June 1996

The other day I was on the phone to the Honda guy who is responsible for fielding all the silly questions from the press, and after tending to business we were chatting about style. I had just seen some photographs of the European version of the CB750, and commented that I liked the Euro-styling of the squarish gas tank much better than the rounded lines on our Nighthawk.

Jim disagreed; he thought the Nighthawk looked better—and therein lies the moral. We each develop our own sense of taste, in movies, clothing, food, motorcycles, wine, everything.

For example, I am usually attired like a K-Mart fashion plate, with jeans, sweatshirt, and inexpensive running shoes. If I have to put on the dog, I go out as a product of Brooks Brothers, with a Harris tweed jacket, button-down shirt, and striped tie.

I see all these men's magazines full of ads from Bill Blass, Giorgio Armani, Ralph Lauren, but I'm not one of those slaves to fashion. Except I do have an Aerostich suit, a Hein Gericke leather jacket, and some other riding gear which I consider to be state of the motorcycling haberdasher's art.

If we all liked the same thing, life could be dull indeed. My wife watches *Home Improvement* on television and reads Stephen King books. I like reruns of *Taxi* and the Robicheaux mysteries.

Back to taste. My taste runs to simplicity, longevity. Which is why my tweed jacket is 15 years old, my main ride has 45,000 on the clock. I might ooh and aah over a 916, and beg for a ride, but unless I possessed an obscene amount of money I wouldn't need one in my garage. My ST1100 does me on the pavement, and a BMW GS is fine on the dirt roads. In both of those form is a distant second to function.

But taste in cruisers—now, there is a hard question, and I have seen some mighty tasty, and tasteless, creations at Daytona and Sturgis and Laughlin and places in between. Beauty is not only in the eyes of the beholders, but is a commodity much sought by motorcycle stylists.

A lot of competition exists in this particular world, a lot of name-calling and other less than tasteful behavior. The first commercial cruiser, as we have come to generically refer to that low-seated styling, appeared only 25 years ago, the Harley FX Super Glide. It was truly a design exercise, and function definitely followed form. It wasn't especially comfortable, not very good at going long distances, had no sporting pretensions, but it looked real fine to a lot of people.

Motorcyclists liked it, bought it. Kawasaki took note and brought out the first Oriental cruiser in 1976, the KZ900 LTD. It sold well, too, but soon the conventionally-minded designers decided that to really be a cruiser, the engine had to be a V-twin. Ergo, the Virago, from Yamaha, soon followed by Shadows, Vulcans, and Intruders.

The Virago immediately elicited complaints of copy-catism from Harley aficionados. Of course, nobody had chastised the American auto industry when it took to building Japanese look-alikes in the seventies. Being a stern advocate of capitalism, I am all in favor of the mercantilist adage: If the customer wants it, build it; just don't violate any patents or trademarks.

But everything changes. The original cruiser concept was leanish and meanish, factory versions of the for-real choppers. A rigid chop may look astoundingly cool, but it is about as comfortable to ride as going over Niagara Falls in a wooden barrel. The OEMs worked hard on selling the illusion of chopperdom, not the real thing.

As ready-made cruisers gained in popularity, so did the demands of the buyers, and trend-setting Harley saw that there were markets both for comparatively spartan Springer Softails and for sybaritic Fat Boys.

The porky, or hoggish, look was in, with big tires, big fenders, big, soft saddles, all curves, comfy.

All is fair in love, war, and motorcycle design, and the 1990s will be known as the Cruiser Decade. Harley led the way, going forward into the past, and everybody following, with the Honda Shadow ACE getting as close as anybody dared.

But this year the Japanese have taken cruiser designing a few steps further along. The low-slung look is the styling target, along with lots of metal, not plastic. As well as giving the owner the possibility of adding little doodads in order to allow him the self-delusional notion that he is creating a genuine custom bike.

Witness the Royal Star (we shall politely ignore the fact that Yamaha does not credit BSA with being the first to use that name, back in 1966). It has cruiser-esque styling, but a V-four engine. The fat look is very much in—with wide tires, acres of sheet metal, bulbous gas tank. And lots of official, Yamaha-approved bolt-on accessories. This is not an effort to copy the Harley so much as a very serious attempt to grab a hold of the styling reins and lead the market in a slightly different direction.

And the Star has been followed by an even more significant design, the new Honda Valkyrie. This is definitely cruiser-styling in bosomy Brunhilde guise, but serving to open up an entirely new look. A flat six engine is a pretty outrageous thought, but enough chrome and fancy paint will capture many an imagination. Nobody can accuse this gussied up and stripped down Gold Wing of being a Harley clone.

The cruiser market is fracturing. Whether these new designs will actually take long-term hold of the buyers' taste buds remains to be seen. The final arbiter in all this is the purchaser, the fellow willing to open his wallet. If motorcyclists are going to buy Stars and Valkyries on a continuing basis, if an aftermarket industry will generate endless products for these machines, then the Japanese will have opened up new styling territory . . . and more power to them.

So back to my phone call. I was saying how much I liked the styling on that GB500 Honda brought in a few years ago, and how maybe he should suggest to the marketing mavens that they think on it.

"Did you buy one?" he asked.

No, I didn't. Point made.

Oh Lord,
Please Don't Let Me Die Out Here!

July 1996

Supposedly I'm a pretty savvy motorcyclist. After a lot of years on the road, I should have learned the tricks of the trade.

Ah, but I do screw up. I know better, but I go ahead and do something suitably stupid anyway. I like to think I'm not the only person who does this, but I might be.

Like last November. I was riding a Harley down the Oregon coast on a typically damp day. Showers; 20 minutes of wet, 40 minutes of dry. Crossed over the line into California and got some weak sunlight; it was time for a late lunch when I neared Eureka. Took the CA 255 turn-off and pulled into the Samoa Cookhouse to eat. Then headed south for Ferndale.

A family friend lives there, Jackie Jett the Jam Queen; the ollalieberry is especially good. I chatted with her over a cup of tea, and after an hour was ready to get back on the road. I had never taken the loop that cuts southwest from Ferndale down to the coast at Cape Mendocino, then comes back into US 101 at the Humboldt Redwoods State Park. Jackie recommended it highly; the locals call it "going 'round the block." About a hundred mile block.

It would put a couple of extra hours on the clock, but so what. My next appointment wasn't until next morning in San Francisco. I headed off for the coast. The afternoon sun was being filtered through the clouds as I crossed over Bear River Ridge and dropped down to the sea.

Mattole Road is the official name of the slender strip of asphalt that runs the 70-odd miles from Ferndale down to the coast and back to US 101. Five miles of it runs along the beach just south of Cape Mendocino, and other than a repair crew working on a bridge there was nobody out there. Nobody at all. Just me and my Electra Glide, and the surf crashing in on unused beaches. I loved it.

Learned something, too. Got to the very little community of Petrolia and found that it was the site of the first oil well in California, back in 1865. They would put the crude in barrels, load it on ships at nearby Mattole Point, and send it down to Los Angeles to be refined into kerosene and lubricants.

Got to the next community, called Honeydew: one store and a phone booth. I looked at the map; a dirt road over Wilder Ridge would save me 25 miles. A fellow using the phone asked if he could help. What about Wilder Ridge? Wouldn't recommend it, he said, too slippery in this weather. Stick with the pavement, and watch out at Panther Pass; they're doing some construction and it's muddy.

A light rain started up on top of the mountain, and I stopped to put on my waterproofs. Then plunged down into the redwoods. Riding among those huge trees on a darkening, damp day was eery, shades of *Star Wars*. I came out on US 101 and headed south.

Now, this is where I screwed up. When I left Coos Bay that morning I had decided that I would spend the night either at Fort Bragg on the coast, or Willetts on 101, depending on the weather.

Fair enough. But I had lost two hours of daylight doing Mattole Road. It had been an exceptionally good ride, no regrets and all that, but my thinking was getting a bit fixated. I could stop anywhere I wanted . . . but I chose to stick to my old plan.

Drizzle. Dusk. Four-lane highway. No problem. I went by Garberville, neon motel signs brightly waving at me in the fast-disappearing light. Now it was getting dark, with raindrops obscuring vision, thin strips of fog licking in through the valleys. It was a long time since I had been up in these woods, and I had clean forgotten how much of 101 was not four-lane.

The road narrowed down to two lanes, wet and shiny, with logging trucks coming in the opposite direction. I was past Piercy by the time I realized this was not such a great idea. A couple of lodges were off in the woods, but I kept on going.

Signs for a detour. Great, exactly what I wanted on a dark and rainy night, just so I wouldn't get bored. Fortunately there were no muddy bits to test my balance and the Dunlops' gripping act. Leggett was coming up, just an intersection in the wilderness, no cheerful lights announcing the Blue Skies Motel. I was certainly not going to head to the coast in this mess. One-Oh-One it would be.

I tried to keep the taillights of the car in front in sight. Big trucks lumbered down as I climbed up to Rattlesnake Pass. I was going too slow and lost the vehicle ahead; I was all alone on a wet, black road. It was okay as long as nothing was coming, but the instant an oncoming headlight beam hit my riding glasses, the light refracting on the countless droplets, mixed in with the fog, I was reduced to focusing on the Botts dots, the reflectors down the middle of the road. Bless Mister Botts.

If a deer came out in front of me, we would both be history. If something had fallen off a vehicle, like a spare tire, I would never see it until I hit it.

No sign anywhere of hospitality alongside the road. Nothing. I could pull off and spend the night shivering under some water-soaked fir tree; I thought about that. This was not fun, this was dangerous. I was riding virtually blind. I was stupid. I could have stopped back in Garberville, gotten a nice room, had a good dinner, and called Cookie to say I'd be an hour late meeting him in San Francisco.

Not me. Oh no. I had to push on regardless. Regardless of what common sense would dictate. I wished Sue were with me; she wouldn't let me get into this mess. We'd be watching the evening news at the Humboldt House Inn, having a steak at the Waterwheel Restaurant, washed down by a bottle of California merlot.

Instead of riding down a rain-soaked road in the dark at 40 mph, slowing to half that when cars and trucks came in my direction, hoping that nothing was in my way, that some drunk local in a speeding frenzy wouldn't run up my tailpipes.

I was completely frazzled as I got to Laytonville. One gas station, one café with no liquor license, three shabby, aged motels. Heaven on earth takes many forms. The old-fashioned motel cabin had a heater that worked, and an attached garage to keep the Harley in. The tough steak and overcooked veggies got washed down with a glass of water, but I was happy. I was alive.

And I'll never let this happen again. . . . Wanna bet?

Counting My Blessings

August 1996

We're early risers around here, up with the dawn. That has nothing to do with commuter problems as I grapple with my word-smithing work at home, sitting at this machine and trying to rearrange the half million words in the English language into acceptable, interesting prose . . . I hope.

It takes a goodly amount of discipline to sit in this chair for many hours on a beautiful day, when several perfectly good motorcycles are under the carport or in the garage.

It's about nine o'clock. Ten minutes ago I decided to make myself a small pot of coffee. I don't much like the semi-automatic drip machines which make a quart or two of coffee at a time and keep the undrunk remainder warm; I like espresso. Which means I grind the beans, put together the little three-piece pot, stick it on the stove, and get back to work.

After putting the pot on I went out on the verandah, which runs the length of the east side of the house. We've just had two days of light rain, and now the sun was shining, with blue skies and some puffy white clouds on the horizon. The scene was a fine example of Mother Nature's work at her finest. I looked across the Salinas River valley to the far ridge, and everything was coming up green.

Knock your eyes out green. Emerald green. Green green. When spring comes to my part of California, it can be a real shocker.

Now, I'm not a religious man, in the conventional sense of going to church and reading the Good Book, but I am a man who knows when he is blessed. Family, friends, and good health are important, but I also consider other blessings. Like the fact that I live in a motorcyclist's paradise.

Truly. I have a thousand miles of nigh-on perfect road to ride within an hour of this house. By nigh-on perfect I mean small roads, curving roads, untrafficked roads, scenic roads, roads which are fun to ride. If I want a big road, there is US 101. Or CA 46. Those roads are useful for getting from Point A to Point B in as short a time as possible. Which is not in my interest when I am out for A Ride. In that case the destination becomes irrelevant; the process of getting there is all-important.

And I can ride these roads 12 months out of the year. This little blessing has a lot to do with my choice of occupations, of course. The minor miracles of computer, modem, fax, and FedEx allow me to process words 150 miles from the office, up here where real estate is less expensive, the countryside less crowded.

Excuse me a moment. From this chair here in my office I can hear the pot make bubbling noises; the coffee is done.

I'm back. That valley view is tempting. If I weren't such a responsible fellow, I'd probably get on a bike and head for Parkfield.

I can see the ride in my mind's eye. Go north on US 101 a few miles, then angle off at Paso Robles to pick up River Road. That runs along the east side of the Salinas River and is little used, with a lot of neat turns and curves as it follows property lines.

When it comes to the Estrella River, one of the main tributaries of the Salinas, there is no bridge, just a ford. Some water will be flowing over the pavement at the crossing after these rains, but nothing unfordable.

A couple of lefts and rights, San Miguel over on the far side of the river, and I'll be on Vineyard Canyon Road. As it goes up the canyon it rises more than 2000 feet. I took a couple of *Ducatisti* up there last month, and by the time we got to the Parkfield Café, 20-odd miles along, they were quite astounded. Living in the rather densely populated southern California, they had not really appreciated that congestion was not necessarily the norm. Scrubbing in untouched rubber on the very edges of their Pirelli Dragons, they thought that it was a fine road indeed.

Parkfield (zip code 93451) had a thousand inhabitants a hundred years ago; nowadays it is more like 40. The café is a last bastion for those of us who choose to ignore the dire warnings of well-intentioned doctors, as the place turns out some exceptionally tasty dead cow, properly charred on the outside, a little bloody on the inside. You can sit inside, outside on the porch, or at a picnic table on the grass. And if you don't feel like leaving, a small inn is right across the road.

Then I'll head south along Cholame Valley Road, 15 blissful miles through ranching country; it's mostly open range, and I'll watch out for cattle. The road connects with CA 46/41 just a hundred yards west of where these two highways split up. It was at this place that James Dean got to meet the Grim Reaper back in 1955, his Porsche colliding with a pickup truck. A mile from this country intersection is the Jack Ranch Café; a small memorial to Dean sits in the parking area, erected by a Japanese fan of the actor. Perhaps if Dean had stuck to riding his Triumph T100 . . .

Just west of the café I'll turn south on Bitterwater Road, 30 miles of little-used county byway where I probably won't see another vehicle, unless it is parked in front of one of the few barns along the way. The road runs right along the San Andreas fault-line—but not to worry. Major damage from earthquakes is done where two or more fault-lines intersect, as in Los Angeles or San Francisco. Along the line itself there is a lot of very slight movement, but nothing to worry about. (Famous last words: Ed.) The Temblor Range is to the east, but as the road passes Bitterwater Spring the country widens out into the Carrisa Plains, a wide, flat, water-challenged grazing land.

Bitterwater ends at CA 58, also known as the Carissa Highway (different cartographers have different notions of how to spell names), a minor east/west state road connecting the San Joaquin and Salinas River valleys. People in a hurry, and trucks, use other, bigger roads. So this will be all mine, and the surface is good, with hills, curves, bridges, lefts, rights, ups, downs—good riding. I'll see the white FAA towers on Black Mountain ahead; I can also see them from my house, which is 18 crow-flying miles further west.

CA 58 ends at Santa Margarita, just south of Atascadero. I'll pick up the old Royal Road, which Spanish horsemen and heavy wagons used to follow from the city of Our Lady of the Angels to the city of Saint Francis. US 101 has taken its place, but the old Camino Real exists in many places, and while not as fast as the four-lane US highway, is certainly a lot more interesting.

Well, I've drunk the coffee. And now that I've thought about it, I've decided we should never take our blessings for granted. I think I'll head to Parkfield; I can finish this tonight.

The Rhythm of the Road

September 1996

Some days are better than others. On Monday the septic tank might implode, on Tuesday I win the lottery. Neither has happened, but I think about such things.

Some days I get on a bike and I am as one with the machine and the road; the next day I might ride the same bike over the same road under the same blue skies, and find myself braking too soon, wobbling through corners, generally acting like a rider with a recent pre-frontal lobotomy.

For every road there is a rhythm. It might be the first time you have ever been down this particular section of State Highway 711, but if everything is precisely on cue, there will be a measure of perfection in the way you ride those 30, 50, 100 miles, each corner carved smoothly, each straightaway a smooth progression through the gears.

Or it could be your Sunday ride, a road you have vulcanized a hundred times or more. And some days are better than others.

Riding a good road is like listening to a live concert. You can always buy a CD of Morissette's *You Oughta Know,* or a toccata and fugue by

Bach, but the replaying is always, inevitably, the same. However, when you listen to musicians actually at work, whether it is a symphony orchestra or a rock group, there are always small differences. No matter how many times Hootie and the Blowfish play *Let Her Cry,* no two renditions will be exactly, precisely alike.

And that is what happens when we go for a ride—we're live.

I'm a lot better at riding a motorcycle than having anything to do with making music. My musical career peaked in the third grade when Mrs. Holloran assigned me the triangle; at appropriate moments I would bang the damn thing, trying to keep time with Mrs. H. as she tinkled the keys on the upright piano and my classmates fluted and drummed and made the sort of noises that might be construed as the rhythm and harmony to *Row, Row, Row Your Boat.*

Life improved when I began riding motorcycles. My first two bikes, an NSU Max and an Indian Chief, had no tachometers, requiring an educated ear to tell when they were putting out maximum horsepower. The learning experience was mildly expensive, as twice I bent a valve by over-revving the Max, and the day after I bought the elderly Chief I sent the rear piston down through the splash-guards—necessitating a new motor.

My ear improved. For mechanical sounds, that is. When I got to college I liked to sing in the shower. One of my roommates was in the Glee Club, and after several weeks of suffering in silence he told me that it actually pained him to hear me trash *Oh, What A Beautiful Morning.* Would I please refrain while he was around? Fair enough.

It turned out that I am tone-deaf. That is not to say I cannot appreciate music, I just cannot, or should not, sing or play an instrument. However, I have eclectic appreciation for those who do. I like the Doors and the Dead, Joan Baez and Seal, the Modern Jazz Quartet and the Allman Brothers, and classical music from Beethoven to Britten.

And I like the sound that a well-ridden motorcycle makes, from the whirring and ticking of valve-train noises to the suitably muffled exhaust note. The rider is the conductor of this little iron and alloy *arpeggio*, and the throttle is his baton. Done right, it is music to my ears.

Probably my most melodious ride, and the one that taught me most about the rhythm of the road, was my Velocette Venom Clubman. It was a sporting 500 single, with no tach, so I had to be attuned to the sound emanating from the fishtail muffler . . . when it hit 6000 rpm, shift. I rode it over the 10,000-foot Tioga Pass in California's Sierra Nevada mountains, and though that ride was 30 years ago, I can remember it as though it were yesterday.

The Velo and I were as one with the road, 60 narrow, twisty miles climbing up out of Mono Lake, shooting over the pass and down into Yosemite Valley; each shift precisely catching just the right rpm, accelerating, slowing, leaning, hardly any braking. It was late afternoon and the sun was casting my moving silhouette on the great rocks by Tenaya Lake; I felt like Mickey Mouse as the sorcerer's apprentice in *Fantasia,* with great shadows leaping along the wall. Then the asphalt led into the woods, the thick soft vegetation soaking up the sounds except for the perfectly pitched exhaust.

An engine certainly does not have to be at redline in order to enjoy a road. Smooth is the key for me, not dissonance, as in a John Cage composition or a grunge band.

A while back a friend and I were camping in the mountains. Great ride up, good campsite, fine fare, excellent sleep—and next morning as we headed off for another day of riding I found I had lost any sense of rhythm. It had just disappeared during the night. I was like a nervous horse, balking at the corners, tearing into the short straights, scalding the brakes whenever the road went out of sight. I was not riding well.

Finally my friend pulled around me and went ahead. He likes a smooth lead, and I was jerky as a garter snake with hiccups. It happens some times.

Each road and each rider and each motorcycle have their own perfect meshing. It is a melding of all three, but while the road and motorcycle stay the same, the rider's mood changes. Sometimes he'll ride *adagio*, leisurely, other times he'll want to be *allegro*, faster. He might find himself slicing a road as clean as a Duke Ellington horn solo, or creaking along like Mose Allison's *Parchman Farm.*

Good music is hard to make; it takes practice and concentration. And it is different music, different rhythms, for different times. Winging my way down the Blue Ridge Parkway can be as soft as a Tammy Wynette vocal, an easy, melodious ride. If I'm in the Rockies and running a Harley over Independence Pass, Bruce Springsteen comes to the ear. Or whisking down the Big Sur Highway on a GSX-R, as hard-edged and fast as Glenn Frey's *The Heat Is On.*

Rhythm is good. Sometimes you got it, sometimes you don't.

An Understanding Guy

December 1996

I'm cursed. Whether it's a lout on a GSX-R, a twit on a Harley, a squid on a BMW, each with his or her own agenda to promote, I can understand "where he's coming from."

Being in Webster's rearguard when it comes to language, I would prefer to say that I can understand "why this person is behaving as he does." However, being an understanding fellow, I'll go along with this slangish shorthand.

Back to motorcycles. I was once sitting in a charming little sidewalk café in Europe, along with half a dozen members of a small tour group. One of our people had chosen to park his Gold Wing on the sidewalk and play a Barry Manilow tape, or something of that ilk, on the sound system.

It was a beautiful afternoon, with birds in the trees, excellent refreshments, good conversation to be had, and there was this stupid tape. So I asked him to turn it off. He got huffy, but obliged.

I didn't approve of his attitude, but I understood it. He was a moderately wealthy fellow who wasn't getting any recognition. Back home folks probably tipped their hats and said, "Morning, Mr. Jones," but here he was just another motorcyclist. Since he had paid big to bring his own machine all the way across the Big Pond, he was going to see to it that passersby were aware that they were in the presence of a Big Man. Or the Ugly American, as the case may be.

I tend not to throw stones, metaphorically speaking, at other riders, because I'm sensitive to what most riders think. I've got a loutish side, a twittish side, a squidly side, so who am I to preach? I also don't like stones being thrown at me.

As long as you don't abuse the children and are kind to animals, I'll pretty much sit and listen to whatever bizarre philosophy you wish to propound, and perhaps make polite comments intimating that you are really some sick/sorry/stupid sumbich.

If anyone wants to leave Seattle, Washington, and ride his Valkerie along 3100 miles of Interstate 90 to Boston, Massachusetts, fine. Please don't invite me along, but I do understand why you want to do it. I'll take US 2, with excursions into our northern neighbor.

If you want to go around the world in the shortest time possible and set some sort of record, that's fine by me. As a matter of fact, you can invite me along on that one. I've even got some excellent route suggestions.

About the squid stuff; I certainly don't approve of, but I can understand, the appeal of risking life and limb on California's Mulholland Highway, Tennessee's Dragon Highway, or other public roads. I've done my share of showing off. Like it or not, many motorcyclists are today's equivalent of the daring young men in their flying machines. Testing one's mettle and tire adhesion can best be done at a race track, but many riders, mostly youthful I might note, prefer to do it in front of an audience of peers, or not to pay the hefty entry fee that a day at the track requires.

On the downside, civilians and insurance companies tend to think poorly of motorcyclists as a result of squidly antics. There is no known way to prevent squidliness, as most young people have to go through it on their way to maturity. We can only offer up small prayers that they will not damage themselves or others as they blunder through this phase.

I can understand bike-bashing by civilians. On the positive side we represent things they lack, like daring and freedom, and they are simply envious. On the negative side the benighted press has rarely made an effort to portray motorcyclists in a positive light. "Too boring," says the editor, when the ace cub reporter comes in with a piece on a Rider Rally; "look, kid, if you want your byline on the front page you're going to have to put a little sex and violence into the story."

Another aspect is the genuinely uncouth, loutish behavior of less than one percent of the motorcycling world; I wouldn't want those guys moving in next door. But even the gang mentality I can understand, the "one for all and all for one!" sort of thing. It has its appeal, especially for people from severely dysfunctional families. Gangs are a fact of contemporary life, a place where immature and insecure boys and girls can find the false courage of group activity.

I understand the Rich Urban Biker, a CPA or dentist in real life, who likes to dress up to look tough, loutish, with the not-so-secret desire to appear a little intimidating. It's the macho thing, gone to a costume party; he gets a small thrill when strutting down the sidewalk and the little old lady steps into the gutter to avoid him.

Or the RUBette who sheds her banker's business suit on Friday evening and works real hard to look like Mata Hari on a motorcycle; she gets a good deal of satisfaction by watching the guys drool over her.

And I do understand brand-bashing among motorcyclists. I cheerfully bashed BSAs when I was riding Triumph, but it was considered a healthy sport back in the sixties. Nobody took it too seriously, and after the Bonneville and Lightning duked it out on a back road, the loser could always blame a fouled plug or bad gas.

Nowadays, though, it is serious stuff. And there is even internecine strife, with BMW owners split between the R- and K-bikes, even Airheads versus Oilheads. Terrible! And genuinely unpleasant words have been known to be exchanged. Serves them right, as they have been smugly even-handed in their Hog- and Jap-bashing.

Really, we motorcyclists are taking ourselves much too seriously. I ride my motorcycle because it is fun. There are serious problems to be concerned with, such as overly big government, the Middle East, AIDS, TWA 800, unemployment, and a long, long list of others, and motorcycling should be a diversion, not a divisive issue.

I know that this column will provoke some irate readers to berate me for not agreeing with their own particular agendas. Ah well, that is the affliction of those accursed with being understanding.

One Hundred Anything

January 1997

This, gentle readers, is the 100th column that I have written for *Rider* magazine. One hundred months, seven and some years.

It doesn't seem like that.

We say time flies; oh no.

Alas, time stays, we go.

. . . So much for rhyming wisdom.

My subject matter has been rather eclectic—though the thread of motorcycling can generally be found. Some readers seem to like the way I string the words together, others charge me with being boring, irrelevant, and politically incorrect.

I am surprised that I've been doing this for so long. It began with the previous publisher, Denis Rouse, and previous editor, Tash Matsuoka, sitting me down to an expensive dinner up on the Monterey peninsula during the Laguna Seca AMA races in 1988. "Write us a column," they asked. "What about?" I asked. "Anything. Preferably to do with motorcycles," they said. Stuff me full of sushi and saki and I'll agree to anything.

The offer was made because I have biking in my blood; riding a motorcycle is what I like to do. I don't necessarily go very fast, but I go far.

So I began. It came easily. Having chosen wordsmithing as a profession, I could hammer out a thousand words with relative ease. I had been riding for more than 30 years, and since I feel that I average one brilliant (25 watt) idea a week, that already gave me some 1500 topics to deal with.

No dearth of material. My first column was about having an adventure. We should all seek adventures, and riding a motorcycle can be adventurous in itself. I do appreciate the transience of our mortal existence, and in this short span between whatever came before and whatever will come after I like to cram as many good memories, motorcycle and otherwise, as possible.

I say memories, because that is what stays with us. I might not be able to tell you what I had for dinner last Thursday, but I do remember that day in 1990, November 10th, when I was hurtling across the Chott El Jerid in North Africa on an R100GS. Or 1980, June 2nd, scrambling down Death Valley's Titus Canyon on a fully dressed CB900C. Or 1970, September 15th, taking a rented Laverda 750 two-up down the old Appian Way outside of Rome.

We had a picnic with us that day, and sat on Roman ruins eating prosciutto and pecorino cheese on fresh bread. After our meal I left my passenger to nap in the Italian sun while I went off for an hour to flog the Laverda through the nearby hills. What neither of us knew was that prostitutes frequented this locale, looking for lunchtime customers; my friend had several offers, which she politely declined.

One of my more academically inclined acquaintances, who writes learned books with lots of footnotes, asked me if I didn't get bored writing about motorcycles. "They don't seem to have much intellectural depth," he commented. True, but motorcycling has a great deal of breadth. It has history, lots of it, some of it is still waiting to be discovered in grandpa's attic. Technology, a hundred and ten years from Daimler's Einspur to Honda's CBR1100RR. Sociology, the tens of millions of RUBs and racers, and occasional rowdies, who ride, the men and women all over the world who make up our sport. Economics; American motorcyclists kick in at least $10 billion to the Gross Domestic Product in pursuit of our avocation. And more.

One hundred . . . the first time the speedo wings past that magic mark. Now, of course, many motorcycles can exceed 150 mph, but in the days of the 883 XLCH and 500 Gold Star, "doing the ton" was big thrills indeed. For me this was back in 1960, and I was in Ireland on my new Triumph Bonneville. I had owned it for two weeks, it was all properly broken in, and I was gingerly exploring the limits of that particular motorized envelope.

I was on a lonely road in County Cavan, angling down from Enniskillen to Dublin. Narrow asphalt, stone walls, sheepy meadows, and nary a vehicle in sight. I put the gearbox down to third and let her rip. Six thousand rpm came up fast, I shifted, the engine kept pulling, the road got narrower, I looked down, saw the speedo needle at 110, and backed off. And heard a funny sound. Not a bad funny sound, just something that wasn't there before.

I stopped and had a look. The factory, bless their environmentally friendly hearts, had stuffed a little perforated cone in the end of each muffler in an effort to reduce decibels, and riveted it in. The right side cone had blown out.

To even things up I had a fellow at the next garage take a hammer and chisel and bust the rivet on the left one as well.

One hundred; $100. The first time I got paid by a motorcycle magazine for my excellent prose was January, 1975. I had submitted a story to "Easyriders" magazine about riding a Harley to Afghanistan . . . a somewhat spurious account, as I had actually ridden there on a BMW. But no never-mind. They published it and sent a check.

It wasn't quite as good as winning a big lottery, but being paid to write about what I liked to do beat the heck out of teaching surly children or driving a hack or whatever else I was doing.

I began free-lancing from the East Coast, and in August, 1979, *Rider* magazine paid me for a story about flying into London, buying a used bike, and going on the road. Life was going to get real good.

A hundred. Nice figure. Even. Smooth. You can get the square root of it with no problem. A one and two zeros.

I may live to be 100. The family seems to have some pretty long-lived genes, but I'm willing to pack it in when I can no longer ride a motorcycle. Or maybe that is when I'll take up skydiving.

But that is all in the murky future. Who knows, some stray mutant asteroid may whack this little planet and knock us all off on February 11th, 2121.

Meanwhile, the publisher will call me a prima donna, the editor will charge me with Pollyanna-ism, the managing editor will condemn my syntax, and the art director will curse my hapless photography.

I imagine some readers will write hostile letters to the editor of this magazine because of this column, saying that they have no desire to read Clement's blathering.

Do it; I love hate mail.

In the meantime I'll get to work on the second hundred.

Packing Problems

May 1997

The first reality of traveling by motorcycle is that there is never enough room to pack everything you want to take. Especially if you are going two-up.

Long ago I met a couple who were traveling overland across Asia from England to Australia on a Suzuki 125. Everything they owned, personal effects, clothes, motorcycle gear, camping equipment, was all strapped and bungied on, using large, home-built pannier bags, a rugged luggage rack stacked high, and a monstrous tankbag. The bike was so overloaded that the sidestand did not work, and the rider had rigged up a little triangular stand that he carried on top of the tankbag and then would lean down and fit to the left footpeg when he stopped.

And I had been complaining about the lack of packing space on my BMW R75/5. How does that moralistic story go? "I was unhappy that I had no shoes, until I met a man who had no feet."

The memory of that 125 is a reminder to me that I have a long way to go before the carrying potential of a motorcycle is truly maxed out. I readily admit that I often grossly violate the GVWR of a bike; that Gross Vehicle Weight Rating is, to my mind, one of those silly legalisms that the motorcycle manufacturers have succumbed to, and can be treated with some indulgence.

In the Bad Old Days you loaded a couple of sacks of fertilizer on the back of your BSA Royal Star, and while the handling might suffer on the way home to the farm, you'd get there.

Nowadays the Politically Correct Squad will chastise me for exceeding the 380-pound load limit that my ST1100 is officially rated for. Shower-weight, Sue and I arrive collectively at 320 pounds (that's roughly a 2 to 1 ratio); helmets, jackets, boots, jeans, and the rest of the clothing we wear is another 30+ pounds. Add ten pounds of rain gear, tire repair stuff, tool kit—and all the baggage we are legally allowed to carry is ten pounds apiece.

However, I'll pack 20 pounds in each saddlebag, 20 on the tank, another 20 on the rack, and we're 60 pounds over GVWR. That's the second reality of motorcycle travel.

Last fall The Wife told me that we were going to Bosnia. BMW kindly offered us an R1100RT for the trip (fully expecting to get it back perforated with shrapnel holes), and all we had to do was to take along the right amount of stuff, including warm clothing and wet-weather gear. When we packed in the States, we were very conscious of the fact that everything, lightweight nylon duffels included, would have to be transferred to the RT. We got off the plane in Munich, Sue collected the bags and I the motorcycle, and we began shifting our load to the bike: her saddlebag, my saddlebag, our top-box and tankbag. By the time we had jammed every crevice and crack, there was still a small pile of stuff we hadn't managed to fit in; we packed it in a box and posted it home.

The RT luggage is frustrating. I am in favor of boxy containers that can be packed easily and find the BMW bags have too many crannies. I also despise those interior locking mechanisms; I understand the aesthetic and anti-theft principles involved, but I defy any RT owner to tell me that he has never bent a locking tang. And when one person has the keys and the other wants to get in a bag . . .

I like simplicity. My favorite pack-mule is the Gold Wing. The saddlebags have slanted openings, making it easy to stuff a stuffed bag inside. The trunk has high sides, so you don't have the contents flowing out as you try to close the lid. My only objection is that no good tankbag will fit up front.

For many years I traveled soft. On my first long trip, ten weeks at the incompetent age of 17, I put everything into a big duffel bag and lashed it to the back of my NSU Max. Two years later I bought a used Indian Chief, with leather bags and strong rack; it had okay carrying capacity, but poor reliability.

I moved on to British iron, and for years made do with a pair of ex-army knapsacks slung over the saddle, whatever I could fit on the tank, and a Craven luggage rack. Ken Craven knew how to build solid; I could put a hook on the rack and winch the motorcycle up. I liked that.

One year I was in Kashmir with a Craven rack on my Beemer and met a New Zealander who had a set of Krauser bags and rack on a similar BMW. The Kiwi was broke, and I liked the look of his setup. We made a deal, which made me a believer in hard bags.

My only untoward moment with the Krausers was about a year later, while crossing the Nullarbor Plain in Australia on a 500-mile stretch of dirt road. I had a small portable typewriter, an Olivetti 22, in one saddlebag, and the bag chose to fall off (those Krausers did suffer from rather weak attachments), hit the road, and bounce completely over the fellow riding behind me. But the saddlebag remained closed and the typewriter wasn't hurt; I strapped it back on and continued. Though my companion did insist on riding in front.

With my next bike I reverted to a Craven rack—and Craven saddlebags, which were big, strong, deep, detachable boxes that you could fill with wet sand if you so desired. Attractive looks ranked low on my list of priorities; I wanted function. With my R60/5 set up this way I went on two long, two-up camping trips, one to Central America, the other to Alaska. I could carry a lot.

A small number of motorcycles in the fifties and sixties could be ordered-up with touring gear. Harleys had offered saddlebags, racks and windshields for generations. BMW had its sources. The Brits had Craven and Rodark and the like. In the sixties and seventies a number of American aftermarket companies like Bates and Beck and Vetter began providing what the manufacturer would not. Which made the OEMs sit up and take notice; there was money to be made here.

Soon came the advent of turn-key touring; plunk your money down and a BMW RT or Honda Interstate was yours for going wherever. Every manufacturer had one in the early eighties. Even Triumph produced the T140 Executive. If a model wouldn't sell (Honda CBX 1000, Yamaha Seca 750, Kawasaki KZ1300), the company would slap on a fairing and bags . . . without much success. Overkill arrived with the Suzuki Cavalcade; it was a two-wheeled Winnebago, poorly conceived, badly marketed. Then Honda showed how to do it right with the GL1500.

Simplification has followed with the latest cruiser-touring models. Harley's FLHS and Road King models set the standards, and now Yamaha has the Royal Star Tour Deluxe, Honda the Valkyrie Tourer (ghastly word). Saddlebags, luggage rack, and a windshield can be mounted on just about any cruiser. Or bolt Nonfango or Givi luggage onto your sport bike. Or a JC Whitney rack on your aged standard. Any bike can be made to carry a traveling load.

Some bikes pack easy, some don't. We all have to cope with, and accept, the finite limits of a motorcycle's carrying capacity. And perhaps learn how to overcome them.

When I overpack a bike, I know the handling will suffer; I take that into account. But when we've set up camp in some mountain meadow, put the stew pot to simmering, opened the bottle of wine, the sun setting over a far ridge . . . I'm glad we carried all that gear along.

If It Ain't Broke . . .

June 1997

Out there between Cleveland and Omaha on I-80 there's a lot of opportunity for ruminating. That is, chewing the mental cud. Sometimes I spend my time contemplating the two, three, four, or six cylinders that are there under me somewhere, chuffing away, sipping gas, four to 24 valves opening and closing, opening and closing, hoping that nothing will go wrong, marveling at the engine's ability to continue to do this repetitive work.

Before the FSSNOC (Four Stroke Singles National Owners Club —a highly estimable organization) militia sets up a hullaballoo to have me tarred, feathered, and run out of town on an Enfield Bullet, let me say that I have cheerfully ridden a single cylinder cross-country. After doing that in 1965 on my new Velocette Venom, I decided I much preferred the lessened vibration of multiple pistons.

These piston, connecting rod, and crankshaft motors have been around for 150 years, and powering vehicles for the last 110. Though not always very reliably; in the not-too-distant 1960s my street bikes would suffer the occasional holed piston, or dropped valve, or broken con-rod, or chewed-up crankshaft. I am glad that our reciprocating, internal-combustion motorcycle engines have evolved to where they are today, even if they are a tad on the old-fashioned side.

People have suggested alternatives to this old up-and-down, up-and-down type of mechanics, such as rotary engines, but as a wise man said to me once—it's simple, it's cheap, and it works. Why mess with success?

If it ain't broke, don't fix it.

There really has not been much in the way of genuinely original thinking concerning motorcycle engines over the past 90 years. What we ride today has been a result of constant improvement in metallurgy, design, and production techniques.

Who actually gets the credit for conceiving the internal-combustion engine seems to be a bit unclear, but the notion was being considered at least 300 years ago. In the 1850s a French fellow, Etienne Lenoir, built a reciprocating motor to serve as an industrial powerplant, with about a 60 rpm redline. But given 60 rpm, some bright fellow could see 600, and then 6000, and then . . .

By the 1880s lots of people were trying to use the idea to build automotive (self-moving) vehicles; Gottlieb Daimler got the credit line. And what we have today is merely a variation on his theme.

I doubt that the Wright brothers foresaw the jet plane, nor James Watt the 200-mph electric trains of today, but Daimler would understand BMW's F650 quite well.

In motorcycle engine terms, much time and effort has been well spent improving on what has gone before. A single cylinder was the first powerplant, and by the turn of the century V-twins, opposed twins, and parallel twins had all been used to motivate two- and three-wheeled vehicles.

While singles and twins are very traditional, it is the multis that I find most interesting. The best-known, and most successful, was probably the Honda 750 of 1969, a knock-your-socks-off accomplishment.

The Japanese, while quite good at mildly creative thinking, are really best recognized for the much harder work of transferring these ideas to a production line, of bringing an entirely new motorcycle to the public. But they did nothing very new. Charles Binks, an Englishman, developed a four-in-line for a motorcycle in the early part of the century, and it could be mounted longitudinally or transversely in the frame, according to the customer's desire. This 385cc sidevalve was adapted by the short-lived Evart-Hall manufacturer (1903-05), and then disappeared.

That was the temporary end of the transverse four, but longitudinal fours marched on and on. On this side of the pond the last Indian 4 was built in 1941, in Europe the Danish Nimbus went on until 1957. And then the concept was restructured and resurrected by BMW in 1983.

Back in 1902 the French Clement company built racing bikes with V-four engines, the terror of the tracks in those bygone days. A generation later, in 1927, Englishman George Brough introduced his short-lived 1000cc V-four. In 1931 the public saw the Matchless Silver Hawk, using a narrow-angle OHC V-four; however, the Depression doomed this creative, and expensive, effort, and it was off the market five years later.

In 1964 Joe Berliner, the American Ducati importer, prevailed on the Italian factory to develop a big engine that could compete with the Harley-Davidson. "*Nessuno problemo,*" said the company, and the 1200cc Apollo was soon readied, with a V-four, cylinders set 90 degrees apart, the crankshaft laying transversely athwart the frame. Nice idea, and nobody has satisfactorily explained why it never went into production. The V-four did not reappear until Honda tried to better its own in-line four with the Sabre in 1982.

We should remember that 1931 also saw the Ariel Square Four come to the showrooms, and this multi had a decent lifespan, staying in the line until 1958.

Just before the turn of the century (to show how long ago this sort of thinking began) a Brit named H. Capel Holden was building flat-four motorcycles, but his design fell into disuse after 1900. In the 1930s several European manufacturers developed opposed fours, laid flat as in the Gold Wing of 1975; the best known were the German Zundapp K-800 and Austrian Puch 800. As an alternative, George Brough built his Golden Dream in 1939, using an opposed four standing up, cylinders out to each side for better cooling. World War II torpedoed that idea.

In the early 1950s Englishman Ron Wooler built some very refined 500cc opposed fours, but the eponymous company priced itself out of existence by 1955.

The late 1920s saw Italian engineers begin developing the transverse in-line four for racing purposes. The DOHC, air-cooled OPRA of 1927 evolved into the liquid-cooled Gilera-Rondine of 1935, and by the end of the decade most serious Italian competitors had a four-banger on the track. MV Agusta picked up the idea after World War II and won an awful lot of races; that company had a street-going prototype in 1949, which did not actually get produced until 1966.

In 1950 a Norton engineer realized that the racing days of the big OHC single were definitely limited, and sketched a lovely 500cc, DOHC, water-cooled, transverse in-line four to replace the Manx—but with money being tight it never got beyond that pencil and paper stage. In 1962 Ariel designer Val Page drew up plans for a transverse, in-line, 700cc four, with electric starter, but the company nixed the notion; no comment.

So I'm motoring along past Des Moines on my in-line four; it's a long way evolved from the Binks of 95 years ago, with double overhead camshafts. liquid-cooling, and a 10,000 rpm redline, but the lineal heritage of the reciprocating internal combustion engine is not to be denied.

What I'm waiting for is something entirely new and different . . . and better. Perhaps by 2030. . . .

How Rude!

October 1997

I'm threading through the traffic in the local Supermarket & Mall parking lot, a car is exiting a parking place, and I pull in. Turn the key off, put the sidestand down, start to get off the bike, and . . .

"You goshdarnedsonofawitch! That's my goshdarned parking place . . .," or words to that effect. I turn my head and see a woman, a well-dressed, well-coiffed woman, leaning out of the window of her shiny new Cherokee, turning the air blue with invective.

Shoppers are stopping to enjoy the show. "You farouking bikers think you can do whatever you farouking want, " she screeches; "I hope you farouking die!"

Dear me. Considering the fact I was on my wife's Seca II, wearing a white polo shirt and a white open-face helmet, I didn't think I quite qualified as a hardcore biker . . . but images can be deceiving.

In the interest of community harmony I would have been happy to withdraw and leave her the parking place, but before I could say more than "Sorry, I . . .," she straightened the three phalangeal bones in the middle finger of her left hand and screeched off.

Let me tell you this—as a civilization the human race is definitely on a downhill run.

Don't get me wrong—I think we can turn the situation around, but first we have to be aware of its gravity.

Ever since *homo* became *sapiens* some hundred thousand years ago, we have been rude to each other. Images of grunting, club-toting neanderthals dragging comely women by their long blonde tresses back to the cave were seared on my boyish memory when I was very young. It is probable that some 2000 years ago my Roman ancestors were busily hauling my Anglo antecedents off to slavery in sunny Italy—which might not have been such a bad deal.

And here in this very country my great-great-great-grandfather Adlard Welby wrote that, during his 1819 journey from Hoboken, New Jersey, to Harmony, Illinois, he found the inn-keepers often unpleasant to the clients . . . because there wasn't much competition. In Chambersburgh, Pennsylvania, one rainy evening he had a disagreement with a tavern-owner, and " . . . the brute landlord, not withstanding the storm, told us we had better drive on to the next town if we disliked his accomodations."

Rude innkeepers. Yes, they are a pain to the old psyche, but occasionally we find them . . . and sometimes have to put up with them. It's not too bad when you can pick up your credit card and go across the road to another sleeping spot, but when the Mouldy Mattress Motel is the only game within 50 miles, and it is a dark and stormy night, things are a bit different.

It is one thing to show up at the Best Western with a straight-piped Boss Hoss and a half empty quart of Jim Beam in your saddlebag, quite another to be a responsible, respectable citizen on a tasteful, quiet motorcycle. Rudeness towards motorcyclists is often directed at who people think we are, rather than who we actually are.

Establishments purveying foodstuffs are another magnet to rudeness. Sometimes the fault is the uppity waiters, who are deigning to offer you a menu, and perhaps will come back for your order, and might even possibly bring you the food within the hour. I always liked the part in the *Five Easy Pieces* movie where Jack Nicholson is trying to order a simple sandwich from an uncooperative waitress . . . oh yes, we've all been there.

Other times it is the customer who is at fault; Joe Schmo is getting no respect from wife, kids, colleagues, so he thinks he can take it out on the wait-person. Bad idea. I mean, rudeness can provoke rudeness, and I remember one of the Beatles reminiscing how in his waiting days he'd expectorate in the food of customers he didn't like.

As my friend Kurt points out, any retail merchant will tell you that a certain percent of his customers are rude people. Kurt thinks that the figure can be as high as 1 in 20, which is quite depressing . . . but that percentage is corroborated by others. Equally depressing is the fact that many rude people are not even aware that they are an unpleasant lot to be with. Not a clue. They don't understand why nobody likes them.

Another place where I have seen glorious examples of rudeness is at a motorcycle shop's parts counter. Most customers, be it for a new bike, parts, or service, are pretty decent folk, pleasant, understanding of pricing structures, overworked mechanics, and back-ordered parts. But a constant minority are genuinely obnoxious, and I admire the calmness with which most shop personnel deal with them. These are customers who are just plain objectionable, which is sometimes a result of ignorance, or serious flaws in the personality.

Like the guy who storms out loudly saying he can buy a new GL for $2000 less if he goes out of state—and shows up two weeks later with a new bike that was improperly prepped, demanding this shop put everything right. Or the guy who wants a widget for an '82 Tempter, and is irate that it is not in stock. Or the guy who brings in a rolling wreck for a new tire, and new tire only, and explodes when he returns and finds that the shop has not tuned the varnished carbs, adjusted the steering head bearings, and washed five years of accumulated filth off.

Rude people are often trying to get a little leverage, and think that rudeness helps to intimidate the other person.

Rudeness really starts at home. I don't think there is a rude gene, it's an acquired trait. Although Kurt would disagree with me on that point. If parents are rude to each other, the child sees it as acceptable behavior. Also, a hundred hours a week of watching rude people on television doesn't help. Child becomes adult, and being rude to family, colleagues, and strangers is a way of life. The opposite of rudeness is good manners, again, an acquired trait. And good manners are an absolute necessity in this rather crowded world we live in.

There are five billion people on this planet, and most of the seriously rude ones seem to be driving on American highways on Friday afternoon. I don't know what it is about "the car," but put an ill-tempered brute behind the wheel and he takes it as his personal mission to endanger as many lives as possible. Don't confuse rudeness with incompetent driving; that is the difference between first-degree murder and manslaughter. The rude fellow driving a car knows full well what he is doing when he cuts you off, when he doesn't allow you to merge, when he speeds up as you try to pass.

And the rude rider isn't much better, except he is potentially far less destructive. The basic element of rudeness is lack of consideration for others, like shattering the early morning neighborhood calm with a loud exhaust, or parking a bike so it blocks a handicapped zone,

I do like the line in the Bible about doing unto others as you would have them do unto you; maybe that is the cure for rudeness. If we adhere to that thought, we might get our civilization back on a well-mannered track.

The Wuss Factor

January 1998

The other day I wussed. It's a terrible thing to admit, but I did.

It all happened this way. I was riding through the middle of Utah, coming down State Route 24 from I-40 to Hanksville, and I saw a sign for Goblin Valley State Park. I had heard of Goblin Valley over the years, and here I was being offered the opportunity to go have a look.

The entrance approach was along about six miles of narrow, unmarked asphalt, and then another six miles of good gravel road. The valley itself is full of wind-sculpted stones which, if you are inclined to half-close your eyes and fuzz your vision, look like legions of ugly, large-headed goblins, the stuff of Halloween nightmares.

Interesting. Utah obviously felt that this bit of real estate out along the San Rafael Reef had limited agricultural or urban use, so why not turn it into a state park. I wandered about for an hour, then remounted.

But first I had a look at my map which, admittedly, was a trifle large-scale at 1,250,000 to 1, about 20 miles to the inch. A light, sectioned line was running from the park southwest to near Caineville on SR 24; the legend told me that the line interpreted to an "earth" road, which I supposed meant it was a pretty crude affair. No distance marked, but the inch and a quarter looked like 25 miles—as opposed to 50 miles going the other way, via Hanksville.

Taking that route seemed reasonable to me, altough it would have been even more reasonable if I had a dual-purpose bike; the Harley Dyna I was riding would just have to do. It was Monday and the park ranger's day off, so there was no one to ask about the condition of the road. Harley and I are going to have a minor adventure.

At the junction a wooden sign pointed me towards MUDDY RIVER 13; no mention of how far SR 24 was. The old Muddy, according to my map, was a longish river stretching down from the Wasatch Plateau to Lake Powell. It had been raining a lot in this part of the country this summer, so the trip could prove to be interesting.

Adventures, even minor ones, are always fun, always stimulate the bloodstream, tickle the old fancy. I started bouncing along around Wild Horse Mesa, heading across a wide valley to where I presumed a series of canyons would start. It was just me, Harley, and Mother Nature. I had two quarts of water with me, and a pair of hiking shoes. Worst came to the worst, I could always walk out.

I've taken a lot of dirt roads in my traveling time, roads that didn't seem to go much of anywhere, but mostly they do get to some place. It is better to be traveling the back country with another bike for company and safety, but if I'm alone, I travel alone.

In Colorado's San Juan Mountains I wanted to get from Telluride to Ouray one afternoon, going over the mountains rather than around. Great trip, scrabbling up a dirt and rock track to Imogene Pass and pitching a tent by Thistledown. Next morning I dropped into Ouray for breakfast, then went up over the Continental Divide at Engineer Pass on a jeep trail to get to Lake City. Superb ride!

Some years ago in Nepal, a considerable remove from the Rockies, a friend and I wanted to go from a village near the Indian border called

Lumbini into the interior of the country. The local police said there was no proper road, and three bridgeless rivers to cross to get to the nearest pavement at Bhairawa. We could see the snowy Himalayas high in the distance, and not feeling like returning to crowded India and taking the conventional roads, Ken and I loaded the bikes and charged forward.

River #1 was less than a foot deep and 50 feet wide; no problem. River #2 was at least a foot deep, and 100 feet across; we managed that one. River #3 was two feet deep and 150 feet from bank to bank. We weren't going to get across on our own, but with the help of a few locals we pushed the motorcycles through and found ourselves where we wanted to be. That was the kind of traveling that one really remembers with infinite pleasure.

Heading down a bad road with no real idea as to how bad things can get is exhilarating. "Push on regardless" is the motto. This is not to recommend a truly stupid attempt at getting from Point A to Point B, like from the Grand Canyon's South Rim to the North Rim via Phantom Ranch—although that has been tried. As a matter of fact for many years there was an old Harley rusting away at the bottom of the canyon, as in the days before the park service frowned on such escapades a half dozen motorcyclists rode down Bright Angel Trail, spent the night at the ranch, and when morning came only five of the six bikes would start. No breakdown service available.

Eventually, what should have remained as a memorable motoring artifact was dragged out of the canyon by the purists; what a shame.

Back to the Goblins. After five miles I come to a rough parking area for a hiking trailhead, with a bulletin board. A large sign read DANGER: FLASH FLOODS. Not a month before a dozen hikers had found themselves trapped in a dry wash west of Grand Canyon and 11 had died. Food and water for thought.

A quarter mile up from the parking area the road dropped into a sandy draw, and the surface was becoming considerably softer. Not good. I looked up at the rim of the reef, and fat white clouds were collecting. I'm no cartographer nor meteorologist, but I presumed I would be following this dry wash for at least five miles, and it might rain. It would be embarassing to have to call Bruce Chubbock, who runs the Harley test fleet, and tell him he can find his bike buried in the Muddy River.

So I turned around. I knew I was a wuss, but that is the price we pay for wisdom. Said I, trying to justify my wussiness. Nevertheless, I felt a bit guilty.

On my way through Hanksville I stopped at the BLM station and asked about the road. "Good thing you didn't try it," said the ranger; "with the wet weather we've been having, the river crossing is a mile of mud, and even four-wheel drives have been getting stuck."

I didn't feel so bad. However, next time I'm out that way, I'll try it again. Preferably on a big dual-purpose machine.

Thieving Scoundrels

February 1998

I got a phone call the other evening, from a friend who had recently had his bike ripped off. Stolen. Illegally appropriated. Liberated by the low-life. Whatever you want to call it. To add injury to insult, he was on vacation at the time, visiting our nation's capital, and the bike was taken out of a parking lot while he was in the Smithsonian Air & Space Museum.

A report was made, but the police did not hold out much hope. The bike wasn't even high on the insurance companies' stealable list (i.e.

Harley-Davidson, CB600F3), being a Triumph Trophy 900, but the cops said this was standard for a D.C. summer. Three or four bad guys go cruising through parking areas in a van, see a likely target, pick it up, toss it in, and they are gone before a concerned passerby can even call for help.

There are times when I think that the Islamic *sharia* legal system is not all bad. Steal something, lose a hand. Not many bike thieves would be in business if they just had one paw to work with.

Now do not get me wrong. I don't believe the chop-it-off approach to sentencing should be applicable to a homeless person who pinches a loaf of bread from a store, but if a guy rips off my tankbag while I'm in the café having a cup of coffee, I just may bust his kneecaps so he'll think twice about doing such mischief again.

Thievery is a problem. Probably the world's second oldest profession, practiced by a goodly number of amateurs and professionals. Magazines are full of ads for anti-theft devices, but the only one I truly trust is a quarter-pound of plastic explosive under the saddle; you might destroy the bike in order to save it, but you'd take the culprit out as well.

I've had my share of bikes stolen, three in point of fact. But that all happened some 30 years ago.

In 1965 I was at college in Cambridge, Massachusetts, living off-campus. One morning I left my Bonneville tucked into its usual parking niche and went to class. Three hours later I came back, and the bike was gone. Anybody who has suffered the miserable nausea prompted by coming around a corner, expecting to see the motorcycle calmly awaiting your return, and finding nothing, knows the feeling of a bottomless stomach. For a moment you try to kid yourself that you must have parked it somewhere else, or maybe you're on the wrong street, but that only lasts about two seconds. Internally there is this sensation that the life force is draining out of you, followed by bile rising in your esophagus, then anger.

Followed by the quick dash all around the block in the hopes that the thief has just finished his dirty work and you can still catch him. Only to draw up panting five minutes later.

I called the cops, did the paperwork, and sent the word out to all my cycling chums: Be on the lookout. One thing about my '64 Bonnie was that it was quite identifiable, with a big crease in the gas tank, the result of a crash. Next afternoon I got a phone call from a friend who had been riding down Storrow Drive and seen my bike, my license plate still on it, with two guys aboard, in company with another bike, also two up. Not willing to duke it out with four hefty dudes, he had taken down the license number of the companion bike.

My apartment mate, Sherlock Fairchild, figured we should solve this ourselves. That was in the blissful days when you could call up the DMV and ask who had the plate. Getting that information, we went off that evening to visit the fellow biker. David and I both stood 6' 3" and looked rather threatening, and he readily told us who his buddy was who had been riding the Bonnie. Then we decided that perhaps we should not take the law into our own unbloodied hands, and presented the Allston police with the information.

Cops and us went over to the culprit's house, who was just some young kid who had been in trouble before. The fuzz took him down to the station, pulled a good guy/bad guy routine, and extracted a confession. I got my bike back, a promise to pay for a new ignition switch (fulfilled), and home we went.

About two years later a friend and I had gone into the import business in a small way, with an English motorcycle merchant sending us over used bikes every now and then. We were keeping them, and my new Triumph TR6, in a garage some distance from where I lived in Boston. One Monday morning I arrived to find the garage door's lock snapped off; the discriminating thieves, obviously professional, had only taken my bike, none of the old stuff. An elderly busybody who kept an eye on things around the garages said he had noticed the door open on Saturday morning, so the dastardly deed was done on Friday, after I'd put the bike away and then gone out of town. I pulled out an old T110 that had recently arrived from Blighty, rode over to the police station, did the paperwork, and muttering curses rode down to Pete Andrew's Triumph/BSA shop to get a couple of bits that the Tiger needed. Pete, an old hand in the New England motorcycle world, listened to my woes and then asked me if I had a Craven luggage rack on the TR6. Yes; he beckoned me to come into a back room, and there sat my bike.

Pete, whose integrity could not be questioned, explained that the low recovery rate for stolen bikes was not good for his business, and he was trying to remedy that a little. He had taken it upon himself to contact known bike thieves when they were about to be released from prison, and since they knew where the pros hid the bikes prior to shipping them out of state, he offered $50, no questions asked, for every bike they brought to him. Fifty bucks did not make it worthwhile to steal, except to steal from the thieves.

Third time I was not so lucky. In 1970 I was living in Arlington, Virginia, in a boring, brick apartment block, and some nasty type nicked my '67 Bonnie. Never saw it again.

Since then I've been luckier, and wiser. I've motorcycled across five continents and never, touch wood, had anything of consequence stolen. Not even a bag bungied to the saddle.

Touring riders are always concerned about theft of baggage, but in Small Town America I don't worry about it. Unfortunately Big City America is quite another matter; there I will find an attended lot and park it right next to the attendant—if he objects, I'm outta there.

When I'm in some more remote locale, like Turkey or Guatemala, and I want to walk around town, I find a friendly shop-keeper and ask him if he'll keep an eye on things. He is usually happy to have this customer-attracting machine on his stoop, as his status will go up in the community, and he assigns some eight-year-old to keep people away. In my many years of traveling I've always been fortunate.

Maybe I'm wiser now, in where I live, where I park a bike. I have an old Kryptonite lock that I use when in doubt, but I know that is merely a slow-down device.

My motto is: When I don't think it's safe, I don't leave it there. But I do want to see the new exhibit at the Smithsonian's American History museum. Maybe I'll go back to that chunk of C4 under the saddle.

Unsafe Touring

March 1998

It's two o'clock on an August afternoon, not quite the best time of day or year to be crossing the Mojave Desert. Heading east, I've just turned off I-40 at the semi-ghostly community of Ludlow and am riding along old Route 66.

I approach a level crossing for the Southern Pacific Railroad, which turns out to be not very level. The Harley Convertible bottoms out and then springs forward, and one and a half seconds later I hear the sound of something banging down the road behind me.

The left saddlebag has just come off. On I-80 south of Chicago I never would have heard it go, what with all the rumble and crash of big trucks, but out here in the dry land the only sound, other than that of the well-muffled Harley, comes from lizards skittering across the sand looking for shade. There being hardly any traffic at all on this byway, maybe one vehicle every five minutes, the bag is in no danger of being run over. I turn around, go back, park the bike, take off my helmet, and pick up the bag. Doesn't seem to be damaged at all.

The attachment system is simple. The bag has a really strong frame that fits over and slides down on two nubs mounted on the bike, and then a gnurled knob screws into a threaded hole in the fender. In the best Milwaukee tradition, this is all rugged, unbending steel, none of that frou-frou plastic stuff.

I slip the bag onto the nubs and try to get the male and female threaded bits to line up; they don't. They appear to be about an eighth of an inch out of alignment, just enough to prevent the connection. That was probably the origin of my problem, of losing the bag in the first place. I get frustrated. After ten minutes under the scorching sun I realize that the brains beneath my bald pate are getting very hot indeed. And I am getting a bit wuzzy.

Screw this, I say, amused by my play on words. I soak my kerchief with water, put it on my head, bungie the bag to my duffle, put on the helmet, and head down to Needles.

It was 109 degrees when I got there; Hell holds no fear for me.

This little saga began with a call from one of the SMSA (State Motorcycle Safety Administrators) folk, asking if I could attend a conference in Denver and talk about touring riders.

Safety conferences are about as exciting as attending my great-aunt Agatha's tea-parties, but that is in the nature of the business. Though Agatha could turn out a mean chocolate cake. Boring or not, safety is important, and the touring rider problem has never been satisfactorily addressed. I would contribute my two bits.

Be delighted, I replied.

We can fly you out if you want, she said.

I'll ride, thanks. After all, if I'm to speak on touring, I should show my touring side.

I would leave home after lunch on Wednesday, ride my bike the 150 miles to the office, pick up the test Convertible, and cross the desert in the cool(!) of the evening. Spend the night in Needles, then take old, old 66 via Oatman, Arizona, the next morning. No sweat (ha, ha); two and a half days would do it.

But things didn't work out that way, as things have a habit of doing. By noon on Wednesday I still had six hours of mandatory work to do. Ah well, plans are made in order to be changed.

I would leave early next morning. It was a 1350-mile trip; that would make a rather pushy two days, with an overnighter in Flagstaff, Arizona.

I got to the office about ten o'clock, nattered a bit with all and sundry, then went down to get the Harley out of The Cage, a security enclosure that makes Fort Knox look like a dime-store piggy bank. It was going on 11 and I was feeling a bit behind. So I did not bother to check tire pressures, oil level—or saddle bag attachments. First mistake.

Three hundred and ten miles after leaving the office I am in Needles, inside an air-conditioned gas-station store, pouring down my throat a liter of over-priced water, but cold, followed by a bottle of cranberry juice. I'm beat, and I still have 250 miles to go to my pre-paid reserved room. The fatigue factor has set in.

Second mistake; being too tired to make wise choices is all too common among long-distance types.

I decide to forsake the twisty road through Oatman and stick to the wide Interstate; good thinking. The multi-laned highway is not an enjoyable ride, but at least I don't have to worry about plummeting off a curve in the Black Mountains and doing boulder billiards. From a mere 500 feet above sea level at Needles I drone up to over 7000 feet at the Arizona divide, where it is pleasantly cool, and on into Flagstaff, glad to be at the Kings House Motel. And to have a T-bone washed down by a half carafe of burgundy at a nearby steakhouse.

In the morning I cadge a bit of wire off the desk clerk—all such places have a toolbox crammed with the most useful stuff—and secure the saddlebag. Then I pick up US 160 out in the Painted Desert, through the Navajo reservation, past Four Corners and Durango, over Wolf Creek and La Veta passes, hook into I-25 at Walsenburg, and north to Exit 198 in Denver. The evening socializing is in full swing.

At the touring-rider panel next day we talk about my own personal BACE concept (Braking, Accelerating, Cornering Exercises, acronymically known as "base") that all riders, touring or not, should become proficient in. However, BACE is not the sort of training that can be done in a parking lot, and each rider has to develop his own drill in finding out just how fast he can slow down, speed up, and get around a bend in the road.

And right alongside BACE are those other two concerns, bike preparation and fatigue.

People who go off on a hundred, thousand or ten-thousand mile trip without first thoroughly checking the motorcycle are damn fools. If you don't trust your own expertise, give the bike to your friendly (we presume) dealer and let a professional mechanic make sure everything is in good shape. A bad or underinflated tire can not only be overwhelmingly inconvenient when it lets you down on some remote road, but downright dangerous. And you don't want stray bits, like a saddlebag, flying off unexpectedly.

Second, watch out for fatigue. Pushing on to cover that extra 100 miles can wear you down more than you realize, and that might take you a longer time to fully recover than you think. Get over-tired today, and tomorrow your judgement can be slightly impaired. And that means you might end up doing something stupidly foolish, like running into a curb and falling down, because you are not paying proper attention. That can do serious damage to the bike . . . and to you.

Touring on a motorcycle is a safe way to travel, as long as the rider is happy and healthy and refreshed when he starts off in the morning. Tired riders are not good riders.

If you do find yourself fatigued, take a day off. Don't forget, we ride motorcycles for fun, not to punish ourselves. Except for the masochists amongst us.

Stuff We Don't Need

April 1998

Out on the road we touring riders tend to be efficient and streamlined in what we take, because we have a very finite amount of space to pack it in. We know what we've got, and where it is. Or at least should have a good idea where we stuck the extra roll of film, or where the rainpants are.

But at home it can be a very different matter. Especially if we have lived in the same place for a few years. The garage, or the shed, or the closet, wherever we keep the motorcycle gear, tends to shrink in size, or else the amount of Stuff we accumulate is growing.

Old helmets are the easiest things to collect. Even if we don't use a crash helmet for the purpose for which it is intended, it does get a bit tatty after a couple of years, with nicks in the paint from when it fell off the saddle, to a rather sordid, moldy lining. We go down to the store and get a new one, but the old one sits on a shelf—alongside three other old ones.

I still have the 1960 Bell open-face that I bought back in the waning months of the Eisenhower administration. I was the first guy in town to have one, and combined with that three-snap bubble shield it was a pretty spacey item. Maybe I could get Bell to do a reconditioning job and wear it to a classic rally. Doubtful; they'll say the shell has deteriorated and it is no longer safe to wear. But will I throw it away? Nope.

Every now and then I turn my toolbox upside down just to see what comes out. Which I did not long ago. I found the little tool for adjusting the primary chain on my unit-construction Triumph Bonneville, long, long since sold. And a steering-head wrench for my BMW R69S, which went off to Japan ten years ago.

Has it been ten years since I've dumped the toolbox? No, it's just that I've always put these useless items—of no use to me, that is—back in the toolbox because I didn't know what else to do with them.

I don't really need these things, but do I chuck them out? Not on your life! I have two cardboard boxes that contain bits and pieces of most motorcycles that I have owned, from an Indian Chief to a string of Brit-bikes, a Harley Servi-Car, several German makes, and an array of Japanese multis. Sidecovers for a '72 BMW. An Amal Monobloc 389 carburetor. Anybody make a bid for a bent sodium-filled valve from my NSU Max?

Pretty useless. Like my collection of inner tubes. When I take a trip on a bike with tube tires, I carry a spare rear tube. It is just a matter of past experience, having torn one up so badly it could not be repaired, and having to hitchhike a hell of a long way to get another. And since I'm on different bikes, and since I, thank God, rarely get to use these items, they pile up. Anybody need a 140/80-17? What is the shelf life of an inner tube, anyway?

The last time I got rid of any sizable amount of Stuff was when Sue and I went off to live in Europe in 1990. We held an infamous garage sale, and mounds of nonessentials went away. But not all of it. And unneeded things accumulate at a most astounding rate. What to do with them. I'd donate them to the annual rummage sale put on by ARF (Animals Requesting Friends) but I don't think there would be any buyers.

The most obvious "unneeded thing" is an unused motorcycle. A lot of one-bike owners will be aghast at this thought, but I can run around my county to at least a hundred garages in which there is an unloved, unwanted motorcycle. Maybe those adjectives are a little strong, but what it amounts to is a bike that is not in running condition, maybe simply for lack of current registration and a new battery, and the owner does not know when, or even if, he will get around to getting it going, or selling it.

I've got a CB400/F I don't know what to do with. It is officially off the road, in the eyes of the law, and when last put away had a front disc caliper that would not retract. Easily fixable. But it sits under a shroud and I know not what to do with it.

I have a few semi-worn out tires. I get ready to leave on a 3000 mile trip, there are 2000 miles left on the rear tire, so I change it before I go. But I keep the old one—just in case. You never know.

Fasteners, as we call nuts and bolts and washers and screws, are another matter. They don't take up much room, and sit in various plastic buckets that originally held Greek olives or calf's liver. My collection is a nice cosmopolitan mixture of American and metric, with a few Whitworth just to keep me on my toes. Trouble is, I usually find it easier to let my parts man run up the microfiche and sell me the right piece, rather than spending an hour in pursuit, and sometimes vain pursuit, of the correct bolt.

Clothes are another "thing" that accumulate. I have three nylon Belstaff jackets, the first one dating from 1972. The waterproofing lasts about eight years, I have figured, and then the jacket is done. At least as far as rain-riding goes. But it is still a good jacket, and I can't really bear to be parted from any one of them. They all have stories to tell, from the leather pads sewn over the holes in the elbows to the old BMWMOA logo of a quarter century ago.

Same with leather jackets. A nice light one from about 1980 hangs in the closet, but the leather is cracked, the lining is torn, and it should be consigned to the dustbin. But I keep it.

Just like I keep the leather pants that shrank over the years. Curious how leather does that. Am I dreaming of returning to a 34-inch waist, or is it that I can't bear to be parted from them?

My sister has an entirely different view of life, as she minimizes possessions. She lives in East Africa where she rides horses and writes books, and her worldly goods fill one small knapsack. Plus a notebook computer. Enviable.

But I like my Stuff, I like pawing through it every few years. It all provokes memories, from the Sportster clutch cable, which broke while tearing along the unused dirt roads around Quabbin Reservoir in Massachusetts, to the aged Whistler radar detector, which bleated its last timely warning near Beaumont, Texas, many years ago.

Sue and I figure we'll stay on this property for the next 40 or so years, so maybe I'll knock together a shed just to put my motorcycle things in.

And on the door I'll write: CLEM'S MOTORCYCLE STUFF - STAY OUT!

The Mysteries of Life

July 1998

Ever weigh a tire? Try it. Twice. First, before you put the petroleum-based doughnut, which we mistakenly refer to as rubber, though probably there is not a drop of rubber in it, on the rim. And then after you've worn the tread down to a mere shadow on the carcass. There should be quite a difference.

A big rear tire weighs more than 15 pounds, and by the time you've scrubbed off that last vestige of tread markings, it is going to weigh a lot less.

Maybe ten percent of that tire's weight has disappeared as you have traveled the highways and byways. Gone. Vanished. We worry about Freon and plutonium and exhaust emissions and our diminishing stratosphere, but nobody, nobody at all, seems to be concerned about these trillions of little particles that have shredded off the tire. I wonder about where that rubber has gone. It's not heaped up in piles by the side of the road. We don't ride through murky clouds of rubber particles. It's just gone.

Maybe our petroleum-based culture has bred a species of particle-eating toads, who thrive beside the highways and byways of the world, sucking up the residue. And then, when they get old and grey and feel ready to pass on to the great Reward of the Everafter, they find a secret tunnel back into the bowels of the earth and replenish our petroleum supply.

I'm thinking of asking the National Council of Scientists to provide me with a $500,000 grant to study the situation.

Does anybody remember the old "elephant graveyard" story? Merchants in the African ivory trade realized that going out and finding live elephants and killing them was costly, time-consuming, and possibly dangerous. They thought that if they could find a deceased tusker, dead of natural causes, they could just pick out the tusks from the piles of bones and go sell them. But no pile of elephant corpses, deceased from disease, old age, whatever, were ever to be found.

So the story developed that there were secret places that elephants went to die. And if you could find one . . . Wow! The riches, the wealth. As good as winning the lottery.

Then some rumor-spoiling naturalist pointed out that when an elephant got old and infirm, rather than traipse across the African savannah he went down to a river, where water and grass was easier to find. And there he would die, and the rains would come, and the rivers would flood, and the remnants would get washed downstream. No elephant graveyards. But what about tire dust?

Here's another mystery. An outfit called the American Association of State Highway Officials crunched some numbers and came to the conclusion that a single loaded 18-wheeler did as much wear and tear to a roadbed as 9600 cars. 9600! I don't have the specific stats at hand, but let's say the average loaded tractor-trailer weighs in at 75,000 pounds, and the average car, with average number of passengers, at 3000. That's a 25 to 1 ratio, and you factor in that 9600 figure, you get the idea that 25 cars are not nearly as destructive to the pavement as is one truck.

Take that one step further, with the average motorcycle on the road weighing maybe 700 pounds, rider included, we bikers barely ruffle the surface of that asphalt.

But do we get a break from the Department of Motor Vehicles for being gentle with the state's precious asphalt? Not a chance! And are the trucking companies constantly lobbying the politicians in Washington and at state capitals to allow bigger, heavier trucks on our highways? You bet they are.

And how many toll booths do you go through that charge you, alone on your motorcycle, as much as a Pontiac Trans Sport with eight people on board? Lots of them. Will any bureaucrat claim the responsibility for that injustice? Not a one.

Figure this. When we see a perfectly clear stretch of road, with a double yellow line preventing any overtaking, you wonder who laid out the lining; 16 miles of straightaway, and no overtaking. Makes me wonder.

An acquaintance I met at a Deadwood bar told me this story. He had wondered about this, too, and asked about it, and somebody told him he should check out the Old Soldier's Home in Hot Springs, South Dakota, ask for Danny D. Well, he was at Sturgis, so he took a little ride one bright and sunny day a few years back and went down to Hot Springs.

Danny D. was sitting on the porch, puffing on a pipe, and ready to tell all. Turned out that he had been a logistics expert in the army, involved in Patton's Red Ball Express and all that, and after World War II and Korea he retired and got a job with the some federal outfit that had to do with building roads. One day he was asked by his supervisor to figure out how to come up with a federal guidelines for this dotted line stuff.

Danny was driving a Studebaker Champion at the time, with that infamous flat six and underpowered overdrive, and he went out on the back roads of Virginia, where the speed limit was "reasonable and prudent" (roughly 60 miles an hour - remember, this is the 1950s) and he waited till he found a truck moving along at 55 mph, and proceeded to overtake it.

The process took a while.

He punched the proceedings into his stop watch, and from that little bit of research we now find ourselves pretty much stuck in an automotive environment which does not legally allow overtaking on a two-lane road.

Danny explained that he had had a lot of remorse over what he did so many years ago, because his twit-witted boss decided to make an absolute out of his little experiment. Danny even developed a complicated equation to demonstrate that not all overtaking situations are the same, having to do with the "footprint" (size) of the vehicle doing the overtaking, the acceleration factor, and a host of other informational tidbits.

The bureaucrats were patently uninterested. They had been given a problem to solve, it had been solved, and now they could go back to drinking coffee and waiting for paychecks. And when the U.S.

Department of Transportation was set up in 1966, the new layer of 'crats just took Danny's figures in and never questioned them.

Of course, this guy at the bar might have been yarning me, and this Danny fellow might be apocryphal, but I've never let the truth get in the way of a good story.

But back to my rubber-eating toad. If nature can recycle tire dust, we should be able to recycle old tires. So I plan on buying a piece of land up north of Cougar, Washington, and I am looking for investors. The plan is to dig a way-deep hole, slightly angled to the northeast, into the Mount St. Helens hot-spot. Then people will pay me a nickel apiece to roll all those worn-out tires into the hole, and the investors will be rich in no time. However, the real money will be in the fact that these tires will revert to being petroleum after being melted down, and I'll soon be richer than Bill Gates after extracting all that fresh oil.

Burnt Toast and Tires

November 1998

I was smearing the marmalade on the toast when The Wife walked in the door. She had been out for a stroll to the mailbox on that early spring morning and come back with the mass of advertising that passes for San Luis Obispo's county newspaper. Enjoying the start of what promised to be a glorious day, she had stopped to smell the flowers and listen to the birds sing; she smelled something else when she came in the door.

"You burnt the toast," she observed. Perceptive woman, The Wife, as I had slightly charred two slices of sourdough bread. However, I am one who likes a charcoally flavor, and that substance works to aid digestion.

"By the way, which bike are you taking up to Laguna Seca?" she asked.

"The BMW," I said.

"Better think about that again; the rear tire is also burnt toast. You are almost through the wear bars." She notices such things because I have grossly inadequate life insurance.

"What!? The bike's only got 3500 miles on it."

"Go look for yourself."

Which I did, slice of marmaladed toast in one hand, large cup of espresso coffee in the other. Sure enough, that tire was very close to being historic landfill, and I still had to get it back to BMW's West Coast headquarters, a little more than 200 miles from our little home in the valley. South end of the Salinas River valley, that is.

I had picked up the K1200RS from BMW just a couple of weeks before, heading down to eastern San Diego county to do a spin through the mountains and deserts. In these remote parts I could do as I wished, like apply a very heavy hand to the throttle. I was quite taken with the bike, a big sport-touring machine with gobs of power and great handling.

Handling is a product of the chassis and the tires, both of which were superb. Climbing up Mt. Palomar, down the Montezuma Grade, along the curves around Mt. Laguna, the K12 was a delight, flipping from side to side with no effort.

I'm talking big-bike handling here, not a 600cc sport bike or a 750 Superbike, and so my idea of a quick transition may be a little different from, say, Miguel Duhamel's or Scott Russell's notion. At 61.2 inches between axles the K12 is a lengthy piece of equipment, with 17-inch wheels, a 120/70 radial on the front, 170/60 on the rear.

I was having a great time on the K12, and being a brand new bike I was not thinking much about the shredding of tires. Until The Wife brought it up. I appreciate that these Z-rated radials must have, perforce, a rather thin tread depth, but this was a bit much; 3500 miles of road riding and the tire was toast? I rode my ST up to Laguna.

I should note that the tires on the magazine's original K12 test-bike went more than 10,000 miles; I did not ride that one. Tearing up tires seems to be my own personal affliction, and has nothing to do with the quality of the rubber I scrub off. You must appreciate that in this narrowly defined profession of moto-journalist we ride, are required to ride, the motorcycles hard, in order to be able to give sound, substantive, subjective reports. We do not abuse, but we use to the max. All I am saying here is that it is possible to wear out a set of very good tires in a very short time.

The next week I took the K12 back to BMW, and on the way home picked up a Harley Road King from the office, which I was to ride to Laughlin, Nevada, for the annual River & Grasshopper Run. The King had some 14,000 miles on the odometer, as it was being used as a test bed; I did not know when the current tires had been mounted, but they seemed to have a reasonable amount of tread left. The Harley has 16-inch wheels, shod with H-rated MT90 bias-ply tires, which equal a 130/90.

I rode it home, and several days later headed due east across the Mojave Desert. It was a nice day, but I had a press conference to make at five o'clock and a lot of miles to go, so I hung into the fast lane on I-40 going across the wasteland, where the accepted speed seemed to be about 85 mph.

After the run I headed to Palm Springs, going down old US 66, a little trafficked road with rather rough pavement. I wanted to do mountain loops around Mt. San Jacinto and over the San Bernardino Mountains, so I signed into a motel. In the morning I took out the tire-pressure gauge to check the tires—and noticed that my rear doughnut had very, very little tread left. The grooves were barely a shadow, about 1/64th of an inch. Oh, dear. Dusted again.

I'm not a rider who is gentle with his tires, but I do play fair. I check the pressures regularly, and keep them inflated to the recommended psi. I don't do burn-outs, but I do ride hard. A lot of Montana work, as we like to say, in reference to that sensible state which places no limit on one's speed in daylight hours.

My point, as there is one to be made, is that tire tread can go away at a most depressingly rapid rate, especially if one freely dispenses the gas. When we prepare to go on a trip we often check the tires, find them okay, lots of tread, and then really don't want to think about them for the next two, three, four thousand miles. Bad idea. Tire wear is my own personal single biggest hang-up when traveling.

I was stranded in the middle of the Yukon with worn-out rubber, and had to limp down to Prince George, British Columbia, with wads of newspaper stuffed between the carcass and the patched inner tube. In India I had to load my bike on a train because the rear tire couldn't take me the last 400 miles to Bombay. In Thessalonika, Greece, I needed to replace a rear tire and all the city had to offer was a block-pattern, unrated tire, which began shedding its tread when I exceeded 90 mph.

I appreciate that I can buy a super-hard tire that will last me the life of the motorcycle and cause me to fall down in the rain. I don't want that. I want that perfect tire that gives me a grippy 40-degree lean angle with perfect composure and will last 10,000 fast miles.

Anyway, I turned in the Harley and Editor Tuttle gave me a Moto Guzzi Centauro to do an evaluation on, with Z-rated radials (160/60 and 120/70) on the 17-inch wheels, barely 2000 miles on the odometer. I found it a great bike, and had a lovely time being chased by the local boys and girls along the local byways.

However, some 900 miles later my friend J.S., a *Guzzista* and vintage racer, seeing this model for the first time, looked it over carefully and commented that he would not want to ride on that rear tire further than the nearest tire shop. Damn! I didn't believe it! The rear rubber was snuffed, worn out, casing showing; I had obviously been having too good a time.

When I asked The Wife if I could borrow her pickup to take the bike back to the office she commented, "Toasting tires again, I suppose." How true!

When Good Things Happen to Bad People

March 1999

I got a speeding ticket the other week. Broad daylight, 8:47 in the morning, clear skies, rural countryside, light traffic, visibility as far as the horizon.

Made me mad!

I was heading south on US 101, coming up on the Nipomo Mesa, on the Central California coast, in one of those sweet empty spots on the road. At this point the highway was four lanes, with a wide divider, and I had traffic a quarter mile in front, a quarter mile in back, but I was all alone. I run the Nipomo three or four times a month, been doing that for a number of years, and I know that it is heavily policed, so I was cool.

A gentle rise ascended to the top of the table (mesa = table), and as I crested, there was a Black & White sitting over in the breakdown lane. I thought nothing of it, until as I went by the whole pinball machine lit up and the cruiser started to move. He must have just got a call; I pulled over to the edge of the slow lane to ease his getting by.

He pulled right in behind me, we stopped, he got out and walked up to the cab; I happened to be in my wife's pickup truck, on my way to pick up a bike. "Morning," he said in a very civil fashion, speaking through the open passenger window; "my radar indicated you were traveling at 77 miles an hour." And he allowed as to how my being in that empty spot, all alone, with that crest keeping any traffic behind me out of sight, meant that his radar could not possibly have been mistaken.

I politely remonstrated, saying I drive this road all the time, know that it is well-policed, have never gotten a ticket, couldn't possibly have been going that fast.

Unmoved by my impromptu defense, he wrote me. Put down a court date.

I accepted the ticket by signing it. What else could one do? I was officially a "bad person," a scofflaw, a quasi-criminal. Too depressing for words.

That afternoon, on my way home, I stopped on the northbound side and contemplated my sin. Admittedly, I did not know how fast I had been going, as I was looking at the road, not the speedometer. But I had not been overtaking anybody, just cruising along the slow lane.

I could cop a plea of guilty, take a traffic school, and get away for about $150. But I did not like that aspect of the law, of making a deal and getting off with a light punishment, of accepting minor guilt because innocence is too hard to prove. I was going to go to court.

I don't like to go to court, having only appeared on two or three occasions to fight the evil forces of injustice. But if it is necessary, it is necessary.

This case was not going to require anything fancy. Come up with a defense, go to court, and hope that I could instill "reasonable doubt" in the mind of the judge. Radar tickets are tough to beat, presuming the policeman has all his paperwork in order. At one time radar readings were treated with the same circumspection as a polygraph (lie detector) chart, but radar technology has gotten really good, and the instruments are checked frequently for accuracy. And most police have to take a 40-hour course before they are let loose with these gadgets.

I still needed a defense strategy. A friend got a ticket while going by our little airport and used the "low-flying aircraft" defense; it didn't work. A lawyer I know got a client off with the "tuning fork" defense, asking for proof that the device used in the daily test of the radar unit had been properly and recently calibrated. The "Santa Claus" defense, used by somebody who received a ticket on Christmas Eve, still makes the rounds of judicial chambers, but has never been known to get anybody off.

Looking north from where the cop had ticketed me, the road dropped away and angled off to the left, leaving a ridge of ranchland less than half a mile away. Of course, there was my defense: While the officer had been focusing on me via his rearview mirror, the radar had picked up a cowboy in his truck tearing along the ridge at 77 mph. A few photographs to establish the physical layout and I was set. Or at least I had some sort of argument in my favor.

I have no problem with policemen ticketing speeders who are a hazard to others on the road. The United States has one of the lowest accident rates in the world, and I am all in favor of that.

I do have problems with tickets that are issued primarily as a source of revenue for a town or county. Any policeman can sit alongside US 101 and pick off five speeders an hour, 40 tickets a day, at $100 a pop, $4000 for an eight-hour day. Ticket money around here goes into the county coffers, and the county likes that, which is why it purchases radar units and donates them to the highway patrol. Although the county authorities will claim that this is in the interest of safety and has absolutely nothing to do with cash flow.

Except if this is in the interest of safety, why are the police cars becoming more and more disguised, with light-bars tucked inside the car rather than up on the roof where everybody can take note of the fact that they are sharing the road with an officer of the law? If that patrolman who ticketed me had been cruising at 65 along the highway, I would never have overtaken him. The police should be on the road, and highly visible, to prevent people from speeding, rather than trying to remain discreetly concealed so that they nab more victims. An ounce of prevention is worth a pound of tickets in terms of safety.

And why is the auto-insurance industry such a proponent of this type of surveillance, to the extent that it happily gives radar units to needy communities? Because it likes to raise the rates on policy-holders who get speeding tickets.

All this makes for general disrespect for the law, as tickets to the general public arrive in a very arbitrary manner, most of them undeserved, but we accept them as a part of living in America. And pay them.

Not me. I honed my defense to a fine edge, which is to say that there might have been that hell-raising rancher on the horizon. Then I put on my best, and only, tie, and went to court.

Sitting there waiting for the procedures to begin was no pleasure, as a courtroom is a pretty cheerless place. The small hope that the policeman wouldn't show up soon disappeared; he was sitting behind me chatting with another officer.

For a moment I thought that maybe I would just discreetly leave, take the rap, be like all the others. No, I had gone to all this trouble, I would see it through. See justice done. Or try to.

The judge appeared. My case was called first. Citing officer and I got up, went to our respective places, and the judge briefed us on the legalisms—briefed me, really, as the cop had heard it all a hundred times before.

The officer got to make his case first, and allowed as to how his cruiser had been involved in an accident after he had cited me, and during the repairs somehow all the paperwork relating to the radar unit, which was kept in the car, had gotten lost.

I am completely and unalterably opposed to the wanton destruction of government property, which is paid for with my taxes, but somehow I could not get too upset at hearing this.

Judge frowned. Case dismissed. The bad guy got off.

The List

April 1999

At least once a month I go off on a trip. It might be a camping weekend, or two weeks in the Alps, or a cross-country voyage. You would probably think that after all this time I have my packing skills polished to perfection. Not a chance.

Something is always forgotten. Sure as God makes little green apples, I'm going to find myself lacking some essential item in my gear.

This last time out it was a towel, a simple rectangle of cloth used for drying oneself after a wash. I was headed to the Sierra Nevadas for a couple of nights in rustic campgrounds (i.e. water faucet and pit toilets) in the Sequoia National Forest, and when I was about to go down to the creek to clean up in anticipation of fixing dinner, no towel.

There must be 30 or more towels at home. Big ones, little ones, thick ones, thin ones. For camping I like a medium-sized thin towel, one that can dry quickly—but I had none. And I was about 5000 feet above the nearest town, 40 gnarly miles of dirt and pavement to get there. A T-shirt would have to suffice.

I sometimes wonder about my ability, or inability, to prepare myself for traveling. I am usually reasonably well organized, but somehow I am not all that good at making sure that everything is packed. Probably because I don't know what I am going to take.

My friend Greg Beemer (who just happens to ride a BMW) has an enviable approach to camping; he keeps a duffle bag on a shelf in his garage, and in it are all the essentials, from air mattress to stove. Me? I'm rooting around trying to find my candle lantern while the others are outside yelling at me to get with it.

Perhaps I should employ the pilot's approach, of having a check-list, of ticking off item after item, from tool-kit to water bottle, shorts to razor. But that means I would have to actually draw up the list, and I'd rather write this column than do that dry, unromantic task. I have been known to go off for a long trip and have everything except, say, extra socks. Which is why my sock drawer is full to bursting.

The actual placement of packed items can be complicated. Most of my traveling seems to be done with a pair of hard bags, a tank bag, and a duffle or trunk behind me. So I have four basic locations, but I still have a hard time remembering where I stuck the Perrier.

Some people pack in three hours, some in three days, I'm more the 30-minute kind of guy. I'll project an ideal departure time, then linger over the newspaper or the computer, and suddenly it's getting late. Cram some clothes in a bag, whisk the bike bits into another bag, stuff this stuff into saddlebags, trunk, or lash it to the luggage rack, kiss The Wife, and I'm gone. Get to wherever it is that night, a friend's house, campsite, motel, and nothing comes to hand. Not even a flashlight.

One thing I do find myself doing on a longer trip, usually the morning after the first frustrating night, is hauling everything, absolutely everything, off the bike, then repacking the whole thing. I get sick and tired of rooting around trying to find this or that, like a corkscrew, and realize that this is the simple solution, done without any distractions and with the hopes that I will remember the layout. Which I usually don't.

I called up a friend, Jeff Brody, one day last summer as I was coming back from a trip to northern California, thinking about making a little detour to his house and having some barbecued chicken that he has long promised. He's the fellow who puts out the intermittent "Back Roads & Barbecue" newsletter, and does a good deal of traveling, as well as BBQing.

"Not this time," he said, "I've got to leave Sunday." I knew he was heading from California to New England for the BMWRA national rally, but Sunday was two days away. However, then I thought that this man is being methodical about the trip, and he is not going to forget anything. He's not going to leave without a towel, or socks, or spare fuses. Maybe I should be more like him.

Maybe I should develop that check-list, but there are really half a dozen lists, such as a Motel Trip List, a Camping List, a Camping-Without-Cooking List, a Cold Weather List, a Foreign Traveling List, but any trip should have a Basic List.

1. Money.
2. Maps.
3. Fuses, just in case.
4. Motorcycle manual, to help find the fuse-box.
5. Flashlight, to read the manual at night.
6. Tool kit, not that you're going to rebuild the engine.
7. Tire gauge.
8. Tire repair and reinflating kit, and know how to use it.
9. Four feet of clear tube (Okie credit card) for siphoning.
10. Spare key, preferably not locked into the saddlebag or fairing pocket.
11. Complete set of raingear, as you never, ever know for sure.
12. More money, to replace whatever it is you forgot.

But beyond that, it is pretty much of a crap shoot. I've tried making lists, anticipating being two weeks on the road, what sort of clothing should I take. I scribble things down, throw a duffle bag on the bed, and start to put things in. Then a cat gets in the bag, so I evict the cat, at which point another cat slips by and crawls inside. And I forget the socks.

As I ride away from the house I try to do a mental checklist, but the devious mind often leaves out exactly what I've forgotten. But occasionally something essential is remembered—like the key for a Harley dresser, which is not necessarily necessary for the ignition, but is useful for opening the gas cap.

I've gone on long, two-up camping trips, like a month in Alaska, two months in Central America. If you asked me how I managed to pack all that was necessary, I have no idea. We did, finding out that what we forgot was not all that necessary. With the motorcycle, nearly everything is optional; a cell phone and a toothbrush can get you from coast to coast.

There are experts out there, like a couple who can pack a tuxedo and an evening gown, with appropriate shoes, into a space the size of a can of Spam. People who take complete fly-fishing gear wherever they go. Me, if I have half a quart of oil I haven't used, I usually end up stuffing it under a cargo net, or leaving it behind.

I was up in some mountains last fall and awoke in my motel to the sound of rain. No problem. Except I had forgotten my waterproof overgloves . . . and in my mind's eye I knew exactly where they were, on a table on the verandah right outside my office. And early Sunday morning there were not many stores open. So I took the plastic-bag liners out of the two wastebaskets; they lasted for all of 15 minutes.

I've learned to live with my forgetfulness. It's easier than learning to remember it all.

The Travel Salesman

June 1999

The occasional insolent, ignorant, and generally benighted sod sometimes has the temerity to ask, "Clement, why are you always traveling? Is everything all right at home?"

Of course everything is all right. I have a wife whom I adore, a nice semi-countrified place to live, a good group of friends, stacks of unread books, music to listen to, and the best local roads in the world to ride. I am, by any standards short of a religous zealot trying to find a shortcut to the hereafter, a happy person.

I also have a lust for travel. On the slimmest of excuses I will jump on a motorcycle and take off on a 3000-mile trip. Or even suffer the indignities of being crammed into an airplane if there is some motorcycle waiting for me in Marrakech or Munich or Mexico City. Traveling is something I like to do.

Not everybody shares this particular passion, as there are many who think that traveling is an unpleasant chore and best avoided. For which I am very grateful. Who would run the gas stations, the restaurants, the motels, if the entire population did what I was doing, if the whole world were on the move.

Deep down, however, I am a travel salesman, trying to sell the joys of traveling to those who might want to go out on the road, but are more than a little nervous about departing the familiar, of riding beyond their area code, their state, their country.

Don't be.

I've been to a lot of places, and there are way more that I haven't been to. And most I'll never get to. A rough estimate of roads on this planet comes to about 60 million miles, most of them unpaved. I'll be quite happy if I can get two percent of that under my wheels before I hang up the old handlebars.

I prefer the small roads. I have ridden I-10 straight through from the Pacific to the Atlantic, and I must say it did not offer much in the way of adventure. Unlike crossing the Banihal Pass in the Himalayas, going from Punjab to Kashmir; no lack of excitement there. Not only was the mountain road a splendid example of a carefree life, unfettered by any silly bureaucratic nonsense such as putting a barrier between me and a thousand-foot drop, but the people along the way were delighted to see me, to offer food and a bed, to ask me why I was traveling on a motorbike in this dangerous country.

"To meet you," I would say, "to sit at this table and talk with you." And they thought that was a sensible reason to travel.

When I was young and unattached, I traveled for the sheer bliss of riding down an unknown road, to an unknown place, to meet unknown persons. I was open for anything. No ties, no need to go to any specific place. It was the kind of travel that few people ever get to enjoy. I could fold my tent in the morning and point the wheel in any direction I wanted. I had no limits, other than what was in my wallet.

In Livingston, New Zealand, a gentleman made a very strong effort to get me to stay, offering a house, a job, and he even had an eligible daughter. I chose to move on. No particular reason, just itchy.

Then I got a staff job with a motorcycle magazine, and while it enabled me to travel a lot, it was only in two or three week stints; there was always that office with a desk to bring me back.

And then Sue came along. Falling in love with her did change my parameters, but before we married we discussed this fully. She likes to travel, and we take at least one trip a year together, sometimes two.

Usually she is on her own motorcycle, but if finances are tight, she'll pack two-up.

But she also likes to have her fingers deep into her gardening soil, or pushing a piece of wood through the table-saw. She has created quite a wonderful place for us to live in, and has absolutely no problem with my being gone a good portion of the time. All it takes is love and trust.

Being married has altered a tiny bit my activity on the road, as I no longer pursue available women, but all the rest remains the same.

Late afternoon and I set up a tent alongside the Buffalo River in the Ozark National Forest. There is no motel as good as this, ever. Steep walls cut by the water eons past are behind me, the bubbling, babbling river ten feet from where I start my fire. A fisherman comes by to chat a few moments, tells me he was born five miles away 76 years ago; he offers me a trout. I wrap a pototo in tin foil and hide it in the coals, and add a little bit of salt to the tomatoes that I bought from the produce stand back up the road a ways. Fish goes on the grill, potato is done, tarted up with a little olive oil and seasoning. Inexpensive bottle of merlot. I couldn't do as well as this for $100 at La Patina in Los Angeles.

I pull into Kalgoorlie in western Australia, one long, wide main street. A couple of bikes are standing outside a pub; I park alongside them. Several beers later I am invited to come home with these bike-riding, hard-rock miners. "No spare room, mate, but the sofa's comfy. Sleep on it myself when the old lady and me aren't getting along." At the house the charcoal of a barbeque is settling into proper heat, and soon the steaks are sizzling. We sit in the warm evening air drinking Swan ale and they tell me about going down the hole, and I talk about going down the road.

It's not that I ever expect to find a revelation on the road, an epiphany, to have the complexities of the universe explained to me. At one point when I was young I did, thinking that if I rode far enough, met enough wise men and women, I would finally understand what this living was all about.

Later I realized what my kind of travel really is: it is an appreciation of humanity. I like to see what people have accomplished . . . the good things, that is. I travel roads, and people made these roads, which take me to see Mayan ruins in Guatemala, castles in Spain, skyscrapers in Malaysia. And food, what is travel without food? Rocky mountain oysters in Wyoming, roast guinea pig in Ecuador, zebra steaks in South Africa.

Every day means meeting people. Maybe just a few words with the cashier in a convenience store in Glennville, West Virginia. Or a rousing debate on helmet laws in Sturgis, South Dakota. Or a stormy night in a Turkish village with a family who invited me in to stay in their small house because it hadn't rained so hard since Noah launched his ark and there wasn't a hotel within 50 miles and the roads were all blocked by mudslides anyway.

I gather all this information into my cranial hard-drive, and then I go home and tell Sue all about what I have done, where I've been, whom I've seen. And I'm very happy to be at home, to lie outside together and watch the stars appear, to light candles and have a long and pleasant dinner.

Weeks, maybe months go by, and I get restless. Got to go. She kisses me goodbye, and I'm away again.

And as an interesting aside, absence does make the heart grow fonder.

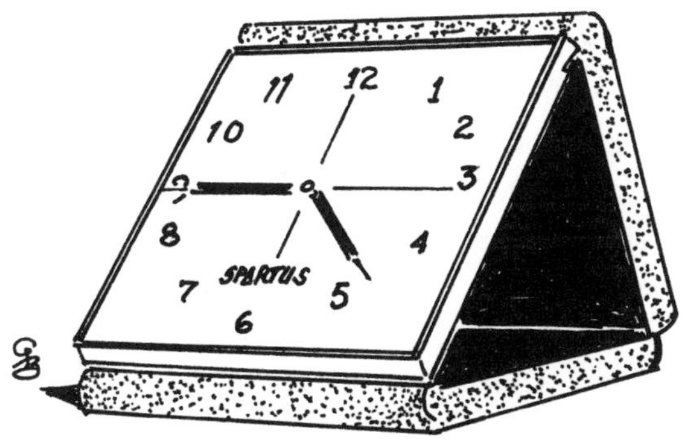

Dawn Patrol

July 1999

Alarm clocks are unpleasant, but they serve a useful purpose. I've got a long day ahead of me, going from Cody, Wyoming, to Hawthorne, Nevada. That's a shade more than 900 miles, and 75 percent of it will be on two-lane back roads.

The paper says that the sun will rise at 6:01. I set my little Spartus alarm for 4:45. I like these quartz-powered watches and clocks; anybody who enjoys winding a watch, or an alarm clock, has got to be a person with too little to do in his life. The bike is pretty much packed.

I pile up the pillows on the bed and settle in to read a chapter of my current travel tome, Jonathan Raban's *Bad Land,* an excellent book about the settling of the northern Great Plains shortly after the turn of the century. That was the railroad era, which preceded the motorcycle era. And it was a tough time.

I tend not to romanticize the past. Certainly, it would have been an adventure to haul across Montana on a Henderson Four around 1914, but the bad roads and questionable mechanical reliability would have kept my daily averages down to under 100 miles. Not the 900 I'm planning tomorrow.

I like modern motorcycles and asphalt highways. I've had a couple of mis-adventures with old-fashioned, breakdown-prone machines and wretched roads, and I am glad these occasions are safely and comfortably stored in my memory bank. Had I known beforehand what I was getting into, I would have changed my plans. Give me electronic ignitions and tubeless tires and good suspensions, thank you very much. And good roads.

Forty pages later I slip in the book-mark, turn off the light, and slide away to slumberland . . . to be awakened some six hours later by the Spartus buzz. I fumble with the ALARM OFF switch; that is a small aspect of these little quartz clocks we often fail to appreciate—the switches are so small that you have to be thoroughly conscious to find them. You can't just whack a button, fall back asleep, and wake up two hours later.

I'm out of bed, start the in-room coffee maker, and do my ablutions. Coffee is ready, the local TV weatherman says it is 47 degrees outside, and going to get into the high seventies. Clear sky. The national report says there is a chance of thunderstorms over the Great Basin, where I'm headed, normal affairs for late summer.

Stuff the toilet kit, book, clock, whatever, in a catch-all and go outside. Chill-willers; Cody is almost a mile above sea level, and nights can be downright brisk. Still dark; the moon is down. Bag goes in the trunk, I go back inside and put on the appropriate layers of clothes, check under the bed for dropped items, leave the key to the room by the remote, turn off the lights, and close the door. The clock in the fairing says 5:07.

Being a decent sort of fellow I paddle the bike away from the room, out to the street, and then start the motor. It's not a noisy machine, and has a stock exhaust, but still, I've been awakened by the sound of diesel pick-ups leaving at ungodly hours, and prefer to let my neighbors sleep.

When I saw the couple next door the evening before, I had said, "Here's the deal; no rowdy parties at your place, no rowdy parties in mine." I think it is always a measure of civility to exchange a word or two with the next-door people, even if they are just one-night neighbors. I find it helps to keep their television volume soft.

Push the button, engine fires, 15 seconds later I pull away, slowly, letting all the component parts of the drive train warm up. The headlight shines along the highway, US 20.

This is my favorite time of day for riding. I am not much of a night rider, but I do love the hour before dawn. Especially if I am headed west. Through the tunnel, past the Buffalo Bill Reservoir, and I am traveling up along the North Fork Shoshone River. I'll be in Yellowstone National Park by six.

The gas tank is full. It's 180 miles to Jackson, where I'll fill up. In this the year of the death of the mom'n'pop gas station, thanks to the overly zealous Environmental Protection Agency, it is wise to calculate distances carefully, to know the amount of gas you have. For those of you who have not recently suffered a SORRY NO GAS crisis, let me remind you that by the time December 1998 rolled into January 1999, more than 15,000 small gas stations had to shut down because the owners had not spent $100,000 or more on renewing their holding tanks.

And it has created a helluva problem in some out of the way places. The fueling spot that was there last year may not be there this year, and if you cannot rely on a station being open, carry a siphon along.

There is an indefinable moment in pre-dawn riding when I realize that I am no longer relying on my headlight to see the road, that the ambient light has increased to the point that it has suffused the landscape with visibility. Distant hillsides studded with trees, rock formations, the river tumbling along, the Shoshone National Forest stretching north and south of me.

Of course, I am considerate of wildlife, and do not wish to injure any deer.

The sun is shining off the top of Grizzly Peak as I climb up through Sylvan Pass, at more than 8500 feet. I am glad I put warm layers on, even if they will come off in a couple of hours. Daylight is here, and I'll be out of Yellowstone by the time the motor-homers have wakened to microwave their instant coffee.

Eight hundred miles later, daylight declines as I turn onto US 95 and head west towards Hawthorne, Nevada. Darkness descends, and I become focused on the long beam of light stretching out in front of me. In days of yore there would have been that noticeable moment when I stretched forward to turn on the headlight, but the US Department of Transportation has taken care of that for me.

I find a motel in Hawthorne, get dinner, set the alarm.

At 5:10 a.m. I'm away in the dark of the night, headed south on NV 369 through the Toiyabe National Forest. As I cross over Anchorite Pass, at a coolish 7626 feet, I appear to be running out of darkness and into light, and a most amazing sight is before me, illuminated by the rising sun, the top of an immense, mile-high granite wall, the east slope of the Sierra Nevada Range. Right ahead of me, along a dead-straight road running across Mono Valley, and 30 miles distant, is Excelsior Mountain, at a lofty 12,442 feet.

This view of the Sierras, rising 6000 vertical feet above the valley floor, is, for my cup of coffee, the best early morning view in North America. Yes, it is a bit nippy out here, but such suffering is good for the soul, and a sight like this makes me a believer in Mother Nature.

The Food Factor

August 1999

Napoleon once remarked that an army marches on its stomach; the same could be said for a traveling motorcyclist. The only question is, "Where's the food?"

For me, the single biggest challenge when I am roaming around this great continent is to find places to eat that are memorable . . . in a positive way, of course. I want a diner that I enjoy being in, a restaurant that serves a meal that lasts much longer in memory than in my stomach. It doesn't matter if the counter is Formica (low bucks) or the napkins made of linen (high bucks), as long as I feel I am getting good gustatorial value for my gastronomical dollar.

Many Interstate off-ramps do offer a large, if uninspiring, choice, with a Denny's, a Fast-Burger or three, and some slightly more formal choices attached to motels belonging to one of the great chains of pillow-purveyors. The convenience store at the 12-pump gas station will have $2 hot dogs, two-quart thirst-quenchers, along with bags of chips of all flavor and contents; never presume that a potato chip is actually made of potato until you have read the list of ingredients on the back of the package.

All this is fine, and very rarely kills you—though there have been a few unpleasant incidents concerning under-cooked ground beef. If I am hungry, and speed is of the essence, I will stop at a Burger King and get a Whopper, my current burger-of-choice; it has bread, meat and salad fixings, a full meal by any standards. I dislike the overly sweetened drinks, and settle for a glass of water; the store manager overhears me asking for H_2O and gives me an arch look, as if to say, "That cheapskate!" At least they should sell O'Douls or some other brand of non-alcholic beer.

Do not misunderstand me; this column is not a negative commentary on the American food industry, which provides better food at lower prices than any other nation on this earth. I remain amazed at how little it costs to eat well in this country, especially compared to places like Europe and Japan. Our most efficient business is agriculture, and we should be damned proud of that. Our grocery store prices are, by first-world standards, very low. As are the costs of eating out in an average restaurant; if you want real menu shock, try Tokyo or Rome.

I am all in favor of the future, and what it promises: better motorcycles, a cure for the common cold, world peace. However, I am not terribly fond of the present trend to corporate aggrandizement in the food business. I appreciate the "economy of scale," but when I can get precisely the same "seafood platter" in Jacksonville, Florida or Jackson, California, I am not happy. Restaurant chains leave me bored . . . and I do hate being bored.

I feel that eating should be an occasion, not just a rapid "keeping body and soul together" sort of thing. And it should embellish whatever place in the country you happen to be. In New England I order Yankee pot roast, in Louisiana, Creole chicken and dumplings, in Colorado, Rocky Mountain oysters.

At the very high end of the prepared-food market there are expensive restaurants, generally in highly urbanized areas, where those in the upper income-tax brackets tend to go and spend a hundred dollars a person for some very tasty fare. And probably get insulted by the *maitre d'* as well. Do not misunderstand, I love to dine out on duck *a l'orange*, or the best Kansas City porterhouse, all manner of fancifully expensive consumables, along with a $70 bottle of wine. Which I do at every opportunity, that being when somebody else is picking up the tab.

Spending $100 on myself for such a passing moment is a little too painful. Which is probably the main difference between the very wealthy and me. I love good good caviar, roast rack of lamb with mint sauce, elaborate desserts—but I am also happy on the meat-and-potatoes circuit, when the beef is of good quality and done medium rare and the potatoes are mashed with the skins on.

What do I do on the road? I am big on picnics, on stopping at a deli and getting a decent loaf of crusty bread, some sliced pastrami, a hunk of Monterey jack, and a jar of Dijon mustard. Add a tomato, and I can ride off to the nearest hilltop, make myself a splendid sandwich, slowly savor it while admiring an unimpeded view, and then take a brisk nap before continuing on.

If I am looking for in-house fare, like a mid-morning breakfast, I will cruise through a town until I come to a café with a half-dozen muddy pickups out front. Or I might stop at a gas station and ask for a recommendation. "I make the best breakfast in town," said one cashier, "but since I'm not going to invite you home to eat, you'd better go over to Bob's, just two blocks along on your left." I'm not saying that Bob's is necessarily going to serve up the finest eggs Benedict this side of New York's Waldorf-Astoria (where the dish was created) but the place will provide honest grub, and with any luck the sausage will be locally made, and the coffee strong enough to suit my jaded taste.

Also Bob, the fellow in the apron and holding the spatula, yelling through the big opening between the counter and the kitchen, will know that he better butter his toast properly or all his daily customers might desert him for the semi-fast food franchisee down on the freeway.

I think, and hope, that there will be a resurgence of individually owned restaurants in the coming century. A lot of people are plain and flat tired of the sameness of corporate cooking. In the California town I live in, there are several chain pizza joints, and one, Nardonne's, that usually has the owner herself spreading on the mozzarella cheese, green peppers, olives, and pepperoni. Nardonne's has what can only be called "the personal touch," and I like the end result.

When I've had a long day and am heading for a mattress, I like to find the motel first and then go out and find dinner. Preferably within a mile of the motel so I can walk. The clerk at the desk might not have the slightest idea what I mean by "a good place to eat," but then again, he might have an uncle who owns an exceptionally fine Italian restaurant. I ask, I see what the response is, and then I stroll along to my destination.

The place doesn't have to be fancy, just clean and with good service.

And I read the menu; I like short menus, with half a dozen selections. If there are 20 choices for entrees, I know they are mostly pre-packaged and in the freezer. I am prone to selecting a special, or taking a wait-person's (ghastly word!) recommendation. And then I say a little prayer, asking that this dinner be absolutely scrumptious.

And sometimes my prayers are answered.

The Tenting Alternative

September 1999

I was traveling in the mountains early last fall and came into a small community that was mostly a quiet place for summer people, and it offered a little restaurant and attached six-room motel. It was getting on to dusk, and there was not much ahead of me that I wanted to see at night . . . although it would be a lot of fun in the daylight.

But the place looked pretty dull. I'd pay my money, get my supper, and go back to the room and watch television or read a book. I asked the girl at the restaurant if there were a campground nearby, and she said there was, a little off the main road, but if I took my second right, first left, and went on for half a mile, I'd find it.

Which I did. Nothing fancy, about an empty acre along the side of a creek, a couple of trees, bathhouse in the middle. Four of the ten or so sites seemed occupied, and two fellows were grilling some kebabs on the barbie. No gate, no office.

I rolled up to the barbie guys and asked what the deal was. "Go back up the road a quarter-mile, you'll see a store. That's where you sign in and pay your five bucks."

Done. I returned and set up my tent, and the neighbors invited me over. We passed a pleasant couple of hours sorting out the political and social questions of the day. They were "operating engineers," which meant they drove trucks for a construction crew that was working on the highway, and lived about 500 miles away. Work was where they found it, and they went home when they could, and lived in their trailers while they were here.

It was a nice evening. A lot more memorable than sitting in a motel room. Cheaper, too. Also, I was meeting people, talking with them, which really is the best part of life.

That is one reason I like camping, the fellowship of a campground. I've never found it intrusive, nor exaggerated, and if I indicate I wish to be left to myself, that's fine. But if I want to spend some time chatting with strangers, that is fine, too.

Another, and quite different, reason for camping is the solitude I sometimes crave. I can go 40 miles from my house, ride up a dead-end dirt road for a couple of miles, and be in the midst of nowhere, part of the Los Padres National Forest, with a view of the ocean, and not a soul within sight or sound. A national forest is public land, and I am the public, and as long as I leave my campsite as clean as when I found it, I feel I have a right to be there.

Nothing fancy about this camping, no campsite with table and drinking water or anything. Just me and an empty hilltop. I set up the tent, blow up the mattress, roll out the sleeping bag, and usually do not bother with cooking. Instead I bring along a sandwich; maybe it is half a loaf of sourdough French bread filled with ripe camembert cheese, or some slices of leftover pork roast between two hefty slabs of pumpernickel, with mustard and tomatoes and lettuce. And a bottle of wine to wash it down, with a Granny Smith apple for dessert. I sit up there for several hours, slowly eating, sipping the juice of the grape, and thinking great thoughts. Perhaps not so great, but often they revolve around how fortunate I am to live in a country in which I can do something as simple as this.

Stars come out, perhaps the moon rises, and I hear nothing but a slight breeze rustling leaves, the occasional night bird. And maybe later the howl of a coyote. Sleep becomes unimportant, but I eventually drift off. To awaken later and note that Orion's Belt has moved along, that the galaxy that surrounds me has shifted. In my limited appreciation of the way things work, I still like to think of the earth as being the center of the universe.

A third variation on the camping theme is best exhibited by one of the more interesting organizations created by our sport, the International Brotherhood of Motorcycle Campers. Started by a fellow named Cliff Boswell 26 years ago, who motorcycled and camped all around North America, the IBMC is a real club in the truest sense of the word, just a bunch of motorcyclists who like to pitch a tent along with some like-minded people. Cliff, who went off to that great campground in the sky a few years back, was one of the original motorcycle touring types, his travel articles appearing in many motorcycle magazines in the fifties and sixties.

Dues are a mere $10 a year, which barely pays for the printing and postage on the bi-monthly *Campfire Ring;* this provides a list of scheduled campouts, from Oregon to Florida, and 46 states in between. The camp-outs are simple affairs, voluntarily organized by members, and the pertinent facts, called *Kindling,* appear in the newsletters. You look at the list and figure you can make Forsyth, Missouri, for the Shadow Rock Campout, and off you go. You bring your own gear, and something to contribute to the traditional "biker's stew," and the newsletter tells you how to get there, how much it will cost, and who to contact if you have questions.

You ride to one of these events, and even though you don't know a single other person when you arrive, you soon will; these are always quite convivial affairs. And several months after the event there will be a small write-up of the campout in the newsletter, called *Embers.*

If this sounds like your way of communing with nature, you can get full information by running up the website at www.ibmc.org—I like that, the computer world meshing with the camping world.

I know some riders who think that camping out is a night at the Motel 6, but for me it is a relief to get away from air-conditioners and ice machines. I'm more of a loner than a group camper, though pitching tents with one or two friends, putting a steak on the grill, and wrapping some potatoes in tin foil is my idea of a good time.

Every year two or three of us go up to a place called Horse Meadows, high in the Sequoia National Forest, in the middle of 100-foot-tall redwoods. Before Memorial Day, and after Labor Day, the place is usually quite empty. A creek runs by, there is water on tap, the campsites have tables and fire-pits, dry toilets, and no trash pickup; pack it in, pack it out.

During the week there is virtually nobody there, but even on the weekends the visitors are sparse. One of us makes dinner, somebody collects firewood from the forest, and we sit around and eat some uncivilized chili, drink beer that has been chilling in the stream, and discuss life, liberty, and the pursuit of motorcycling.

Camping is a healthy way to expand our lives. A great, big world is all around us, and setting up a tent in the forest reminds us how insignificant and transitory we really are—and when you go back to your city or suburb or town, chances are you will be a slightly nicer person for having had the experience.

The Mossbacks Amongst Us

October 1999

Every time I hear a motorcyclist refer to "the good old days," I tend to cringe. This is based on the relevant fact that one person's "good old days" might well be another person's "bad old days," and I, for one, am more attuned to next year's offerings than to the relics of the past, be it computers, cars . . . or motorcycles.

I am far more interested in performance, reliability and safety than I am in painting the machines of yore in nostalgic colors.

De mortuis nil nisi bonum—speak only well of the dead. Or to paraphrase and reverse Willie Shakespeare: The good that motorcycles do lives after them, the evil is oft interred in the junkyard. In the sixties I always sold my British-made bikes before they had 20,000 miles on the odometer, so I would not have to think about the inevitable major rebuild expenses.

And my travels were inhibited by the fact that motorcycles often broke down, and I was generally quite inept at fixing important things . . . like a dropped valve or rear wheel bearing race that became welded to the axle.

I happen to think the new CBR600F4 is a superb motorcycle—with power brakes and handling that weren't even dreamt of when Honda introduced the CB750 back in 1969. This machine is a triumph of the human ability to make good things better.

And speaking of triumph, let me refer to that noted motorcycle of 1959, the Triumph Bonneville. The other day I was in the parking lot of a local motorcycle shop, and a young mossback (look that word up in your *Webster's* if you're not familiar with it), 30-ish, was pouring oil into the wretched Umberslade Hall frame that the Bonnevilles of the seventies suffered. The frame holds the oil, which was not a good idea on a bike whose engine was prone to self-destruction, as the system was hard to flush properly; after any internal disintegration tiny bits of metal could get caught up in some little crannies in the frame, to come floating back into the system a thousand miles later to lodge in a bearing. This was a pretty tatty looking bike, and young mossy, born about the time the bike was built, was riding it from Los Angeles up to San Francisco. It has such wonderful handling, he claimed, and is so perfect for hare-ing along the Big Sur.

Hare-ing, ha! Better to say turtle-ing. My Triumph TR6R (pre-Umberslade) and I were a regular feature on the Big Sur in the late sixties, and what I considered fast then would be downright less than modest by the standards of today's Suzuki 600 Bandit.

I did not have the heart to say, "Absolute balderdash!," which is very much of a mossback word, because the chassis, especially matched to those skinny tires on tall wheels, was never noted for its handling, generally giving the rider a sense that he was always about a second and a half late in reading input. Now, if young mossy had said that he liked riding older bikes because of the sound, the look, the experience, I would have accepted that, but he was trying to promote his 25-year-old twin as being the equal of, if not better than, what is available today.

No way, Jose. Anyone who loves and rides old bikes because they are old, not because they are contemporaneously competitive, is a classicist in my lexicon, and worthy of considerable respect. In my neck of the California woods are a group of pre-1916 buffs who love nothing better than to take a Henderson Four or a Flying Merkel out for a spin on the country roads; they derive great pleasure from mastering the riding techniques of yesteryear, but they also drive fuel-injected pickups with ABS. On the other hand, a mossback is a genuine throwback, an irrational type who believes that a telephone with a rotary dial is better than all this new-fangled push-button stuff. I disagree.

The riders who most appreciate the constant flow of technology are the sport bikers, the ones looking for a Yamaha R1 or a Ducati 996, experienced (we hope) types who can understand the subtleties in airbox volume, sag measurements, and shaving of grams from valves and connecting rods.

Trick new stuff can become old in a matter of months, especially in that sporting category. The differences between a 1985 GSX-R750 and the 1999 version can best be seen on the microfiche, where the name stays the same and all the parts' numbers change. The mossy 1985 Gixxer promoter might have bolted on every single piece of go-fast equipment made in the intervening 15 years, but the newer model will lap any racetrack a bit more quickly, presuming equal riding ability.

Mossbacks occur also in the touring and cruising worlds, where the old guard maintains that the Cavalcade was the greatest sea-to-sea bike ever, or the GV700 Madura (R.I.P., along with that unfortunate name) was the best dawdling machine ever built outside of this country, and that Harley's 1980 Sturgis Twin-Belt model could run 100,000 miles without having to do more than change the oil.

Witness the latest GL1500 and the K1200LT, which are the motorcycling equivalents of $200,000 motorhomes. Compare them to a GL1100I or R100RT—those early versions were like a 1960 18-foot Airstream or John Steinbeck's camper when he traveled with Charley. These new single-track RVs may be big, but their handling belies their size.

And the accoutrements, from cruise-control mechanisms to reverse gear to sound systems that would blow the woofers out of a 1960 Pioneer hi-fi.

Mossbacks often refer disparagingly to the "complications" of all these new motorcycles, how it is hard to fix them in one's own garage. Well, old green-spine, let me tell you that these new bikes usually don't need to be fixed, as opposed to a Norton Commando or Harley Shovelhead or Ducati bevel-drive 750SS.

Brakes and tires? I would not consider going back to a double-leading-shoe drum brake or All-Traction Goodyear tires, not that these weren't considered state of the art products in the late sixties, but they are only distantly related to a current disc brake with a four-piston caliper, or an Avon Azaro.

I think the mossback problem comes from several sources. One, a lot of people get bogged down as they flounder along the uncharted path we call life, and decide to decide that wherever they get stuck is as good as it will get, and everything after this point is useless . . . what that fable-telling Aesop fellow would have called the sour-grapes approach. Others believe that taking this proto-Luddite attitude will make them more interesting, but that is only because they are dull folk to begin with. Third, there are the "slow dogs" amongst us, who genuinely find that a 1973 Kawasaki Z1 is quite as good as a 1999 ZRX1100, because they are in no way interested in pushing the performance envelope of either of these machines.

Me, I'm more interested in the Aprilia Mille than a Vincent Black Shadow. And find that BMW's R1100S has a lot more appeal than my old R69S.

The Moss family can sit around the fire and discuss the family tree; I want to know what the next generation will do.

Thru The Windshield Darkly

November 1999

Last spring I drove across this great country, from Massachusetts to California, in a middling-sized truck. It was a humbling experience, but even in the midst of such adversity there were important nuggets of useful knowledge to be learned.

We tend to ride our motorcycles with cheerful freedom and muted exhilaration, and often gaze upon those soul-less creatures locked in their metal boxes with a mixture of pity and scorn. Not a good idea; these unfortunates, hands firmly clamped to the steering-wheel, body strapped to the seat by webbed belts, trapped for days and weeks in a rolling carpet of tin-roofed Mercurys and Mercedes, Toyotas and Kenworths, are an unpredictable lot at best. Their minds are often far from realities of what is happening a hundred yards in front of them, being more concerned with getting a dial tone or sneaking a look at a spread sheet while speeding along at 70 mph. Scary. And for four and a half days I was one of them.

Sue and I needed to shift a lot of books and paintings from the East Coast to the West, and the local moving company gave us an estimate that would have made Bill Gates blanche. Sue, ever the one to cut through the smarmy smiles of (excess) profit-minded companies turned to me and said, "Let's get a truck and do it ourselves." And within the hour we were behind the wheel of a 15-foot Penske rental.

Have you ever wondered why many rental trucks—Penske, U-Haul, Ryder, etc.—are often painted yellow? For the same reason that warning signs on highways are painted yellow: Watch out when you see this color!

Especially if the driver is accustomed to the small size, brilliant accelerative power, and stunning braking ability of a good motorcycle.

We packed the box full, had a good night's sleep, and were away as dawn cracked. My first enlightenment concerned those REST STOP: 1 MILE signs. On a motorcycle I avoid such oil-soaked parking lots, as they are full of noise and clamor and about as restful as a construction site. But with the truck they provided delicious moments of relief while not interfering with the schedule too terribly much.

I've gone cross-country on a motorcycle 15 or more times, but rarely on four wheels. Of course there was the mandatory see-America trip with my sister and our parents when I was 11, but I shan't count that.

My first four-wheel odyssey was in '65. I had just ridden my 500cc Velocette over field, plain, and mountain, from Massachusetts to Georgia to California, and as I was leaving Yosemite National Park a gawking tourist (from New York), came around a bend on my side of the road, and I glanced off his rear fender, breaking my left foot in the process.

I got out of the hospital with a large cast, which rather precluded riding, bought an elderly Chevrolet sedan for $50, tossed out the rear seat, took the bike's front wheel off and tucked the Velo in the back, and away I went. My main memories of that trip are watching needles in the gauges slowly move, indicating imminent despair, visits to junkyards to find working generators, and buying reconstituted oil in gallon jugs. But the clunker got me to New England, my cast came off, the bike went back together, and I sold the car for $35.

Two years later I was headed west again, this time to go to graduate school. The Monterey Institute of International Studies had an excellent Masters program, which the GI Bill would pay for, but what really interested me was that Monterey was located at the north end of the Big

Sur—motorcycling nirvana. However, just before I was to leave Massachusetts, the US Army insisted on reclaiming some metal that it had used to pin my right femur back in '64. When the doctor came to see me after the operation, I asked him how soon would I be able to bend my joints enough to ride my Triumph TR6R. "Probably not for the better part of a month," he said, "unless you like suffering." So I crutched around and found a Rambler American convertible for sale for $200, white with bright red vinyl interior. I loaded the bike in a trailer, hooked the trailer to the bumper (not wise, in retrospect, but it held), tossed in my books and clothes, and headed towards the setting sun. At the west end of the Pennsylvania Turnpike I picked up a bearded hitchhiker who, it turned out, lived in Monterey. How convenient! The car worked flawlessly, if a bit slowly when climbing over Berthoud Pass in the Rockies on US 40. But with two of us driving and putting in long hours, we were there in five days. I kept the Rambler, though using it little, until I got my degree, at which point I sold it for $100. I remember it fondly.

Scrapiron, for that was the hitchhiker's moniker, and I became fast friends and riding buddies, and we attended the last official Death Valley Motorcycle Rally together, in the fall of '67. Which has nothing to do with this story, but I just threw it in for historical purposes.

From then on cross-countrying was done strictly on motorcycles. Wherein I tended to stay away from anything more than two lanes. I can run from just about anywhere to anywhere on this continent without hardly ever putting wheel to even a four-laner, let alone a super-slab. It might take me a while longer, but it is a lot more enjoyable.

However, back to last spring, there I was looking through the big windshield in this Penske, while Sue plotted out thousands of miles of Interstate. It was a drone, but we had acceptable company in each other. Most frustrating was the truck's governor, which limited us to 70 mph, while rural Interstate traffic moves along at 80. However, I could feel my generally benign Dr. Jekyll personality turning to Mr. Hyde's angry persona as I would get stuck in the fast lane while trying to overtake a 65-mph vehicle that had edged up to the 70-mph mark just as I began to pass (ever notice how a driver seems to speed up when he realizes he is being overtaken?), and traffic piling up behind me. "Ha," I would snort, "I have just as much right to this space on the road as anybody else. Let them wait." And Sue would awaken from a semi-slumber and ask, "Clement, was that you snorting or did I dream it?"

Most unnerving was making lane changes, as I never did acquire any real competence in using the rearview mirrors. Crossing the bridge into St. Louis at rush hour was like being in a demolition derby, with nobody allowing me any leeway as I desperately tried to maneuver into the correct lanes, cutting off Mustangs and Suburbans with great, and necessary, abandon. The only highway users who seemed to understand that this Penske was a potential lethal weapon were the motorcyclists, who always appeared to give me a wide berth. Smart folk.

It was a nice trip, I suppose, since we were going through a perfect American springtime, the roadsides abloom with flowers. But every time I saw a motorcycle the bile of frustration would leak into my mouth; I knew I was not cut out to be a teamster.

I was very thankful to arrive home, unload the truck, run Sue's little Yamaha into the box, and then drive down to the nearest Penske outfit. It was 40 miles away, but it took me three hours to get home again, as I took the long, long way back. I needed that.

With some luck and good planning, I hope I won't ever have to do a long haul in a cage again.

When I was a Young Man . . .

December 1999

Twenty-five years ago, a quarter of a century past . . . what was I doing? Where was I?

Ah, yes, I remember! I had just spent ten days cruising across the Indian Ocean, from Cape Town, South Africa, to Fremantle, the seaport for Perth, the capital city of West Australia. On a Chandris Line ship. In those good old days this Greek shipping line had four ships, one of which departed on a three-month 'round the world trip every month, carrying freight and lots of passengers. Airplane transport had not proliferated the way it has today, and ships were still the cheapest way to travel across an ocean. And useful for carrying motorcycles.

When I arranged for the ticket in Cape Town the gent in the booking office asked me how much my motorcycle weighed. Four hundred pounds, I said, being a BMW R75/5. "Ah," he replied, "your baggage limit is 400 pounds, so we shall merely list it as personal possessions; you will not have to pay extra." Done. It was ten pleasant days aboard, and I was bunked into a large cabin with seven Brits emigrating to Oz to seek their fortune, and who were determined to party the entire way.

After we arrived in Fremantle I got off the ship, was frisked thoroughly by Australian customs, the bike was steam-cleaned (nice of them) to prevent any African bugs from immigrating, and I rode off alongside the Swan River to Perth, a few miles away. A motorcycling friend was living and working there, to reconstitute his traveling funds; this was Ken Gawenda, a fellow from Detroit out to see what lay beyond Michigan.

Traveling the world was becoming popular in the early 1970s, but motorcycle-mounted wanderers were few. I had met Ken in Iran, we traveled from Afghanistan to Nepal together, and then split up in India, as he was headed to Southeast Asia, while I was going to Africa. We kept in touch, sending a postcard every couple of months to some General Delivery in a far-off city, and that is how I knew he was in Perth.

He and a couple of other travelers had rented a house and I was invited to stay. It was a good city, with good beer, good people—I spent a happy couple of weeks fettling the bike, getting my kit in order, doing what people do when they roam around the world with no need to be anywhere in particular at any time. This is traveling at its best.

But the urge to move on was strong. I left one day, headed east 1600 miles to see some friends in Adelaide. The directions were easy, with only three turns: go east 350 miles to Kalgoorlie, south a hundred to Norseman, and then it's a straight thousand miles east across the Nullarbor Plain ("Half of road's dirt, mate, so best be wary of the 'roos.") to Port Augusta, hang a right and it was 150 more miles to Adelaide. Lots of adventures, lots of good times.

In the middle of the Nullarbor, at a gas station just where the pavement turned to dirt, I was mounting a new tire, when a motorcyclist heading west stopped to exchange information. Geoff Lea, for that was his name, was out doing a lap of the continent during his vacation, and I gave him Ken's address.

From Adelaide I went north to Alice Springs, which at that time was more than a thousand miles of dirt road, including a side trip to Ayers Rock. My Adelaide hosts had given me three bottles of good wine to take on this section of the trip, and each night I camped in the absolute solitude of the outback, building a fire and drinking my wine. I loved it. Maybe I'm a solitary sort of fellow, but those three nights, plus a raucously drunken evening in the opal-mining town of Coober Pedy, were magnificent.

I pushed north into the tropics to Tennant Creek, then east to Mt. Isa, where I had been told I could get a job in the mines. However, I'm a claustrophobic type, and I still had enough money to exist without, so I headed up to the Gulf of Carpentaria. That stretch from Cloncurry to Normanton was the longest single stretch without gas I have every covered on a motorcycle, 240 miles; I carried a small can to augment my 20-liter tank, but ambling along that red dirt road for six hours at a leisurely pace, the engine just sipped the fuel and didn't even need the extra.

Then it was east to Cairns, on the Great Barrier Reef, and a wonderful place to camp on the beach. I met three Australian motorcyclists and we decided to go up together to Cape Tribulation. The only trouble with Cape Trib was that to get there we had to cross the Daintree River, and the ferry only ran at high tide on Sunday. Once across we were committed for seven days. Good fun; we'd live off the land, and our sidecar man had a fishing rod, crab trap, and even a .22 in his hack. No problem, and we all scoffed at our companion who bought twenty pounds of granola.

On the dirt road to the ferry we met some motorcyclists camping, including Geoff Lea, who had beat me there by going from Perth over the top of Australia. Small world. But he had places to go to the south, we had to catch the ferry, so the meeting was short.

We crossed the Daintree, got our front wheels jammed on sticky muddy roads, and camped in the most beautiful places. We ended up eating the granola quite thankfully, as rod, trap, and rifle produced nothing. However, the fields were full of hallucinogenic mushrooms, which added marvelously to the effect of the granola chapatis that were every evening's fare.

We left Cape Trib a week later, and I went south, through Bambaroo, Eton, Gladstone, Gympie, and a score of other towns, with several days on Brisbane's Gold Coast to admire the beaches and the nubility. South of Brisbane I pulled into the remote, semi-deserted mining town of Nimbin on a rainy day, stomped into the café—and there was Geoff. Small world indeed.

Eventually I made it to Sydney, and booked my passage out to New Zealand on another ship. This time they charged me for the motorcycle, but not much.

Geoff lives in Tasmania now, Ken returned to the States, then moved back to Perth where he married an Aussie and become a brewmaster. I haven't seen Geoff since he visited me in Boston 20 years ago, but we stay in touch thanks to the efforts of the postal services and E-mail. I saw Ken at the Laguna Seca World Superbike races last summer, when he was back for a family reunion.

For me, one of the greatest benefits of travel is the people I meet . . . and stay in touch with. Memories are good, and sitting in the shade with Ken and talking about the week we spent on a houseboat in Kashmir—very good.

Simple Pleasures

January 2000

There are three parts to a life: drama, simplicity, and sleep. Leaving the sleep part for another column, I will deal here with drama versus simplicity.

Which I shall start by describing one of my favorite local rides. Three or four times a month I scoot up California Route 58, heading out of Santa Margarita. I especially like the ten-twist, up-hill chicane going east from the Parkfield Road turn-off; it is quite short, less than half a mile, and I sometimes go up, stop at the top and turn around, go back down, and then up again. This little section is the primary reason that the outside edges of my boots are always beveled to a 45-degree angle.

My stretch of Route 58 is the western end of the road, running from the San Joaquin Valley to the Central Coast; it is a small two-laner, with not much traffic due to some severe curves and bends in the asphalt, not to mention a wickedly lovely little range of hills, the Temblors, that has a lot of seriously twisty bits. Usually only locals use 58, although the occasional tourist can be found, either hopelessly lost or looking for spring flowers in California Valley. I love the road. I'll often take it all the way to McKittrick, 75 miles away, where the McKittrick Hotel offers a breakfast worthy of an oil-field worker. And it is those hard-hatted fellows who keep gas in my tank who constitute the primary clientele at the establishment.

And then an equally delightful 75 miles back home.

An acquaintance who is infatuated with computer electronics rather than internal combustion engines asked me the other day, "Don't you get bored doing the same road over and over? At least what I do is always changing."

Since I am not even sure of what he does, other than stare at a screen for days and weeks on end, I could not discuss that point. But about the road . . . "No," I said, "I don't get bored. I'll probably ride that road for the next 40 years, and I'll know every foot of its surface, and each ride will give me just as much satisfaction as the ride before. Maybe a little more."

If the truth be known, it is the simple pleasures in a life, like riding an oft-ridden road, that I find the most rewarding. How many parents have looked at a child doing something quite ordinary, like turning a somersault on a grassy slope, and been overwhelmed with emotion, wishing the grandparents were there at that very moment, that they had the video camera with them. Then they have to tell their friends about this most amazing little feat, who politely listen, and even those having children of their own wonder what the ruckus is about. Because they know that these simple things cannot fully be explained.

I can better convey to a listener the excitement of riding across the Andes Mountains than I can the pleasure of riding Route 58. The first is drama, the second is simplicity.

My life has had, by most standards, a good deal of drama in it, especially in the motorcycling part. I rode around the world when I was young. Now I occasionally get to ride motorcycles in odd spots about the world, like Morocco and India, and less odd places, like the Alps and the Rockies. Last year I did a 12,000-mile loop of North America, which gave me many fine memories. But if I were denied my Route 58, those extravagant trips would taste like saltless food.

My life here at Cat Crossing might well be considered dull by many urban denizens, who brave the asphalt jungles of Manhattan and Chicago and San Francisco every day and night. Here, the wife and I are early risers and the coffee is started before the sun is up. I open the door and walk out into the dawn, accompanied by a cat or three, and slowly stroll the hundred yards to the mail box, where awaits the local paper—a miserable Knight-Ridder rag, but it has good comics. Along the way I'll see some of the nine deer who really own the place, and the family of kit foxes may be drinking from the tub that Sue keeps full by the garden; maybe a wild turkey. No lions, no tigers, no muggers, no drama here. I bring back the paper, drink the caffeine, and if work is not seriously pressing, I might just go out to Route 58, shoot up Shell Creek Road, and come back on Route 41. That takes less than an hour, and then I'm back at work. What Sue generously calls a loop commute.

Late in the afternoon I could decide to give a motorcycle a once-over, rolling it into the cool, cement-floored garage. I check the tire pressures, the oil level, the battery if it is not a sealed unit. If I'm really feeling feisty I might give the paint and chrome a light shine. These are uncomplicated, and essential, chores, and I derive a satisfaction from doing them. I will leave it to others to rip engines apart and put them back together; that, for me, is drama.

So much of my motorcycling involves, I find, these simple pleasures. The Sunday ride. Meet at Hoover's, the same men and women I've ridden with for the last few years; maybe a new face. Where to? Somebody, anybody, the person who made the first phone call, is the decision-maker. We have half a dozen rides that I've done thirty, forty or more times; I've lived here nigh on ten years, which is 500 Sundays. Pozo, Parkfield, Big Sur; two, four, six hours, depending on the choice. There is no real competition amongst us, and the fast riders are happy following each other, not dicing; the group strings out according to each individual's notion of a good speed. Dennis could be leading on his R1, Kurt sweeping on his KLR650; Diane may be on her Monster, Becky, her Radian.

We ride, we stop, maybe for a soda, maybe for breakfast or lunch. We talk, not about presidential elections nor the situation in the Balkans, but about families, friends, work, vacations. And, of course, about motorcycles. What's new? What are you buying? What does the rumor mill have to offer? We love our motorcycles, but even more, we love riding them, braking hard for the sharp corner, angling over into the curves, accelerating up the hill.

We're not awed by our bikes; we ride them as often as possible, whether it's a commute to work or a trip to the store. I know that some guys genuinely feel it is a dramatic moment when they roll out the Ducati 996 or Arlen Ness special and ride it up to Alice's Restaurant or the Marcus Dairy . . . but that's not us.

"Tis a gift to be simple, 'tis a gift to be free. . ."

That is an opening line from an old Quaker hymn, and it applies to the way I think about motorcycling. So, having said all that, I think I will print this out, pop it in an envelope, get on the bike and ride to the post office, then do a little half-hour ride before stopping by the market to get some salmon for supper.

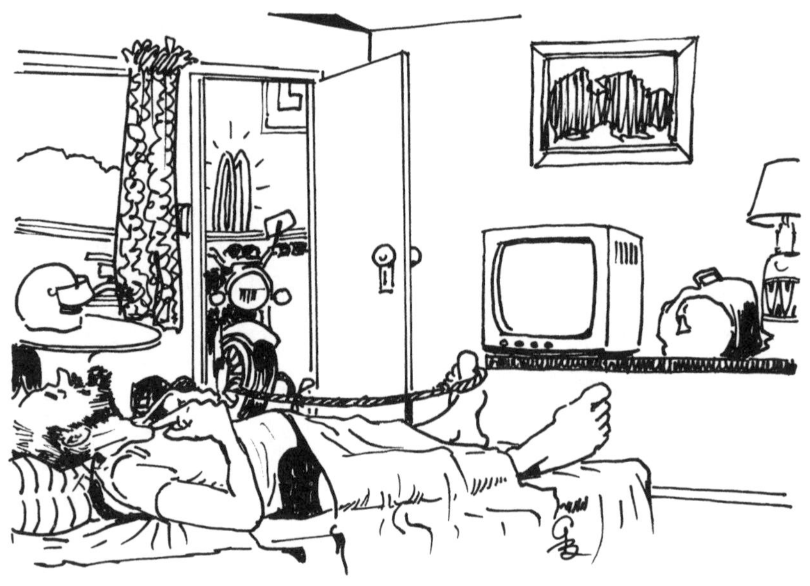

Sleepless on the Road

March 2000

One of the most treasured aspects of my mortal existence is "a good night's sleep." Without sufficient sleep I tend to be a witless, worthless soul, unpleasant to have around. And when I am on the road, a sleepy self is a hazard to me and others.

In most of my traveling, I stay at motels—or the closest thing I can find to a motel. A motor-hotel should have but a single story, where you can park the bike right in front of the door to your room, any carrying of bags is absolutely minimized, and if you are paranoid about theft, you can tie a piece of string to the front wheel and run it inside to attach to your big toe.

Unfortunately, that old-fashioned motel is on the 21st-century endangered list, and about the only place you can find them these days is on the old highways. Today, because of property prices, motels have had to double- or triple-up, stacking at least two layers of rooms, and making the motorcyclist who is not fortunate enough to get a ground-floor room to hike up and down some outside steps.

About those ground-floor rooms—they are convenient, unless you have an insomniac above you who paces the floor in hob-nailed boots from two to four in the morning. Or an early-riser who gets up at five o'clock and does not care who knows it.

And forget those new "inns" that are now proliferating at highway interchanges, where you actually go into a lobby and walk along inside corridors, with the individual rooms having no access to the outside. These are like the hotels of yore, except they have no bellboys, no room service, no concierges. If I want a sleeping establishment of that sort, I'll stay at the Pierre in Manhattan or the Mark Hopkins in San Francisco.

When I start looking for a motel, I'm quite diligent. I know what I want, and I usually know where to find it. If I'm in a rush and on an Interstate, I know that the exit ramps will be staked out by chain motels of the two-story variety. So I heed the small green sign that says: I-40 BUSINESS. You can run through Gallup, New Mexico, on old US 66, which is the business side of the interstate highway, and find 30 motels, most of which haven't seen a coat of paint since Jimmy Carter was president. But that is okay by me, because I am always in search of the funky.

Two reasons. First, I like funky. These motel chains that advertise that there won't be any surprises in Motel Ten between Jacksonville, Florida, and Tacoma, Washington, that every room in every one of the 400 motels in the chain is exactly alike, won't get me as a customer. I do want different; I don't want to wake up and have to ponder which city, which state, or country, I'm in. Also, I know that funky sometimes offers pleasant little bits of nostalgia, like finding a genuine bathtub in the bathroom, not one of those elongated footbaths most places offer.

Second, I like inexpensive. If all I want is a room with a bed and bath for ten or twelve hours, I don't need the Ritz. Just a clean bed, hot water, and it shouldn't cost more than $50, which is my notion of the upper level of cheap. Granted, you don't get that in Manhattan, New York, but certainly in Manhattan, Kansas. Even the infamous Motel Half Dozen is starting to price itself into the middling category ($50 to $100) these days, while lots of individually owned motels are still in the $30 dollar range, even the $20s.

As a digression, let me speak for a few words on the AMERICAN OWNED signs that I sometimes see outside an old-fashioned motel. I go in, and usually there is a sour couple watching television in the room behind the desk, and one of them grudgingly comes out and does the necessary. Not long ago I chatted one of these people up; he had a very Irish name, and feeling feisty I asked him if he remembered his history, when a hundred and some years ago signs at job-sites read: NO IRISH NEED APPLY.

"Yeah, I've heard about that," he replied.

And I pointed out that his sign was the modern equivalent, intimating that Asian Indians were not held in high esteem. He grunted, told me to leave the key in the room when I left, and went back to his re-runs of *Death Valley Days.*

Many of the bottom-of-the-line motels are now owned by Indian immigrants, mostly belonging to the Patel patronymic. Thirty or more years ago a newcomer to this country found that he could buy an old motel quite cheaply, and while the immediate financial returns were a bit meager, it provided a place for the family to live, and they could do the work, and the value of the property would eventually rise. For a great many Patels, this has become their path to the American dream. Just as the Irish of yore went into construction or the police. For me, to walk into a motel and have the slight smell of curry at the desk is a pleasure. I just wish they would open restaurants as well.

Expensive places are fine, even quite preferable, but to tell the truth, if I am spending $100 of my own money just to lay my head for a few hours, I consider it a bit of a waste. Should I be traveling with Sue, and we want to stop early and enjoy the late afternoon and then sit on the deck with a bottle of cabernet to watch the sun set, a pricey place is in order. But for a dusk to dawn stopover, give me inexpensive.

I have a list of over-nighter motels that I consider exceptional by my crude standards, and that I will likely revisit. Like Scott's Shady Court Motel in Winnemucca, Nevada; it is old, it is off the noisy main drag, the rooms have windows at both ends, the place is well-maintained, and the price is $32 on up. And there are two Basque restaurants within walking distance. I can make Winnemucca in one long day from the house, so should I be heading in that northeasterly direction, it is a goal.

As an historical note, the original motel claims to be in San Luis Obispo, California, some 15 miles from my house, where I once stayed in the early 1980s. The Milestone Mo-Tel was inaugurated in 1925, and welcomed the travelers going from Los Angeles to San Francisco on US

101. The architect, one Arthur Heineman, actually registered the "Mo-Tel" name that year, but use of that expression has long-since passed into the public domain. A largish building at the front housed the office and the restaurant, and behind were a series of small structures, each one consisting of four separate rooms, spread out in a garden-like setting. I parked the motorcycle right next to the door, and felt that this is the way motels should be. The place, name changed to the Motel Inn, has been closed for a dozen years or more, and what the future holds for this historic sight remains moot.

However, I remember that I got a good night's sleep, and I value such things beyond mere gold.

Heat, Cold, Wind, and Rain

April 2000

The four apocalyptic aspects of motorcycling are the product of extreme weather: too much sun, too much cold, too much wind, too much rain. Too much of any one of these can make a smart rider stupid, and that ain't good.

If wishes came true we would always ride when the temperature is in the seventies and the wind at our back. Dream on! Maybe in Camelot, but not in most parts of this large green earth.

On one trip I was leaving Death Valley in July, which is not a good time to visit that place but I had wanted to see the 4th of July parade at Furnace Creek; good parade, by the way, done very early in the morning. The bike was heading south on CA 127 towards Baker; suitably named, because by the time I got there the humongous Bun Boy thermometer was reading 112 degrees.

That's hot. I can operate quite well up to 95 degrees, and beyond that my faculties begin to melt, my decision-making gets skewed, I'm a hazard to myself and to those around me. I went into the Mad Greek's, where the air-conditioning must have been running at full throttle, keeping the temp in the sixties, and sloshed down about six quarts of juice and water.

Do I continue, or do I stay put until evening?

I figured I was good for no more than an hour at a time with this heat, with a dew rag under my helmet and a soaking wet T-shirt under my jacket. I could make it to Amboy in less than an hour, hang out in Roy's Café for a while, push on to 29 Palms, pause a while for refreshment, and get to Palm Springs by late afternoon. It was either that or check into a Baker motel and watch Pat Robertson ask for money.

I pushed on. Most of us have heard about wind-chill factors, but there is also a wind-heat factor. Since my body was regulated to 98.6 degrees, and not wanting to blow my thermostat, I stayed tucked in behind the windshield. Not a fun day, but I had places to go, people to meet.

Not much you can do about the weather. If it's a day trip, and you can choose your day, you might have a perfect ride. But on a two-week trip? Be prepared, as the Boy Scouts would say. And be prepared on a day trip, too, is my sage advice.

Tough weather is not only unpleasant to ride in, it is also dangerous. If there is too much in the way of heat or cold, wind or rain, it can grind you down physically and mentally, turn your once-witty self into a stupid lout, and you might make a dumb mistake. If you are riding along in a rainstorm, with the temperature down to 40 degrees, wind gusting to 40 mph, you can be in a heap of hurt if you are not at your smartest.

Heat . . . there is not much you can do about it. Except to stop often, to drink a lot, and maybe try to keep some moisture on your head and torso. You do not want to get dehydrated, because that will really fry your neurological computer. Our bodies are quite sophisticated little machines, but they can get messed up. Try running your Gold Wing without any coolant in the system and see what happens.

Cold you can deal with, if you are prepared. I advise people to always, always stick an electric vest in the tank bag, even on a day trip. Do I heed my own advice. Ha!

I took off one morning when the temperature was already 75 degrees at the house, and headed up to Monterey, about 150 miles away. I decided to take the picturesque route up along the Pacific, only to find the coast was fogged in, the temperature in the fifties, and I was not prepared. As the cold seeped in I could actually feel myself coming unglued, so to speak; there was quite a bit of debris from spring storms on the road, and I was not doing well dodging rocks. I got the shivers, and probably suffered a mild touch of hypothermia on that trip, because it took me a good three hours of sitting in the hot sun in Carmel Valley before I felt really good again.

If I'm prepared for cold, if I'm carrying all the gear, I can ride all day at 40 degrees. If I don't have the clothing, I can be in big trouble. And don't rely on your local meteorologist, because he or she will not have all the answers.

And then there is rain, which is more than just a bother to a rider. Staying reasonably dry is not a real problem. If I'm going to take off on a rainy day, I sit in the warmth of the house and put on the rainsuit, the rain gloves, the rain boots, wrap a big kerchief around my neck to catch those drips, and I'm away. But I might be out on the highway, and want to move into the passing lane, and will I turn my head to see if some low-slung micro-car has moved into my blind spot? Nah, I might get water down my neck if I twist around. Bad thinking, very bad thinking.

Let me advise you, and I have it on the best authority, it is better to be a little damp than a lot dead.

Rain is not only making your life less than pleasant, but it can slicken the pavement and hinder other drivers from seeing well—even if they have a good set of windshield wipers, which fewer than half the cars seem to have. Most drivers end up peering myopically through smeary windshields, and they think that little red light on your rear fender is way, way up the road—when in truth it is right in front of them.

I got stuck in the cold and rain in the mountains of Colorado one time. I'd left my gear at a cousin's house in Carbondale and was heading over the Continental Divide on a dirt road to Leadville, via 11,982-foot Hagerman Pass. It was only 60, 70 miles, and it was hot in Carbondale, so all I had was a light leather jacket. I got up to about 10,000 feet and ran into a thunderstorm which left me soaked and freezing. And I had nothing with me to put on. If it weren't for the heated grips on the Beemer, I might have been in serious difficulties. I gripped those grips really tightly, and could feel the warmth running up my arms; just that little bit seemed to help a lot.

And then there is wind. A tail wind is great. A head wind you can put up with, especially behind a fairing, even though gas consumption will increase. But a strong cross-wind? That is a misery. I've battled cross-winds for hundreds of miles out in the prairies, where roads go straight and there aren't many trees. A wind like that can beat you to pieces, wear you down, make you stupid.

The key to a long, happy motorcycling life is to always be 100 percent ON mentally when you are behind the handlebars. And if cruel weather smacks you when you are not properly prepared, it is easy to turn into a clumsy duffer.

Take it from one who has been a clumsy duffer, and who works very hard at not being one again.

Rally Rats

July 2000

You've seen them; we've all seen them. The greybeard on his 12-year-old Wing, pushing 150,000 miles on the odometer, paint pitted and scratched, but there he is, anytime more than 500 bikes gather in one place, greeting the scores of people he knows, picking up another long-distance award. Or the younger version, maybe on an R100RT, two big duffles on the back seat, bound and determined to hit every BMW event he can between the time school lets out and the day he has to go back to teaching.

These are the rally rats, the cheerful, peripatetic few who live to ride to every major, and minor, motorcycling event they can possibly get to. They make friends easily, just like any accomplished bar-fly (that's a compliment, by the way), and are a pleasure to have at any campsite, full of good stories, always knowing where to get a pile of firewood, appreciative of the most basic stone soup. These compulsives suffer a mild, and benign, obsession, notching up a new rally every week for as long as they can.

Of course there are the extremes, the quasi-neurotic on the scuffed and scraped FJ1100 who puts up a pup tent in the most remote corner of the campsite, socializes with no one, has a 20-word mono-syllabic vocabulary, and eats a can of Spam and a loaf of white bread every day; but he's at all the rallys. Or the European who shipped his Moto Guzzi over and figures he has six months before the money runs out, and in that time he's going to every rally, race and rendezvous he can find on the map, with the high point being the MGNOC National. Of course, this is also a good way to meet hospitable people who will invite him home for a night or two and let him use the washing machine.

To qualify as a novice rally rat you have to hit at least 10 events in a year. Amateur status means your face is seen at least 15 times. Expert, you are out there every weekend from May through October, and you are on a first-name basis with most of the vendors.

Rally-ratting has become quite a sport onto itself in the last dozen or so years, men and women who get on a circuit and spend an entire summer doing little else other than riding to different venues. And since there are now dozens and dozens of motorcycle get-togethers every week, scattered across these United States, and Canada, a rider with a valid gasoline credit card can tick off an impressive number of meets.

The term "rally" has been expanded in my lexicon to include any large gathering of motorcycles. In these latitudes, you can say the motorcycle season starts with Daytona Speed Week in early March, and then moves on through a thousand rallys big and small, and ends with a slew of toy runs in December. My little county, San Luis Obispo, is no great mover and shaker in the motorcycle world, but there were an estimated 1500 bikes on our last Xmas charity ride.

When I was an 18-year-old, a short time ago, I went to my first rally, although back then it was called a gypsy tour. A friend, Sandy Sheehan, and I traveled about a hundred miles from home to get to Laconia, New Hampshire, late one Friday night. We camped out in the woods at the Belknap Recreation Area, along with a few thousand others, it seemed. For a couple of guys just out of high school, this was a pretty exciting world. Best part may have been the informal Saturday night drags, done in the parking lot in front of the concession stands, with the two bikes heading off into what appeared to be a solid mass of humanity which would, rather like the Red Sea of yore, miraculously push back to let the bikes pass.

Official statistics said that Sandy and I were just two of 20,000 spectators who had bought tickets that weekend to watch the likes of Brad Andres, Dick Mann, and Dick Klamforth battle it out on the 100-mile national. And a kid hardly older than we were, Roger Reiman, won the 50-mile amateur. But more than the racing, it was the fraternal feeling of those thousands of riders that appealed to me.

Had I not been offered a scholarship to get some elevated education, I might have given Roger some competition; that's a joke. As it was, I rode my motorcycle to college, did the army, graduate school, got a job, and then went traveling (on a motorcycle) for a few years, during which time I did not take part in the rally world much. However, in the early summer of '76 I left San Miguel de Allende, Mexico, where I had been living for a year, rode up to Alaska, and was heading over to Massachusetts when I stopped to see a BMW-riding friend in Iowa; Steve recommended that we go to the BMWMOA rally over in Oshkosh, Wisconsin. As I rolled into this huge encampment, I began to get a repeat of that little thrill I had felt at Laconia.

Since then I've hit every big, and most middling, and quite a few small, events that this continent puts on. The old Til Thompson Aspencade in Ruidoso, New Mexico (now renamed the Quaking Aspen Rally, I believe); Americade in New York; Sturgis, South Dakota, where 100,000 or more bikes roll through during the ten days of activity; the world GP, now Superbike, races at Laguna Seca, California; the ecumenical Honda Hoot in North Carolina; the constantly moving club nationals, big like the MOA and GWRRA, less big like Norton or the Kawasaki Voyager association; and the latest events, the rolling rallys, like the ones put on by the BMW Oilheads and the Concours Owners Group, where the rally has no fixed point but rolls on for 5000 or more miles, picking up participants for a day or a week, dropping them off. I do like the concept.

I've done some of the big European events. I was at the FIM (Federation Internationale Motocyclistes) rally in Yugoslavia in 1990, the first time that Americans were officially participating. And at the Isle of Man TT in 1978, when the immortal Mike Hailwood reappeared after many years absence and rode his Ducati to victory. And the Assen Grand Prix in Holland, where 40,000 motorcycles were parked in an orderly manner in one large field while the riders watched the races.

And I've been to a lot of gypsy tours, rallys, events where hundreds of riders gather, where the mandatory cloisonné proof that you were indeed present at the 44th annual Jawa Owners Group national rally is given out and pinned to the already burdened denim vest.

Maybe I'll become a bonafide rally rat some year. Start at Americade in June, and work my way through the summer without ever getting nearer to home than Hollister. Or maybe do 20 HOG events in a row, ending up at the national in Milwaukee.

"Yup, here comes Clem again. That boy does need a haircut. And a new rear tire. Let's have him over for supper; he's probably got some good tales to tell. Those rats always do."

The Stepford Motorcycles

November 2000

I am generally a tolerant fellow, but I am getting sick and bloody tired of hearing a wimpish minority amongst us bleating about "practicality," "usability," "comfort," using those anodyne words in an effort to change our culture into the equivalent of a Marie Callender's chicken pot pie. If you don't know what Marie's pie tastes like, it is a perfectly healthy, quite uninspired mixture of diced poultry, boiled veg, and cream sauce poured into a forgettable crust.

Some people love it. Good; I'm glad. I'll take a plate of *penna arrabiata* myself, which happens to be a very spicy pasta dish. And speaking of pasta, let me segue into Italian bikes. I recently rode both a Guzzi V11 Sport and a Ducati 996. Those motorcycles are immense fun to ride; I might not recommend either for a stop-and-go commute, but I do think that on a back road they are superb instruments for gauging lean angles. Granted, the only similarity that the two have is that they are Italian-made V-twins, but they do serve as excellent examples of Italian impracticality. Now, if you are one of those people who is now whimpering about ergonomics and chiropractors, buy a Guzzi Jackal or a Ducati Monster, offering much more composed seating positions and reduced performance; nobody is forcing you to choose one of these sportily inclined bikes.

Italian men of fashion still carry purses because the cut and hang of a good Brioni suit would be deteriorated by the presence of a wallet or handkerchief. And we can make a comparison with super-sporting Italian motorcycles.

I am the first to say that there is no good reason to run a race-bred 996 down a public road, but if you are incautious enough to promote that line of thought, then inevitably you have to arrive at the conclusion that there is no good reason to own a motorcycle. So watch where you tread.

We ride what we want to because we like to, and we don't need no stinkin' reason.

Years ago a movie came out called *The Stepford Wives,* in which a young couple moves into a community and the wife soon realizes that all these other women are a bit too perfect, too much the same. And then her husband starts to like this cookie-cutter approach, which makes her really nervous. Good flick; rent it. And now I segue again, to the fact that many motorcyclists want those Stepford motorcycles, which are good-looking, trouble-free, inexpensive, powerful, great in the corners, comfortable—I've got a couple in the garage.

But there is more to motorcycling than that. And I find it is the softies who tend to poo-poo the extremists.

The other morning half a dozen of us went on a 100-mile, back-road ride; it was a mixture of Japanese fours and Euro-twins, but also included "King" Kahn on his '47 Indian Chief. He has his own small stable, from a chopped Ariel Square Four to a Triumph Sprint ST, but his ride of choice that day was the three-speed flathead. He likes it. A good bump in the road will bounce him off the saddle, but that's fine. And braking is better done in anticipation rather than in real need.

He's not suffering; he's having a good time. And as my great-aunt Agatha was wont to say, suffering builds character, which, by the way, seems to be a key word in describing these "impractical" machines . . . but that is another story. And one person's idea of a good time might not be another's idea.

Take clothing, for example. Especially with the fashion-conscious cruiser riders. At the Laughlin River Run this year I saw an attractive woman in the tightest imaginable leather pants ("intraveneously applied," a friend opined), and tall, high-heeled boots. I adroitly engaged her in idle chat and worked the conversation around to the fact that her get-up looked a trifle uncomfortable, and was it? "Yes," she said, "but don't I look great!?" She did, and I commended her for suffering in a worthy cause.

As a young man I was reading a book about post-revolutionary France, and the author dwelt at length on the loosening of sexual mores, and the advent of the rather comely empire-style dress, popularized by Napoleon's wife Josephine. At parties young women would sprinkle water on the bosom of their thin dresses in order to enhance their attributes; the result was that many died of pneumonia, which is sort of taking suffering for style to an illogical end.

A more modern, and less drastic, equivalent to that can be found in Richard LaPlante's book, *Hog Fever,* in which he describes a rainy ride from England down to Spain on his highly customized Harley. Wishing to look super-cool, he did not want to spoil the lines of his machine by carrying baggage, and had not even packed a rainsuit. Good story.

If you want to ride from Chicago to Sturgis in jeans, fringed chaps, and a leather vest, with a toothbrush being your only baggage (I insist on that, in case I end up standing next to you in a bar)—that is fine with me. If you want to do it on your Eagle hardtail, that is fine, too.

If you want to take that same trip on your Gold Wing, that is also good. But as you put your GL on cruise-control and sip the soda that has been hanging in the gimbel from the handlebars, powering down I-90's fast lane at 80 mph, do not sneer at the rider on the '55 Panhead lumping along at a steady 65. He is having his own good time.

I don't find the chopper or hard-edged sport bike rider any different from the person who likes to camp. A tent and sleeping bag in the George Washington National Forest will never be as comfortable as the nearest Hilton Hotel with 60 channels on the television, but so what? Nor will Honda's RC-51 be as easy to ride as a CBR600F4. But there is a pleasure to be found in camping, and riding an RC-51, that only those who do it know about.

I'm glad there are riders out there who like to suffer a bit. Nothing against Stepford motorcyclists, but when you hear them rail against the harder-edged machines, I know that they know they are missing something.

Fast Guys, Slow Guys

December 2000

As my friend Fireball likes to say, there are four speeds: slow, fast, very fast, and absurdly fast. And I promise you that when you are a thousand miles from home, on a road you have never been on before, your speed will be somewhere between slow and fast.

Leave the very fast for your well-known local road, and save the absurdly fast for track day.

A while back I was going west through New Mexico on US 64, just past Cimarron where the road gets nicely curvaceous, chugging along on a Harley bagger at a very little more than the 55 mph limit, and two sport bikes came up behind, stayed for a moment, and then passed when the way was clear. The riders, both brightly leathered with their gear neatly stashed in tankbags and tailpacks, waved and moved along about ten mph faster than I was going. I was into scenery that day.

A couple of minutes later I heard a tootle from behind and before I could look in the mirrors a Gold Wing went by me like a Dodge Viper passing a Plymouth Colt, stereo full on with some country and western station playing. He waved, and wailed off into the distance, leaning deep into the next curve, going a good 25 mph faster than I was. I hoped he knew what he was doing, because I knew he would hate to scuff up all that pretty chrome.

Later that day I saw the sport bikers, both on 600s, up in Red River, and talked to them for a moment. Yes, the Wing had nearly blown them off the road, too. We figured the rider was either suicidal or commuted over that road regularly.

It is one thing to speed along pleasantly, always staying within the boundaries of line-of-sight stoppability, quite another to go into a totally unknown bend in the road, already at maximum lean, only to find out the curve has a decreasing radius, or that the hillside has dumped a load of rock on the pavement, or that a station wagon full of tourists has decided to make a U-turn. Happy touring means not having an accident, and that means a sensible approach to speed.

I would say that at responsible touring speeds, a Gold Wing will keep up with any sport bike. For that matter, my Harley bagger didn't do badly up to 90 mph. Yes, an RC-51 or YZF-R1 will go a whole lot faster on the straights and around the curves, but if you are crossing New Mexico on US 64 from Clayton to Farmington, with the sheriff's department and the highway patrol eager to add to local revenues, my single-track motorhome would not be far behind.

Some of us don't like to go fast at all, adhering to the posted speed limits because that is the speed we like to go. Others of us are seriously deficient in monoamine oxidase (MAO), and the lack thereof supposedly causes us to operate in a somewhat more reckless manner. If you are not familiar with MAO, back in the 1970s researchers at the National Institute of Mental Health found that people with low levels of this enzyme in their brains are more likely to do fool-hardy things, to be risk-takers. I haven't heard of anyone using that defense in defending a speeding ticket in court, but it will happen.

I sometimes wonder about my MAO level. I've gone absurdly fast maybe twice in my life, and both of these were when I was old enough to know better.

The first time was in 1981, very early one spring Saturday morning (one remembers when one does such things), and I was up at The Lookout on the Ortega Highway, one of Southern California's Racer Roads, on a new Suzuki GS750E. I'd been riding that road for the better part of a year, but I was still fresh meat, a newbie, to the regulars. We were kicking tires and drinking coffee, and the current King of the Road said that he was about to do a run down the mountain to the fire station, and would I like to ride back down with him. Here it was, my test for entry into the informal club.

Sure. We saddled up, only the two of us, and off we went, just for a quick ride. This was not a race, merely a little rite of passage, and the unspoken rules said that all I had to do was stay within a hundred or so feet of his taillight for the ten or so miles to the bottom. I had to figure that the King knew what he was doing, and that my bike could do what his bike could do, and off we went. I wanted acceptance into this little group, and so I stuck with him, helped along by a good push of adrenalin.

We got to the forest fire station and stopped. "Not bad," he said, and turned around to go back up. Passed.

The other time was at California's Laguna Seca Raceway some five years later, when BMWMOA held a national rally there, and Kawasaki had just come out with the Concours model. Reg Pridmore was running a CLASS school and I was out on the track on a test Concours, just coming out of Turn 9 (now 11) onto the front straight, and I looked over to see that my friend Craig Erion was right beside me on a mildly hotted-up K100RS. We both nodded and screwed those throttles tight. The Concours apparently had a few more horses to call on as I came over Turn 1 first, going way too fast for my comfort and skill level, but I kept going. This is the sort of informal competitive event which is not conducive to long life and uncrashed motorcycles, but it is part of growing up. I came up the hill on the back stretch, slammed on all brakes just before dropping into the corkscrew, and then jammed the throttle wide open. Only to find myself still upright but sliding sideways down the hill. Not a good thing, I was reminded, as a full load of adrenalin jolted my system. I gently backed off on the gas, Craig went by, I got things under control, and proceeded to continue lapping the track at a somewhat slower pace.

I still like speed, still like to go fast. But I am more judicious about when and where I go fast, and how fast. I stick to my own well-known county backroads when I want to wring out a bike. Like Shell Creek Road, an absolutely blissful ten-mile stretch of smooth asphalt running through ranch country. Maybe one pickup along the way. Or a herd of cattle in the road. Good fun.

I think Sue hopes that somebody will come up with a herbal supplement to boost ones MAO, and she'll sneak it into my orange juice in the morning.

Centennial Apologies

April 2001

We are well tucked into the 21st century . . . which in calendarial fact began this last January 1st, and not the year before. A new dude is in the White House, the economy seems strong, the Middle East seethes along, oil prices rise. My bike runs well, as does Sue's, and we go for rides. And pick up the bills and catalogues and occasional letters six days a week (excepting holidays) from our mail-box beside the road. The world seems much the same as it was in the 20th century.

But it is not. If any of you readers called me up last week and left a message on my answering machine, you had better call again. The recording mechanism broke down. While, I might add, the machine I was riding, a Ducati ST4, was behaving flawlessly even as the rider was behaving a bit recklessly.

Two recent incidents have forever changed my view of how our civilization functions. First, I picked up my morning newspaper, turned to the comics, and Dagwood was using a cell phone to call Blondie; that rattled my fuddy-duddy cage, and almost caused me to rush out and buy one. Next thing I know, Dagwood will be commuting to work on a Honda Reflex scooter.

Second, a buddy of mine in the motorcycle aftermarket trade gave me a call the other day to tell me about his latest foray into the world of three-martini lunches. He is L.A.-based, but was in New York City with a couple of clients, and after an expensive dinner to celebrate The Deal they took a cab to a truly non-descript neighborhood on Second Avenue. There was a door, just an ordinary door, and they went in, walked upstairs, and into a really fine bar, all polished wood, backdropped by several hundred bottles of scotch. Where you could buy a shot of Bowman 40 for about a thousand bucks.

A grand—for a single shot of whiskey. Although the owner of the "Hole In One" bar claims that he gives exceptionally big shots. I must not have kept up with how much things cost. Premium gas is two bucks a gallon out here in the West, and not likely to get any cheaper. And our property taxes just went up. However, the price of 2001 bikes is really going down. A Bandit 1200 for $6999?! Wowzer! A Shadow Spirit 750 for $5999!? Double wowser!! For five shots of Bowman 40 I can have a new KLR650 ($4999).

What happened this last New Year's Eve? Nothing much, really, no Y2K+1 fuss. According to the Gregorian calendar we moved into the 21st century and the third millenium—though the Jews, Buddhists, Moslems, et cetera, all have their own dating systems. And I cleaned off my desk. Which had accumulated a lot of paper. My *modus operandi* is to take all the letters and faxes that come in and put them in an IN box. When I answer one, I put it in the OUT box, from where it goes, if I get around to it, into the files. Unfortunately, more comes IN then goes OUT, and there is some horrendously old correspondence that I have never dealt with. When either box gets overloaded, I carefully move the contents to a cardboard box which gets put under my desk. Which eventually gets moved to a high shelf in the garage, next to the old Venturer fairing and saddlebags.

So all you people who wrote me letters and have awaited a reply for the last five or ten years, you now understand why you have never gotten an answer. And some gifts have never gotten thank-you notes, which in my mother's book of etiquette was a most grievous sin. On my map shelf is a boxed set of excellent maps for Argentina that a *Rider* reader who was working down there sent me after reading a column I had written about maps. I have always meant to thank him, but have lost his address.

Whoever he is, I trust you are still reading this magazine and consider yourself well thanked.

By the way, The Wife takes care of the bills, which is why the water and electricity are still functioning here, and the motorcycles get re-registered every year.

I tried to get into the new century reasonably unencumbered, except with the inevitable guilt, but I retain my right to be fuzzily confused. I am still having some difficulty understanding the usefulness of on-board GPS gadgets when most people in SUVs are stuck in traffic jams on Friday evening. Which brings me back to Dagwood—I consider the cell phone to be an extremely useful device, though why the much more efficient satellite phone concept failed beats the heck out of me.

My biggest problem with any phone is this insidious need that most Americans have to "be connected." They can't bear the thought that Snookums can't reach them at any moment in the day or night, whereas my idea of 21st century heaven is to leave all that stuff behind, to get on a Yamaha FJR1300 (I wish!) and ride off to some remote valley and spend a day watching wild-flowers grow.

But I accept the inevitable presence of more gadgetry and gimmickry and techonological trickery. I loved disc brakes and CDI ignition and tubeless tires, all of which came about in the last third of the last century. What is next?

I've got enough horsepower, enough handling, give me light weight. Having recently dropped an 800-pound behemouth while U-turning on a bad dirt road in a remote woods, and not been able to pick it up, I was again reminded that I should always ride a bike that I can pick up by myself. After contemplating my stupidity for a few moments, and just as I began to strip everything off in an effort to lighten the lift, I heard a chugga-chugga in the distance, and within a minute a very old Dodge pickup, with a skinny, semi-toothless fellow at the wheel, came around the trees.

"Yup, usta have me a motosickle. Couldn't pick the sumbich up neither. Let's give 'er a heave." And away I went. Carefully.

Now I'm looking at the next 100 years, although I probably won't make it to the next century. However, one resolution I have made is that I am going to try to respond to my correspondence better. I have a new system; the new stuff goes to the bottom of the IN box, and the oldest letters will be on top. Which might work. Or it could just mean more cardboard boxes full of paper.

And I'll write to my local newspaper and get them to drop *Blondie* and pick-up reruns of *Li'l Abner;* no cell phones in that world. And as for that $1000 shot of whiskey—I can buy a lot of palatable wine for that money. Or a good used Nighthawk.

Banning Boorish Behavior

May 2001

We motorcyclists are often our own worst enemies. We complain that we are discriminated against, that people don't like us, that we are misunderstood. Poor us. But we often fail to appreciate that we just alienated half a dozen innocuous right-turning cagers when we cut along the bicycle lane so that we could make the light ahead of them.

They got rattled by our unexpected presence, as suddenly a motorcycle is where they didn't expect one to be. And where the law, in protecting bicyclists, says there should not be one. So that evening at the dinner table the 16-year-old child says, "Dad, I want to get a motorcycle license," and Dad responds, "Not on your life!" or words to that effect.

We've done it again, we've been mindless slobs who do things without thinking about the effect it will have on others. A slob, according to my *Webster's*, is a boorish person, and a boor is defined as being rude and insensitive.

When is the last time eight of you barged into Denny's on a rainy day, spread your wet gear all over three booths, drank coffee for two hours, and left the waitress a three-dollar tip? Think about that when next you get a surly look as your gang comes into a diner.

Or you are very proud of the set of Gatling Gun pipes on your cruiser, and took off from your buddy's new house in that nice development at one o'clock in the morning in a manner that allowed the whole neighborhood to sit up and take notice of how cool you sound? You aren't cool; you're a horse's ass. And if your buddy has any sense, he won't invite you back again. Unless you drive your Ford Pinto.

Or you wake up in the morning after a good night's sleep in the Bide-A-Wee Motel, and find it's rained a little. Going into the bathroom you get a couple of clean, fluffy towels and proceed to wipe your saddle down, and the tank, and so on. Your bike was pretty dirty when you pulled in last night, and now these towels are filthy to the point that they can't be used again. Do you think the motel proprietor is happy? You've just cost him any profit he might have made on your room, and then some.

You are, in a few carefully chosen words, a stupid, selfish, thoughtless slob if you abuse a motel like that. Just because you don't ever plan on coming this way again, and don't give a damn what the motel owner thinks, doesn't mean this won't affect the next rider to come through.

And such boorishness is really quite unnecessary. When staying at a motel or hotel, every time I have gone to the desk and asked for something with which to clean the bike, or my boots, I have cheerfully been given old towels or torn-up sheets which were retired from active duty to the rag box. You just flat do not use the new ones you find in your room.

Personally, I have a great deal of difficulty understanding such boorish behavior. Sure, if a kid throws a tantrum, that is part of growing up. Or your teenager becomes insolent and hostile . . . this is done to teach parents grace and patience. But once a man or woman has achieved maturity, all those childish things should be put aside.

Manners make the motorcyclist. Good manners, that is, not bad. I was up at the Laguna Seca races last year, talking with a friend whom I had not seen in many months, when this Bob Boor-type connected my beard and beret with *Rider* magazine, walked up and rudely interrupted the conversation, starting on a rant about how magazines are failing to meet the motorcyclists' needs, et cetera. Friend Dean looked at me, shook his head, and left. I, being a weak-willed and cowardly type, stood and listened to the dolt for four full minutes before excusing myself, saying my presence was immediately required in some small Central American country.

This Bob Boor had not a clue. There is a word somewhere in the English lexicon (which escapes me now) for a person who is convinced that other people like him, find him interesting, when in truth they don't. Such a person trundles through life, boring everyone he meets by talking endlessly about the mudflap he recently riveted on the front fender of his machine, and how manufacturers, if they had any sense at all, would do the same. Ad nauseum.

On the other hand, I know of many more motorcyclists, the great, great majority, who are excellent examples of what the human race could and should be like. They help little old gents across the street, donate time and money to their charitable works, pay their taxes without complaining, vote even when they think all the candidates are twits, and are good, up-standing citizens. However, these are not the ones who stay in the non-motorcyclist's mind.

The one the non-riders remember is the loud-piped, over-stuffed slob with the XXXL T-shirt pulled tight over his obscene belly, his lint-filled navel showing. The way-too-cool dude riding his sport-bike in shorts and sneakers who scares the motorist almost into a ditch by overtaking on a blind curve. And the parking-place biker/thief who, as a cautious driver backs his '89 Oldsmobile slowly out of a spot in a crowded mall for which some Taurus-navigator has been waiting several minutes, sneaks in quick-like and then jumps off and rapidly walks away, pretending never to have seen the Taurus. The jerk who makes rude gestures at wide-eyed kids who are staring at him from a Dodge Caravan. The club that takes up half the pumps at a gas station, and after filling up they all walk off to have a soda and chat in the shade, leaving their bikes to block the pumps. Two riders cruising slowly down the Interstate in the fast lane while traffic backs up behind them.

It is the action of the boorish rider that will be remembered and talked about by non-riders, not the charity run that raised $10,000 for a needy family. That is just in the nature of things.

I realize that the intelligence quotient rating of 100 is the median, with half the people below, half above, but I like to think that the great majority of riders are at the three-digit level. In truth I think that an IQ test is more important than a conventional licensing test, and perhaps motorcyclists should have to pass the 100+ mark . . . though to achieve that my slow-witted self would have to take a cram session. I also think any would-be rider should have to take a course in proper motorcycling etiquette before he is allowed to roam the highways.

We motorcyclists are a minority. Minorities have equal rights in this great nation of ours, but the truthful reality is that a minority (us) has to be concerned with how the majority thinks of it if we want to expand our sport, bring more people into it, if not as riders, then at least as supporters.

So do not be a slob. And if you know one, tell him, or her, to shape up.

How many times do I have to say this before this sinks in? Again, and again, and again. A few of you will never learn, will always give motorcycling, and motorcyclists, a bad name. And I hope that you thoughtless morons will sell your bikes and take up golf real soon.

For the rest, this is just a reminder to be considerate. Be thoughtful. Realize that in your actions you are representing five to six million motorcyclists, and if you act like a stupid, selfish, thoughtless slob, that is how much of the public will think of the rest of us.

And, dammit!, do not use those motel towels to wipe down your bike!

Overcoming Inertia

August 2001

We were up at Ragged Point, a bluff overlooking the Pacific Ocean on the south end of Big Sur. It is a beautiful place, and being beautiful the aesthetically inclined entrepreneurial spirit has built a motel, restaurant, café and small gas station. At the café window the counterman slid two disposable cups full of coffee over to us and we walked across the grass to the bluffs where we could look down and see the waves crashing on the rocky shore.

And my friend began to speak of regrets. About the trip he never took many years ago. He was young, he and his buddy had Triumphs, a little money, no commitments or responsibilities, and they decided that they would just get on the road and ride until they had seen every place and thing they wanted to see. They'd roll out sleeping bags at night, cook trout caught in mountain streams, maybe eat one meal a day in some little diner. Travel cheap, travel far.

They'd see the Grand Canyon and the Mississippi River, the fall foliage of New England, the blue grass of Virginia. They'd meet interesting people, think thoughts they'd never had before. See what life was like on Bourbon Street, see the skyline of Manhattan at dawn. Eat fried chicken in Kentucky, pizza in Chicago. It would be an adventure.

I imagine that most of you reading this have wanted to do the same. Wanted to get on your bike, whatever it is, and head east, west, north or south. Just get on the road, just go. And it really is easy. You can load your Venture or Voyager in 15 minutes, or toss the necessary in a duffel and bungie the bag to the back seat of your Nighthawk or Bandit, and be gone.

But we usually don't. Not even when we can, when we have the opportunity, when we don't have to worry about getting the kids to school, feeding the dog, mowing the lawn, keeping the boss off our back. For whatever reasons, we most often choose not to go, whether it is for a year, or something as simple as a weekend ride. We're mired, stuck, as though our boots are trapped in thick mud. Or, like Lemuel Gulliver, M.D., a thousand tiny strands hold us down; admittedly, Doctor Gulliver had not wanted to travel to Lilliput, had never even heard of the place, but the fateful storm had swept him there.

Here is my presumption, if you can imagine this: you have the metaphorical window of opportunity ahead of you, a month without having to answer the phone, pay the bills, fix the roof. All you have to do is roll your bike out, tuck a rainsuit and flat-fix kit in the tankbag, and you can be gone.

Don't worry about reservations. Don't call your sister up, who lives clear across the country, and tell her you'll be there in a week. This is your moment of opportunity, your chance to slip through the door of everyday constraints and out into the wide world. Do it! Don't even finish reading this; put on the jacket and boots and the helmet and get out there. Now! Quick!

• • •

Didn't do it, did you? You're still sitting at the kitchen table, looking at this page. Maybe for a few fleeting seconds you had that urge, that "Yes! I will do it!" moment, and then it vanished. Inertia has a hold of you.

Inertia is powerful stuff. In a slightly warped view of celestial physics, our entire planet is a product of inertia. We just keep on spinning around our sun, and our galaxy cheerfully rotates through the universe, and it takes an almighty whack, like the boost in a Jupiter rocket, to get free of the place.

And the same thing happens to us in our daily lives. It can be hard to break free. Friday evening, the phone rings; it's Harry. "Let's go for a ride tomorrow. Eight o'clock at the store in Creston." And you can come up with eight reasons why not; not good reasons, but good enough not to accept the invitation.

And three days later you see Harry at the supermarket, and he describes a magnificent 300-mile ride with four others, great roads, great lunch, great camaraderie, all the stuff of great motorcycling. And what did you do? Can't really remember. Oh yes, I cleaned up a corner of the basement.

That day is gone forever. And it certainly did not enhance your memory bank, though it did Harry's.

Have you made that long-promised (to yourself) trip to Americade, or Sturgis? Many of us need planning, need organization, need preparation in order to achieve lift-off. Or departure. For a ride to Lake George or the Black Hills the two weeks may be planned well beforehand, with routes and motels lined up, a set number of days on the road, and then you're home again. If that is what it takes to get you out of town, good. Any trip is better than no trip, and whatever it takes to overcome inertia is good.

However, here I am promoting spontaneity. *Carpe diem,* as they used to say in old Rome, or "Seize the day!," as might be heard in St. Louis. With long-range planning you have merely blipped into a temporary deviation from the normal course of your life, which is good, but not as good as coming home on Friday evening, telling the spouse you've had a rotten week and need a ride. You line up a dog/cat/child sitter, and next morning the two of you head off to where the sky is bluest.

A hundred miles of two-lane road go by, then another hundred. You stop in a small village, fill the gas tanks, have a soda. Ask the woman at the counter if she knows of any nice place to stay. "There's a little resort up on that mountain," she says, pointing; "my cousin works there and says its pretty comfy, with hot tubs and all that. Let me call and make sure they got a room."

They do. And by the time you get home Sunday afternoon, your whole attitude towards the world has changed. "Bring on Monday!" you say. "We'll teach it a little respect!"

We want spontaneity. We need spontaneity. And our daily lives tend to be just the opposite, well programmed, inert. But all it takes to change that is to put the key in the ignition, push the button, and go for a long ride.

Gaining Attitude

September 2001

Back in the mid-eighties a friend of mine, who had been riding European and Japanese bikes for many years, decided to try out this new Evo Harley that the motorcycle magazines were talking up. He rode down to a dealership, chatted up the salesman who then put him on a Big Twin for a test ride, and away he went. To return in less than half an hour, not terribly enthused.

"What's the deal?" he asked this fellow who was responsible for moving these Harleys off the showroom floor and onto the street. "My bike goes faster, handles better, stops quicker, and costs less. Why would I want to buy this one?"

The salesman, who had obviously heard this line before, was quick on the response: "Hey, to want to ride a Harley, you've got to have attitude."

As if to say that attitude was a prized possession, and that my friend sadly lacked it. With the not-too-subtle intimation being that maybe if he bought a Harley . . .

Move forward to the spring of 2001, and I am at the Furnace Creek gas station out in Death Valley. It's early morning, the weather is perfect, and the only other clients are a pleasant-looking couple, grey-haired, sixtyish, getting on a big metric cruiser, as we have come to refer to the Japanese versions of a Harley. They seem to be very nice, poster-worthy grandparents, and tell me they belong to a cruiser club in Los Angeles and about a dozen of the gang have come out for the weekend. I admire the bike, which had some mild customizing done, and after a few minutes of talk they say, "Gotta go."

He pushes the starter button . . . and I am about blown off my feet from the noise emanating from the unmuffled exhaust. Jesus Lord, have mercy on my eardrums! The straight pipes end just beyond the passenger pegs, and the full blast of sound had to be blowing out the tympanic membrances of the good woman on behind, though she looked quite beatific and very comfortable as they pulled away, racketing up to 110 decibels or better. That sucker was loud!

Why do they do it? I have no idea. Perhaps it does have something to do with riders wishing to appear attitudinous, rather like those tattoo decals that some riders sport on weekends. The business of aftermarket pipes is booming (good pun!) like never before, and I seriously doubt that there is a single replacement exhaust system on the market which makes less noise than the stock. Okay, I can understand somebody wanting to mellow out the exhaust sound, to make it a little more syncopated, to create a more melodious passage.

I felt that way on the Yamaha Venture I rode recently; nice bike and all, but the exhaust note was so muted it was like listening to a noisy air conditioner. Were I to buy a Venture I might well be in the market for a set of aftermarket mufflers. Note the use of the word "mufflers," as in to muffle the sound. If the stock Venture puts out 80 decibels, I might go as high as 85, but no higher.

But noise for the sake of noise? Forget it. Except that I am working on a theory that when a person is subjected to a lot of noise, he develops an attitude. And I'm not talking about that smarmy Webster's dictionary type of attitude, but the loud-pipe attitude, so that when you pull up in front of the Bucket of Blood Saloon, blip your throttle one last time, the pipes pointing straight at the open door, people will know you've arrived. And are not to be messed with.

That's the attitude. I'm tough. I'm mean. Don't mess with me. I've got a splitting headache because of these pipes, and nobody should get in my way.

I admit that I had one brief foray into loud pipes, or I should say, a loud pipe. When I was in high school I owned an NSU 250 Max, a properly muffled bike, as even back then the Germans were cracking down on such things. One day a well-meaning friend gave me a cheap chromed megaphone, just a straight-through echo-can that would fit on the end of the header pipe. I unbolted the 15-pound muffler and slipped the megaphone on after school, and that evening rode the ten miles to the Aces Up M/C clubhouse, which was in Stan's garage. I liked hanging out with Stan because he knew a lot, and not just because he had a BSA Gold Star 500 at the time, which I coveted greatly, but could not possibly come up with the money to purchase such magnificence.

He made some comment about my noisy bike, and opined that my sorry excuse for an exhaust system had probably cost me a couple of the Max's precious 18.2 horsepower, as advertised by NSU. When I left I looped over the nearby hill and came down a straightaway about a mile from Stan's house wound out to the very max (another pun!), which usually meant about 85 mph, but this time I could hardly creep beyond 80 mph. Maybe I had lost horsepower, but I had gained attitude, because I thought it was cool to be disturbing the sleep of everyone whose house I passed. Until I got word that Stan had said I would not be welcome around his neighborhood until I had put the stock muffler back on. Which I did, and also got a stinging lecture about nasty punks who give motorcycling a bad name.

Life rolls on, and I rolled into Laughlin, Nevada, this past April, for the 19th version of the River Run. During the rally's four days this place is loud-pipe heaven, because there is nothing to do there other than to gamble and to ride up and down the two miles of main street in front of the nine casinos. And see who has the loudest pipes. Burn-outs at 3 a.m. are popular, with Gatling Gun and Shotgun exhausts battling it out, not for speed but for noise.

It seemed that if a River Runner did not have that seemingly essential quality called attitude, he could disguise the fact with minimal muffling.

At dinner one night the publisher of this esteemed magazine was dissecting his crab legs and boiled crayfish, and he said that during the day he had been walking along and stopped to admire a new Harley parked by the curb. While he was looking at it the owner fired the beast up . . . and it had a stock exhaust.

"Nice to hear a bike quiet like that," said Jim, sincerely.

But the rider obviously felt that this was a not-so-discreet put-down and responded, "Yeah, I gotta get a set of pipes for this baby."

Obviously our well-meaning Jim had just made a sale for the aftermarket exhaust world. And he didn't even get a cut.

Nuts and Bolts

October 2001

In times past I used to wander down the narrow aisles behind the counter at Randy's Cycle Sales, with row upon row of the parts, small and large, that went into the construction of a motorcycle, from an assortment of jets for Amal Monobloc carburetors to a Velocette Viper gas tank. R. G. Wilson was a motorcycle dealer in West Boylston, Massachusetts, whom I used to frequent back when LBJ was president, and he had a pretty *laissez faire* attitude about his long-time clientele, giving them the run of the shop. An array of British bikes and parts were always on hand, anything from the popular Triumph to the off-beat Panther and Greeves, and parts to fit just about anything that came from the Old Sod.

With hundreds of little boxes that held every size of nut and bolt and washer to fit these machines.

I loved to handle these fasteners, to touch the threads, feel the cold metal, marvel at the way they would match, male to female. Granted, the simplicity of design may have had something to do with this, as I'm a simple fellow, and any number of things amaze me. Like that international space station orbiting way up over our heads. Or the fact that it takes heat to make ice and have air-conditioning. That a Boeing 747 can even get off the ground. That today's motorcycles are as reliable as they are, thanks to nuts and bolts.

I appreciate the technological march that moves us forward inexorably, from the steam train to the jet plane. And the psychological advances as well—when that IQ (Intelligence Quotient) testing was popularized in the 1920s, the norm was 100; in the 21st century that has moved up to 112. Times, they are a'changing. Or else we have become better at test-taking.

As are the construction techniques in building motorcycles. In 1958 I bought a very used 1951 Indian Chief, and in my own personal reliability-rating system it scored about a 3, as opposed to the 2-minus of a '48 Harley Panhead, compared to, say, the 9-plus of a 2001 Kawasaki Nomad. That old Indian shook, and as a result of that shaking, just about anything that could fall off did. It came with windshield and saddlebags and spotlights and bits of chrome, and in the eight months I owned the bike just about all of that fell off. Not to mention blown head-gaskets.

On more than one occasion I have been castigated by readers for having written an article that struck the reader as being more than a mite old-fashioned—which apparently is a sin in the eyes of many of these 21st century chalupa-chomping dot.commers and the like. I prefer to think of myself as being historically minded. After all, it is said that those who do not know their history are doomed to repeat it. I don't think the Hanlon brothers, of Excelsior infamy, had properly read their history.

I consider most of the current crop of motorcycles, from Aprilia to Yamaha, to be very much 21st century machines, but if we are to look down the road to where the next generation of machines are waiting to be seen, then maybe we should look back to the 19th century . . . or even earlier.

All bikes are held together by nuts and bolts and screws and washers, metallic things that many of us take for granted. Who has not got a jar of odd-sized fastners somewhere in the garage or the basement? It is in the nature of the mechanical age that after you take something apart and then put it back together, a few pieces will be left over. Put them in the jar.

The concept of using a threaded device to apply pressure goes back to the ancient Greeks. That was an intricately carved wooden design, intended to apply pressure and squeeze the juices out of a vat full of grapes or olives. The first metal nuts and bolts appeared around the 15th century, handmade items used in the construction of suits of armour, which allowed for some measure of adjustment should the knight partake of too many banquets.

Move forward to the early 1800s when Brit Henry Maudslay developed a screw-cutting machine, and in 1841 a fellow named Joseph Whitworth (a name all British nostalgists are familiar with), who had worked in one of Maudslay's shops, proposed a uniform measuring of screw threads. In 1845 an American, Stephen Fitch, patented his turret lathe that he used for cutting threads, known more formally as "creating continuous helical ribs on a cylindrical flank." And thanks to Whitworth's notion a manufacturer could standardize production, and, like the present Crown Bolt, Inc., make a good living selling these little bits.

Today the International Standards Organization has accepted both inch and metric standards (the Whitworth standard is long gone, thank goodness, although I still have a collection of Whitworth box, open and socket wrenches, as well as the invaluable Whitworth adjustable wrench) in determining the pitch of a screw's threads—now usually set at coarse, fine, and extra fine. Naturally the material used in the creation of a bolt has a great deal to do with its strength. It might be carbon steel, or alloy, or a stainless steel. Or zinc-plated pot metal.

Years ago I was in Mexico City, and one of the centerstand bolts on my BMW R75/5 had vibrated its way to freedom. I went to a shop and got a new bolt—it fit, looked shiny, and lasted less than a month before shearing through. Too soft; probably Grade 2. Never underestimate what your fastener is made of.

In my not-too-distant, Brit-riding past, I traveled with an assortment of nuts and bolts in a small bag, because sure as Elizabeth Regina's minions made motorcycles, those fastners would drop off on a regular basis. On any trip there would be the morning vetting, going over the whole bike with a handful of wrenches and screwdrivers, tightening everything that had loosened up the previous day, replacing anything lost.

Today, it hardly occurs to me. As an engineer friend patiently explained to me, there might be a lot of reasons for that. First, fasteners come with more precise threads, which can be snugged more tightly. Second, we build less vibratory engines, like multi-cylinder machines, and make good use of counter-balancers. Third, we use enough nuts and bolts to actually hold whatever it is together, as opposed to the hit or miss notions of old. Four, the proper torquing of a bolt is no longer a dark science; generally, a bike fresh from the factory will have no problems, and it is only after a mechanic without a good torque wrench has worked on it that fasteners might come loose.

We also have the wondrous chemicals that can glue a bolt into place, the most popular being Loctite, available in blue, red, and other hues. Do not confuse the colors, or you might never rend asunder what you just put together.

I still check the odd nut and bolt, especially on my lawn-mower. Sadly, Randy and his type have long retired, and when I need a tactile hit, I cannot go down to my local dealer, where all these fasteners now come sealed in little plastic bags with MADE IN TAIWAN or something on the outside. However, I can go to my local hardware store with its scores of small, open boxes. And I might buy a buggle-head ¼ x1 bolt just because it looks good. Or a pound of Grade 8 Rockford mixed nuts and bolts for a mere $2.99, because you never know when you might need one.

The Basics of Geography

November 2001

There is no such thing as an entirely free lunch, or dinner, as you are going to pay for it somewhere down the line. And I usually try to repay repastian hospitality by bringing along a good bottle of wine and entertaining my hosts with tales of travel. The other week some friends, knowing Sue was out of town and my can-opener might not be working, invited me over, so I was dressed up in my Tuesday evening best, jeans and a T-shirt, and regaling the table with stories of my adventures in crossing Tibet on a motorcycle. Their 15-year-old looked at me and asked, "Clement, where's Tibet?"

Darn! And here I was presuming that everybody in these United States would have known where Tibet was. "Look at the back of my shirt," I said, which had a nice little map of my expedition. "It is up there between India and China, where the Himalaya Mountains are. You've heard of Mount Everest, haven't you?"

"Yes, that's the tallest mountain in the world. But I'm not sure where it is." Back when I was 14, Mr. Rand had each and every one of us in his civics class point out the whereabouts of Mt. Everest on a big map. And Mt. McKinley, too, I should add.

Obviously Mr. Rand and his kind of teaching have long since been retired from the public school system. My freshman year at Northampton (Massachusetts) High School he made darned sure that we knew the location of all the the places that were talked about on the front page of *The Daily Hampshire Gazette,* the local paper. He pulled down his roll-up map every Friday, and we knew where China and Indochina and Korea were, where Argentina and South Africa were located, and how big the Soviet Union was, stretching across ten (if I remember correctly) time zones, with all the clocks being on Moscow time.

I got my geography lessons early on, and they have been invaluable in helping me in my travels. But apparently geography seems to have pretty much disappeared from school classrooms, according to an article I read recently; maybe those learned folk who determine curriculum think that this GPS technology makes knowing where you are obsolete. I disagree.

When I'm riding around North America, it doesn't interest me much what the capitals of the 50 states are, but I do have a good idea of where these states are located. Can you tell me what states border Kansas, which is about in the center of this country?

That's not meant to be a trick question, just a little thought-provoker—and maybe win a bet or two. There's Missouri to the east, Colorado to the west, Nebraska north, Oklahoma south. I had one of those 48-state puzzles as a child, which helped me learn such stuff. But knowing the lay of the land is useful information, because when I am thinking of doing a cross-country trip, I have a good mental image of possible routes. I know where the mountain ranges and the deserts are, which can mean cold weather and snow, or boiling hot temperatures, all good things to be aware of when planning a trip.

I've been riding on six of the seven continents (I leave Antarctica to more adventuresome types), but I must admit I cannot really keep up with the number of separate countries there are today. In the past ten years, with the break-up of the Soviet Union and of Yugoslavia, we've got a bunch more nations that fly their own flag and make their own stamps. As of last (2000) September, the United Nations had 189 members, which does not include the traditionally neutral Switzerland.

I have two drawers full of maps, one dealing with the U.S. of A., the other of the rest of the world. In the first I have maps of the entire country, scores of state maps, down to county and city maps. You can never, ever have too many maps. My most-used maps are those that cover the 200-mile radius from my house, and there are still some, a few, roads I have not been on, despite my having lived here for ten years. I've yet to do Rancheria Road paralleling the Kern River canyon; I just have to get off my lazy duff.

The global collection goes way back, as I haven't thrown away a map in more than 30 years. Being alphabetically arranged, it starts with a large map of Afghanistan, with lots of photos on the back. I picked that up from the tourist office in Herat in 1973, and it guided me around that then-kingdom; unfortunately, I look at the pictures of the giant statues of the Buddha at Bamiyan and realize that those are gone forever, blown to pieces by local fundamentalists. The world changes, and we had better change with it. There's a good Michelin map of Algeria and Tunisia, not that I'll be going back to Algeria for a while; too much strife. A bright, shiny, government-issue, 25-year-old map of the Republic of Guatemala indicates that the neighboring country of Belize is also a part of Guatemala, though the Belizians would strongly disagree. There are several maps of New Zealand, which has the advantage of consisting mainly of two large islands all alone in the South Pacific, and the only danger there is from the Japanese wanting to buy the whole place, lock, stock, and sheep. Under "R," for Russia, is an Intourist "Scheme of Automobile Tours" for the western Soviet Union, showing one big happy family that is now sub-divided into a least seven different countries.

A good sense of geography, combined with a proper appreciation for the weather differences in the tropics and in the temperate zones, allow for some leisurely long-distance traveling. Of course these days travel complications have more to do with politics than geography. This year an acquaintance of mine was intending to ride with his son all the way to the tip of South America, but by the time he got to Panama he was so thoroughly disgusted with the border hassles in Central America, and anticipating more of the same south of the Darien Gap, that they shipped the bikes back home. Bureaucrats are today's biggest problem.

Some travelers seem to get target fixation, as in getting on I-90 in Boston and never deviating from that highway until you get to Seattle; you don't even need a map for that trip. Down in Baja Mexico a while back I met a German motorcyclist who had just one map combining Mexico and Central America, figuring that would get him to Panama. It would, but he would also miss out on a lot of great roads and great sights. I showed him the deviously indirect route that I would take, and we parted company. I never heard from him again, but I think he probably ignored my suggestions. He seemed to be a man in a hurry, and just wanted "to get there," wherever "there" might be.

Perhaps those of us interested in geography, who have lots of maps, are the more laid-back, mellow, Type B personalities. We don't really want to get to the end of the road, we just want to enjoy what we find along the way.

Packing Lite

December 2001

How many of us go off on a trip, having carefully prepared a minimal packing list, and come home two weeks later with 10 or 20 percent of the stuff unused?

It is really easy to take too much, says one who has taken many trips over many years and still tends to come home with some clean clothes. If you have a Ford Expedition or 35' motorhome, that's fine. But packing for a motorcycle trip is a more refined art. Sometimes. It all depends on how you approach the trip.

I see people cruising through Colorado's Glenwood Canyon on I-70, two-up on a full-boat touring bike, towing a trailer, and know that this

couple will have all the comforts of home no matter where they are for the night, in a posh suite in a four-star hotel in Aspen, or camping out in the Gunnison National Forest.

Then there is the minimalist approach, a leather-clad sport-biker with a tank bag and a pillion pack, carving byways during the day, finding an inexpensive motel at night. No need for much other than a toothbrush, and toothpaste, and a change of socks. You might want a swimsuit in case there's a pool.

I do believe that one of the things that prompted me to propose to my girlfriend, now and forever known as The Wife, was when I was in Europe for a couple of months, and she could squeeze only two weeks of vacation out of her employer (the Motorcycle Safety Foundation). But two weeks was better than nothing, and she was going to fly to Rome to meet me and see a bit of the Italian countryside. "We'll be traveling light," I told her, "on a ZX-10 with just a pair of throwover saddlebags and a tankbag." And she walked out of the Leonardo da Vinci Airport with her helmet in one hand, a small carry-on in the other. My kind of traveler, and we had a great trip.

Or the dual-purpose rider, out to see as much of unpaved America as he can in two short weeks, with camping gear and mosquito repellant, tools and a towel. That is the most difficult packing chore, as you need to haul gear, and still want to be able to have fun riding the dirt roads.

I've done two long two-up camping trips, one to Central America, the other to Alaska. Both involved many miles of bad roads, both were great successes, and neither gave me the satisfaction of knowing exactly what I should take. Two sleeping bags, two mattresses, a tent, and enough cooking gear to turn out an enviable meal takes some space. So the rest has to be minimalized.

Clothes? That all depends on how spiffy you wish to look. With laundromats in every town in the US, I really don't feel the need to take more than a week's worth of duds. If you are on one of those two-week foreign trips, wherein the tour-company recommends black tie for the man, evening gown for the lady, be glad that a van is carrying your baggage.

Speaking of foreign, a few months back I was reading a piece by the estimable Greg Frazier, who appears to motorcycle around the world on a biennial basis, in which he was describing what he takes on a globe-circling trip. Lots, quite the opposite of me. For his dual-purpose BMW he carries at least 30 pounds worth of tools, and easily that much weight again in spare parts. And has large metal panniers to carry this stuff in. Well and good, but with all that load running down a muddy road in Kenya's northern territory would terrify me, as the major benefit of a d-p bike, which is light weight, would be lost. I would prefer to travel light and presume there is an alternative to packing my own well-equipped workshop.

I did come a cropper in East Africa once, and I attribute that to the fact that I was overloaded, to the extent of carrying a new spare tire strapped to the top of the duffle bag which was bungied onto the rear seat. I was taking a little-trafficked dirt road, hit some serious bumps, the load shifted, forcing me towards the tank, shifting my weight forward, the front wheel nosed in and Crash! When I came to there was nobody anywhere in sight, and the bike was laying on is side—not seriously damaged, but with a dead short in the electrical system.

Eventually an absolutely full-beyond-capacity pickup truck came by and the driver, worried that I might be eaten by lions, strung out a piece of rope and towed me to a nearby village. And in time a larger truck carried me back to the main road, where the only mechanic in town had a tool kit consisting of a large hammer, a very worn adjustable wrench, and two big screwdrivers. Eventually we fixed the problem, but I also put the new tire on and gave him the old one. I did not want to be overly burdened ever again.

In this day and age I usually restrict my toolkit to whatever comes with the bike, but my tire-repair kit is complete, for tube-type or tubeless tires, depending what I am traveling on. A well-maintained bike should not break down, although inevitably there is that possibility. However, being well aware of the severe limits of my mechanical expertise, I know that there is little that I am actually capable of fixing.

Many years ago, traveling two-up on a BMW R75/5, I felt the bike go into a severe wobble in a curve, and managed to pull up safely to a stop. The tires were fine, but the bearings in the rear wheel had heated up and self-destructed, welding one inner race to the axle. I don't care how many tools and spare parts I might have had along, this was not self-fixable. A truck came along, we loaded the bike, the driver dropped us off at the nearest train station, and eventually we got to a BMW dealership that could fix the problem.

I travel light. That's my personal choice. If somebody else wants to take along the kitchen sink, that's fine, too. But he probably won't be riding the same roads that I do.

Of course, I could knock 20 pounds off the load by going on a diet . . . but that's another story.

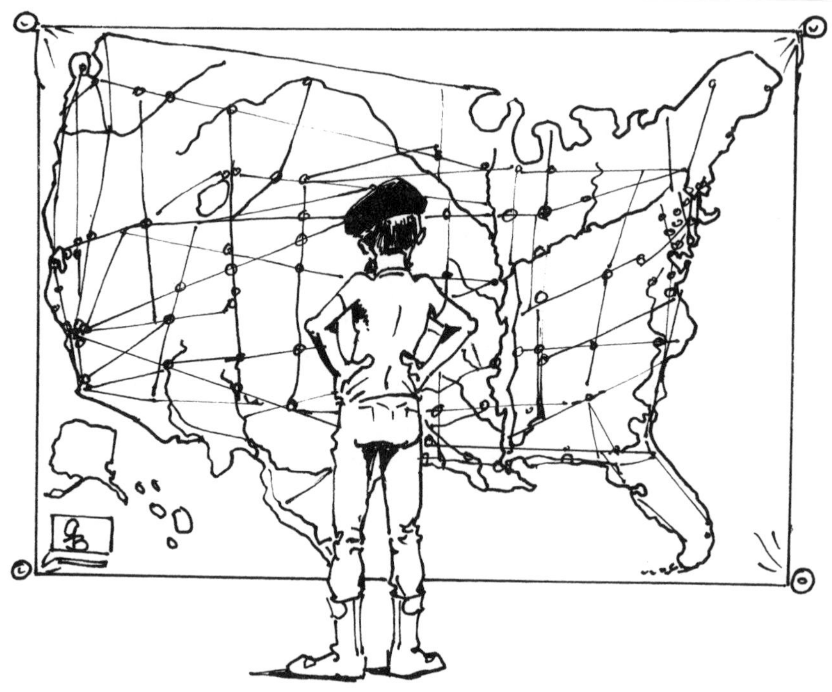

For Love of Roads

January 2002

Roads are good, be they big roads or little roads, paved or dirt. I like ten-lane Interstates slicing through huge megalopolises; cut-bank logging roads in national forests; twisty little two-laners climbing through the mountains; arrow-straight asphalt across the great plains; gravelly byways slithering over hill and into dale; long U.S.-marked highways running from city to city, state to state, coast to coast; short country roads used only by the occasional pickup-driving rancher or farmer.

I'm a road rider; I need roads to ride.

All in all, our 50 states are traversed by the better part of four million miles of road. A lot of us take these roads for granted, not thinking much about why they were built in the first place, who maintains them now. Unless, of course, we get stuck in some construction zone on US 50 in

August, at which point we rail (unfairly) against the orange-vested workers for having inconvenienced us.

Personally, I feel that the authorities responsible for maintaining our roads do a damned good job in keeping these millions of miles in good riding order. Manhattan is plagued by potholes, so what? The intersection of I-10 and I-405 in Los Angeles is jammed up 20 hours a day, so what? And the bridge on Bisbee Road over the Mill River has been out of commission for six months; live with it. The nice thing about so many roads is that there is always an alternative route, officially called a detour.

I have a genuine affection for roads, and try to find out a little bit about the roads I travel. I love riding the Natchez Trace, which began life as a footpath 200 years ago. Or the bits and pieces left of old US 66, the "Mother Road." I'm a conservative fellow by nature, a man who lives in the present and understands that we really do have enough roads to accommodate our 150 million motor vehicles; we just have to utilize these transportation routes more efficiently. You won't often find me riding off-road, real off-road, meaning no road at all, though occasionally I have gone bouncing across deserts in the West or been trailing through wooded sections in the East—all on our communally owned public land, mind you. I'm the essential road-rider, though it matters not if I am Gold-Winging along a smooth strip of pavement, or taking a Triumph Tiger along a grumpy section of mud-holes and dirt.

Roads have long been a mark of civilization . . . and power. The original premise of a road was to be able to hold an empire together, and 3000 years ago roads were being built in Persia and the Middle East so that troops could be moved quickly to keep invaders out, or rebellious citizens in line. And increased commerce inevitably followed. One should note that the construction of our Interstate system was a result of General (later President) Eisenhower's having seen how easily the Germans could move their armies around on the *Autobahnen* during World War II, to help keep the Third Reich together, and Ike felt that this country should have the same sort of high-speed, uninterrupted highways. Now we have 45,000 miles of Interstate, and you can ride 3400 miles from Miami, Florida, to Bellingham, Washington, without ever coming across a traffic light. That is, to my simple mind, quite amazing.

Not that I am a personal aficionado of Interstates. What I like best about these big freeways is that they take the traffic away from the small roads I like to be on. And they are useful for getting across or around large urban expanses, like Oklahoma City or Denver.

Probably the most famous ancient road system is that of the Roman Empire. Since the legions marched on foot, the shortest distance was the best, and these roads were designed to get from Rome to wherever in the quickest manner possible. No curving around a hill, no bends, just straight. My father, who bicycled in Europe a lot as a teenager, said he could get up in the morning and look down the road and see where he would be that evening.

The mountains did require some re-thinking, and anybody who rides over the Little St. Bernard Pass in the Alps should be aware that the original road was ordered built by Emperor Augustus 2,000 years ago.

In this hemisphere the most noted road builders were the Incas who ran a large empire in the Andean Mountains. But since they did not have any wheeled transport, these stone-paved roads were pretty narrow. That all changed after 1492, and the first trans-continental highway was built in Panama in the 1530s. This allowed Spanish ships to off-load their booty on the Pacific side, which would then be carted over to the Caribbean coast to be reloaded and sent to Spain.

Up north in the British colonies roads were considered essential to maintain order and bolster the economy, and after the Revolutionary War the Americans continued to expand the highways. Though at times the work was a bit rustic. When a great-great-great-grandfather of mine went from Hoboken, New Jersey, to Harmony, Illinois, in 1820, he wrote in his journal that many of the roads merely had the trees cut down to less than carriage-axle height, with the stumps being left in the ground.

Major changes took place a hundred years ago, as motorcycles and cars proliferated. And often got stuck. Motorcycles were quite popular as they could be hauled out of a mud-hole with relative ease, while an early Model T or Oldsmobile would need the assistance of a team of horses. Back then speed traps were unknown, but enterprising farmers sometimes enhanced local sticking spots, and charged a goodly sum to unstick the luckless motorist.

The first motorized vehicle to make a cross-country run was a "Regular 1903 Model 1- 1/2 H.P. California Motor Bicycle," ridden by one George Wyman who left San Francisco on May 16, 1903, and got to New York City 50 days later—beating the first four-wheeler by more than a month. The roads he covered were pretty minimal and patchwork, and he sometimes had to bounce along the ties of the railroad lines. The first semi-official trans-continental road, the Lincoln Highway, was not inaugurated until ten years later, and much of that work was done by private citizens.

In this 21st century we have come to view good roads as our right and our due, constructed and maintained by our tax dollars. In effect, it is a socialized transportation system, and a rather commendable one at that. And the best part of it all is that while trucks and motorhomes clutter up a lot of the more popular roads, there are hundreds of thousands of miles of pavement and gravel which seemed to have been designed by engineers who love motorcycles.

The Church of the Open Road

May 2002

The weekend ride is undoubtedly the basis of our particular faith, the ability to go out on a Sunday or Saturday - or both - and whisk briskly along some country roads for 50, 100 miles, perhaps have a pleasant lunch at some friendly café, and then head on home. We can do this alone, but it is generally more fun to do it with some other riders.

Around this neck of the woods that I inhabit it is easy to get a ride together. We have a couple of Internet-savvy groups in the area, and all someone has to do is to type in that he's leaving from the Templeton park at nine o'clock on Saturday morning, and two to ten people will probably show up. Unless it is raining.

More immediate, of course, is the telephone. Of an evening, having just seen that the morrow's forecast is bright and sunny, I can call up Larry or John or whomever and say that I am going to McKittrick for chicken-fried steak, want to come along? I usually get company. Riding buddies are nice; on a day run they make the whole scene a little more interesting. And when I stop, they are there to race benches with me.

I don't always like company. If I have to go 2000 miles in three days, I'll go by myself, thank you very much; he who travels alone travels fastest.

However, this column is about local rides . . . and about one of the problems that we should deal with.

You men and women reading this magazine are what the churchly types would call the choir. And preaching to the choir is easy; we all love our motorcycling, and we will continue to ride no matter what. However, it will benefit us to increase the size of our congregation, which may sometimes take a little effort on our part.

Our little Church of the Open Road always has its doors open, and many people come in to find out what we have to say. They sit in the pews and listen, and like what they hear, but they are also looking for a sense of belonging. Too many of us in the choir, when the service is over, just grab our helmets, get on the bike, and go for a ride. We often do not pay enough attention to the new guy who is sitting in the back row, hoping to be invited.

A lot of people are attracted to motorcycling, for any number of good reasons. It might be by having a friend who rides, which is a great help when it comes to enjoying the social aspects of our church. However, sometimes a new rider does not know anybody who has a bike, but just knows that he wants to ride. So he signs up for an MSF course, gets trained, gets a license, goes down to the dealer, and pays out hard-earned bucks for a bike. And he goes for a ride, hoping to meet some like-minded people.

When you are new to the faith, you like some company. And sometimes a new motorcyclist doesn't find that company. He goes out riding on a weekend, he sees other riders, he goes to the local motorcycle haunts, but he never quite feels as though anyone wants to talk to this newbie. A lot of us choir members are well connected in our own little gangs and groups, and we prefer to hang out with those we are familiar with, rather than to go through the whole "getting to know you" routine. In truth most of us, by the time we reach the late youth of 40 years, know more people than we can comfortably deal with, and while we would always like to make new friends, we flat do not have much time for that. So we do not introduce ourselves to the new guy in church, at the hang-out.

Maybe he won't fit in with the regulars, we think. Maybe he doesn't ride well enough and will slow us down. Maybe he's got bad breath. We can rationalize our actions a thousand ways.

But if that person does not feel welcome by our church, our fraternity, he gets lonely. Six months, a year, goes by, the bike is parked in the garage more and more, not because he doesn't want to ride, but it is just not as much fun as he thought it would be. So he sells the bike.

Bummer! We just missed our chance to keep a new member in the fold.

There are any number of organizations that a motorcyclist can join, but not all of them are useful to the recent convert, not all of them help the new rider make contacts. The most successful organization in this respect is the Harley Owners Group, famously and acronymously known as "HOG." This is a company-sponsored club, with more than half a million members, and any member can be guaranteed of having people to ride with. Harley understood the problem of disenchanted ownership, and has put the enchantment back in.

Another commendable, but much smaller, club is the BMW Motorcycle Owners Association; BMWMOA was founded by a bunch of enthusiasts and offers a lot to its members, with never a dearth of things to do and riders to do them with. However, new riders are more likely to buy Japanese product, often because it both is cheaper and has better dealer networks, and so far none of the Japanese OEMs have had the success that HOG has enjoyed. Although Honda's Red Rider club is working hard at changing this.

Perhaps our greatest failure is the AMA, the American Motorcyclist Association; membership is now around 275,000, but it should be at least ten times larger. The association does good lobbying work, representing us in Washington D.C. and at state level, but other than dealing with legal rights the organization is so fixated on the racing side that it has never really dealt with the concerns of road riders. Which irritates me greatly; the AMA is motorcycling's one truly ecumenical association, and it simply has not done enough for the average street rider. They try, they do try, but they never seem to get it right. If more riders join we might be able to change that.

There are some five million street riders, plus well over a million off-road types, plus another million or so of people who may not be riding at this moment, but are enthusiasts. My rounded figure for American motorcyclists comes close to eight million, all potential worshippers at our church.

And I want that church membership to grow. So next time you see somebody sitting alone at the café, in that last pew, make the effort to go over and chat him up. Invite him along. Make him feel good. He does belong; he wants to be one of us.

Cops

June 2002

The other morning two friends and I were out for a ride, rolling down a little-used back road at a cheerful velocity. I'm leading, when half a mile ahead I see a solo light come around a curve—followed by eight others. Oh, a little club ride, I think.

Our closing speed is probably about 150 mph, and as I approach the first bike I see POLICE written across the Electra Glide's fairing. Whoops! It's the police academy taking a bunch of motor officer trainees off on their long ride. I wave, and looking in the rearview mirror wonder if the officer in charge might decide to give his recruits a little impromptu lesson in giving chase.

They keep on going. Whew!

Seeing a policeman, on the beat, in a car, on a bike, can provoke several very different reactions in me. If I'm walking down a street in town I think, "Oh good, the boys and girls in blue are out there protecting me from the evils of the world." Police officers, for the most part, have my respect and admiration. It's an important job, and we often fail to appreciate just how important.

If all the cops suddenly disappeared, went on strike or something, I think you would be surprised at how many low-lifers there are in our population. Especially in the larger urban areas. You get some disaffected slum-dwellers who decide that smashing windows and looting is a good way to improve their lifestyles, and the police all go out with the blue flu, you have problems.

As a counterpoint there was a police strike in the upscale seaside city of Santa Barbara, California, some 20 years ago, which, if memory holds true, lasted about a month—during which the crime rate actually went down. The locals realized they had to fend for themselves and did so with aplomb. I do not support vigilante actions, but Neighborhood Watch is a good idea.

But back to the police and the motorcycling lifestyle. I can detail every time that I got stopped by a cop that really got my goat. Here's one: Back in the old double-nickel days I was running south through the rolling country of central Nebraska on US 83, on Veterans Day. Hardly a car to be seen, visibility to the horizon, and I come over a slight hill—and the highway patrolman parked by the road down below the rise locks me on radar at 66. The trooper was tall and lean and mean, with creases in his pants you could cut yourself on. Big brimmed hat, dark glasses, the very image of authoritarian rectitude.

"Hey. Howdy. I'm a vet. This is my day. There's nobody out here. Not bothering anybody." Never a smile, just handed me my ticket. That one has always stuck in my craw. It was the kind of citation that makes me not like cops.

We have roughly a million officers of the law in this great nation of ours, from the Transit Authority Police in New York City to the California Highway Patrol, from Florida's Dade County Sheriff's Department to the harbor patrol in Seattle. These are all men and women who have been trained to do their job, have sworn to respect the rights of the citizens, to be polite when they can, and sometimes to put themselves in harm's way.

There are more than 40,000 police jurisdictions in this country, with the FBI and other agencies covering the federal angle, down to state and county and local. My town of 24,000 denizens has 29 sworn officers on the payroll, providing protection 24 hours a day, seven days a week. And after ten years, I have not gotten a ticket in this town.

Although I did get stopped one evening, with that stomach-sinking feeling as my mirrors turned red. Oh, my God! What have I done? What am I in for? How much is this going to cost? All that negative stuff. But the cop only stopped me to tell me my taillight was out—no fix-it ticket, no nothing, he just wanted to make sure I didn't get rear-ended.

There can be a lot of friction between motorcyclists and cops. The classic contretemps was when the BMW Riders' Association, as do-gooding, law-abiding, authority-respecting a lot as ever twisted a throttle, held its annual bash down in Graham County, North Carolina, a few years ago, and the sheriff decided that these were a bunch of bad dudes and dudettes who should be harassed out of the place. He was a stupid cop.

And stupidity has a lot to do with our image of the police. Here is my breakdown of good cops, not-so-good cops, and bad cops, which is based on nothing more than my analytical imagination. Bad cops get the headlines, appear in the movies, but I would say that only one percent of cops qualify as bad, those who are criminals in uniform or who enjoy brutalizing citizens. In the not-so-good category we have stupid cops, cops who became cops because they like to be in a position of power, cops who abuse their authority; I'd say three or four percent fall into that slot. Maybe that is way too many . . . or way too few.

But for me the real cop is the good cop, the other 95 or more percent. He's the cop who resolves a family feud with the husband wielding a meat cleaver. The cop who goes into a dark alley looking for a perp who has a gun. The cop at the accident scene who pulls the bloody driver from the burning car.

And occasionally he might write me a ticket for breaking some road law. I'll say I didn't deserve it, because I was riding in a safe and sane, if a little fast, manner—but I will have to admit that I broke the law, inane as the law might be.

I like cops. I wave at them when I go by, which is a friendly thing to do, and I want them to know they have a friend in me. I'm very glad they are a highly visible part of this country . . . but I just hope they're not around when I crack the throttle.

Doing Good by Going Riding

August 2002

When tens of thousands of bikes show up for California's annual Love Ride and donate hundreds of thousands of dollars to the Muscular Dystrophy Association, and the National Pediatric Tumor Association can raise several million dollars annually from motorcycle riders, and the San Luis Obispo Toys for Tots Ride delivers truck-loads of gifts to underprivileged children, it appears that we have figured out an excellent way to contribute to those in need while also having some fun. Which is a win/win combination.

What is it about these charity rides? Nothing new. Way back when I belonged to the Aces Up Motorcycle Club, headquartered at Stan Djuba's garage in Amherst, Massachusetts, we would ride over to the Cooley-Dickinson Hospital *en masse* and donate blood, and the local

Daily Hampshire Gazette would take our picture and give us a little write-up in the paper. Somewhere I still have a clipping from one of those events many years ago.

That sort of thing upped motorcycling's reputation in the Connecticut River valley, where I lived. "Golly gee, Maude, look at this picture! Those motorcyclists aren't as rough a bunch as we thought they were." That's the secondary effect of doing good works, of having that reflect positively on us motorcyclists.

But the primary reason is helping others, whether they be the families of those who died in the 9/11 disaster, or a child with a deadly disease that will take his young life before he can ever fully know the joys that this world offers. Including riding a motorcycle. We Americans are a generous society, and I would say that we motorcyclists are among the most generous. Every weekend, somewhere, a crowd of riders is getting together to have a good time and to do good.

Motorcyclists are a bunch of men and women who like to ride, like to fraternize with other riders, and, for the most part, like to contribute to charitable causes. As a matter of newsworthy fact, I would say that motorcyclists are the most prominent of the do-gooders out there, far more so than, say the golfing mob or sailing set. And that, perhaps, is due to our attachment to the realities of life.

We, and I speak in generalities, are not what I would describe as a typical country-club lot, though I am sure that many of us do belong to the Middletown CC. But that is a different facet of our existence. What we really like to do is to ride our bikes, and that means getting out on the road. As a result we witness life as it really is, waving at a child in a wheelchair, seeing run-down houses in a pocket of rural poverty. These sights make us sad; we want to help. And if we can combine the joy of the ride with that warm feeling of having done someone some good, all the better.

There is the old saying, charity begins at home. Three thousand years ago Greece was pretty much divided up amongst city-states, like Athens or Corinth or Thebes, and if you were the citizen of one of these places who had suffered some tragedy, whether it was an earthquake leveling a house, or a family impoverished by the death of its main provider, all the other citizens would rally around and help. Religion has always been a purveyor of charity, especially the expansive faiths like the Buddhists and Christians and Moslems; you joined up, you got help when it was needed.

All the way to the 21st century when charitable efforts are often directed to people and places we will never see, never go to. Motorcycling's biggest one-day charity event may be that Love Ride, run out of Oliver Shokouh's Harley-Davidson shop in Glendale, California. Shokouh has been sponsoring this for 18 years, and puts a lot of his own sweat into the affair. The event has gotten a little bigger than he anticipated back in 1984 and now requires a small staff to manage—most of which is volunteer work. When you line up bands like Steppenwolf and Creedence Clearwater, and get the donated services of celebs like Jay Leno and Peter Fonda, you know you have moved into the big time.

With big-time results. Last year more than 20,000 riders made the 50-mile run (slowly) from Glendale to Castaic Lake, and contributed more than $1.25 million dollars towards funding research to find a cure for muscular dystrophy. That is a particularly nasty disease, and with enough financial backing I bet we can find a remedy within the next 20 years.

There is something about helping others that brings out the best in all of us—perhaps there are some mean-spirited types who like to see others suffer, like the grinch who stole Christmas, but they are in a small minority.

Speaking of minorities, my local one-percent-er club here on California's Central Coast, the Molochs, ran a charity drive not too long ago, and ended up donating a truck-load of canned food to a do-good grocery outfit called Loaves & Fishes, and gave $1000 to a hospice operation. I applaud.

Our President has said that we should all donate 4000 hours of our life to doing good things for our country, whether it means being a Big Brother or Sister to an unhappy child, volunteer work down at the animal pound, mowing the lawn of the house-bound elderly, or going to visit sick kids in the hospital. And there is also the need for money, as well as time, to pay for research into finding cures for terrible diseases. In which case my own preference is, rather than sending off a check in the mail, to look around for a charity ride, pay $30 for a participant's ticket, go on a 60-mile run, have some barbecued tri-tip, see a lot of friends, and the designated recipient gets a check for $5000.

Doing good can be fun.

The Motorcycling Menu

November 2002

Over the last 4th of July weekend I went up to Hollister, California, to watch the Harleys (mostly) parade slowly, very slowly, along San Benito Street; tens of thousands of motorcyclists had ridden to "The Birthplace of the American Biker" in order to be a part of the annual Independence Rally. And downtown 150 vendors were selling everything from T-shirts to tattoos to tri-tip. On aptly mis-named Gourmet Alley, breathing the grease in the air was enough to add pounds to a body . . . though it was good grease, with great barbecued pork ribs.

About a week later I was at Laguna Seca Raceway for the Superbike World Championship, enthralled by some seriously fast riders hurtling around the track at speeds that defy the laws of physics. For the Sunday of the big race some 50,000 tickets were sold; these boys and girls had to be fed, and two or three dozen food and drink vendors had set up. Calamari and chablis, anybody?

Fun, both of the events. And they took place about 50 miles from each other. I can't imagine more disparate examples of motorcyclists than the fellow in a "distressed" leather jacket, chaps, and non-DOT-approved beanie crash-hat, on his Softail, versus the rider of a Ducati 998 with one-piece custom-made multi-colored leathers and a $500 "signature" helmet.

I love 'em both. I love being them both. I love cruising the main streets of America on an Indian Chief, I love blitzing the back roads on a Ninja 900. I'm omniverous in terms of my taste for motorcycling; I like just about everything. The same goes for food; it can be a hard call between a Phillie cheese steak and some Rocky Mountain oysters.

It's all choice. I have friends who own both cruisers and sport bikes. Some mornings they choose to put on the many-zippered Brando jacket and putt out to the Pozo Saloon for a glass of sarsaparilla, other days they want to slide into an Aerostich suit and run up the coast or around the mountains. I look at them like I do the restaurants in town. We could stop in at the Old Vienna and order sauerbraten, or the Oasis Moroccan for some couscous with lamb stew, or maybe Juan's Oaxacan for a bowl of red menudo.

I understand that there are some people who are happy eating hamburgers every day; that's fine with me, but I do think they are missing out by not considering the tasty joys of *tandoori* chicken, or tuna sushi.

In the magazines, and at my nearby dealers, I look at all the bikes lining up for the 2003 year, coming from more than 30 manufacturers, and it really is like a huge international menu. There are bikes for every taste, every aesthetic appreciation, every (nearly) wallet. And no one style of motorcycle is any better, or worse, than any other; it all depends on what you want to do with it.

Sport-bikers often sneer at cruising riders; dual-purpose, single-cylinder buffs look down at mono-bago touring types; the daily commuting rider thinks he's better than the person who only gets out for a few hours on Sunday. No need for all this internal dissension; if it has a motor and two wheels, it is good.

I look at the array of different motorcycling possibilities the way I do a very extensive menu. And the long list of restaurants in the local *Yellow Pages*. If my stomach is set on a medium-rare T-bone and baked potato, I might consider the Big Sky Café. If I am lusting after meatloaf and mashed, I go to Margie's Diner. If it's genuine Polish *pierogi* I am after, I'll visit my mother-in-law . . . nice excuse for a trip.

My own stable is small, essentially a sport-touring bike and a 650cc dual-purpose machine. But I have, and do, find a lot of pleasure in all the other motorcycles that I get to ride for fun and business. I can cruise with the best of the boys, a dozen big V-twins rumbling along for an hour or two, then stopping under a tree by a lonesome mini-mart for a long break and talking trash, eating hot dogs. Or get on a finally honed sport bike and follow a couple of like-mounted friends up the Pacific coast to Big Sur for an "Ambrosiaburger" at Nepenthe's.

The motorcycling menu is long, and we should sample everything. Perhaps not all at one sitting, but over one's life. My taste buds hanker sometimes for *osso buco* (braised veal shanks in English), sometimes for pork fried rice. Not much disagrees with me, and I figure if the chef is going to put it on his list of dishes, he knows customers will like it.

There are limits, of course; once I was offered a small bowl of what looked rather like an avocado dip. Since I knew that avocado trees did not grow in the highlands of Vietnam I asked my host what it was. The undigested contents of a goat's stomach, a real delicacy, he said via my interpreter; I declined.

Which is sort of what I do these days when Brad asks me to go dirt riding. About 30 miles from my house is a very technical off-road area called Turkey Flats, and the last time I went Brad loaned me an XR400. Good bike, but I am not a good dirt rider; when things get seriously gnarly instead of gassing it I sometimes try to stop and put my foot down . . . not a good idea on an extremely steep downhill run. I ended up with the XR on top of me. So this is one kind of fare that I do not indulge in much. I could say that it is too rich for my blood, like fried eel; very tasty, that dish, but in very small amounts.

My own personal preference, if I were to be restricted to one kind of riding, is to be on a fast, comfortable machine with 500 miles of two-lane road weaving through the countryside. But I like change, variation. I can also understand the pleasure that other riders get from their own chosen style of riding, from trials to drag-racing. While I can appreciate both a dish of Spanish *paella* and a good chicken-fried steak.

And there is always something else to try. I haven't been on one of those KTM V-twins yet, and nor have I sampled haggis.

Trivial Pursuits

December 2002

Next to this keyboard on the desk is a little leatherette container that holds a commemorative one-crown coin, struck by the Pobjoy Mint in England. On one side is a rather unflattering right profile of Her Majesty, Elizabeth II, and on the other is the commemoree, Honda-mounted Joey Dunlop, both wheels in the air, as he hurtles around the Isle of Man. He was the winningest rider ever on the island, until he came to his untimely end in a small, rainy race in Estonia in 2000.

I watched him ride at the Isle years ago; I never got to meet him, but from everything I have heard, he was a thoroughly good fellow. For years his name was a constant in European race results, and it was a sad day for our sport when he died. A few months ago a friend gave me this coin, and it has sat by the computer since then.

But eventually it will get put away, and years may go by before it ever sees the light of day again. That's the way of it. We accumulate such trinkets, admire them for a while, and then they go in a carton, which gets tucked away in some dark recess.

I've got lots of little bits and pieces related to my motorcycling past, all of which eventually ends up in various boxes. And because we recently had a flood in the garage, due to a broken water filter, not heavy rain, I was going through a number of boxes I haven't looked at for ages.

An old pocket watch came to light, with a chain, and on the chain is a small brass and enamel medallion celebrating the West Ealing Motor and Motorcycle Club, with a bas-relief motorcycle that looks like a 1930s sloper single. On the back are engraved the words: Hospital Cup Trial, 2nd, H. Nickless. I know that Ealing is part of greater London, but I have no recollection of ever knowing anyone by the name of Nickless, and have no idea how I came by that award.

The timepiece, an Elgin, was already pretty aged when it was given to me on my 30th birthday; it still works. The watch alone weighs more than a quarter of a pound, so I can see why it got put away.

More watches, but inexpensive ones. The *Ninja* watch probably came my way in the Ninja 900 intro back in 1984, and is still in its gold-trimmed suede-like case with the information that: "Your Ninja watch contains a fine Japanese quartz battery." The *BMW Grand Prix Edition* watch comes from, I imagine, roughly the same era . . . though what BMW was touting the GP for, I have no idea. Of historical note, this timepiece may exemplify the last effort for a wind-up to compete with a quartz. Watch and strap are plastic, weighing less than an ounce, with the only metal being in the very small mechanism—which doesn't work any more.

There is a photograph cube, about five inches square, which my longest term riding crony, Dick Tatlock, must have done back in the late sixties, when he was in his photography stage. The six black and whites are shots of details on a Greeves, an Ossa, and a Bultaco, artfully showing things like a rear wheel, front forks, an engine; those were his early dual-purpose days. Dick and I first met when I was five, we rode his Harley 125 in the woods when we were 15, and we still go riding together just about every year—although we live 3000 miles apart.

There is non-motorcycling trivia, too. What's that? A tiny bear in a little cage, with YELLOWSTONE actually burnt into the wood; that must have been from the family trip out West when I was 11. A three-inch tall replica of the Eiffel Tower probably dates from when I was quite young and Papa worked at NATO headquarters in Paris. And a small cannon with a tiny brass plate reading: OLD NORTH CHURCH, BOSTON, MASS.; another childish souvenir. I can see myself threatening to throw a tantrum unless I get what I want.

The motorcycling fraternity loves pins, and I have a jumble of them in an old Caballeros cigar box; 20 CENTS EA is written on the lid, which means those Brazilian cigars were quite affordable when the box sat on a tobacconist's shelf. A tiny frying-pan pin reads 14TH ANNUAL DEATH VALLEY MOTORCYCLE TOUR 1967. A very nice cloisonné pin has a graciously draped lady standing in front of the VELOCE sign, circled by VELOCETTE OWNERS CLUB OF NORTH AMERICA; since my Velo-owning days were back in the mid-sixties, that must be its dating. I hope that the current club has an equally attractive pin. My Isle of Man pin from the 1978 TT has BENEVOLENT FUND written at the top; obviously somebody benefited from my contribution.

I see a triangulated AMA 2 pin next to an AMA 23 pin. And an un-numbered AMA pin with a sort of triple Nike-ish swoosh symbol in the middle may have been the first year. Being a life member these days, I don't seem to be getting any more pins; just as well, as the money is better spent on lobbying efforts. A winged pin from BMWMOA is to remember my first 100,000 BMW MILES; I imagine I was awarded that sometime in the late seventies.

Here is a strange pin, quite large, looking quite old. A very futuristic-looking motorcycle, with fully enclosed Buck Rogers-ish styling, appears to be riding around the world. But there is no writing to explain what it is, what it celebrates. On the back is the tiny imprimatur: Hartnett Co. Boston, obviously the manufacturer. But not a clue as to what this pin is about.

I see a stamped key marked LUCAS ENGLAND, attached by a rusty little chain to a small oval medallion with a picture of the Empire State Building on one side, the words, TALLEST BUILDING IN THE WORLD 1472 FEET on the other. Those Lucas ignition keys were pretty simple things, and for all I know it may have come from my 1960 Bonneville . . . or any number of Brit bikes I have owned. The medallion is chronologically mis-matched, as I remember going up the ESB when I was eight, and I didn't buy that first Bonnie until I was 20.

And what's this? Another little presentation box which looks like it could hold a set of cufflinks. No . . . it's one troy ounce of .999 fine silver, a gift from U.S. Suzuki back in 1981. I don't have a clue why I was given this, but at least the value of this is doing better than most of my stocks.

Anyway, all this stuff is going back in the box, and the box back in the garage. The bits and pieces don't really mean anything to anybody but me, but it's been fun rummaging through them.

The Joey Dunlop commemorative will stay out here on the desk for the foreseeable; it's a nice way to remember him. For a while; some day the coin will end up with the rest of the trivia. That's the way life is.

Traveling Solo

January 2003

If you happen to see a solo rider, sleeping bag strapped to the luggage rack, running rapidly down a road somewhere in the Rocky Mountains, or dawdling through the Shenandoah Valley, or crossing a pass in Washington's Kettle River Range, that might be me. I like to travel alone.

Riding companions are okay, but if I am going any serious distance, like a thousand miles or more, I generally choose to saddle up by myself. Which has nothing to do with the time element, though we all know the inevitable slowing factor of having even one more rider along.

No, solo traveling has to do with the "me" element. I enjoy the solitude, and the unexpected company . . . which presents itself as a contradictory notion.

Solitude has to do with pulling off the road in some country setting, doffing the helmet and jacket, stretching out under a tree with a blade of grass between my teeth, and watching the cumulus clouds drift by. Nobody expects me to be anywhere, nobody even knows where I am. Nobody is getting restless and wanting to move on.

In this 21st century we seem to get little enough time all by our very own selves. Time to do just as much, or as little, as we damn well please. I might pull off my boots and fall asleep for half an hour. Or maybe get back on the bike and burn off a quick 200 miles.

When traveling alone I stop when I'm tired, eat when I'm hungry, and I do not have to consider anyone else. Which may sound selfish to some, but the whole reason I am doing this is so that I do not inconvenience anyone else. I think it would be selfish and inconsiderate if I told whomever I was with that I did not care that he was hungry, that I was not stopping to eat.

Not that I don't enjoy riding buddies; there is lots to be said for them. Probably the number one reason is that you like his or her company a whole lot, and conversation is easy and interesting. Number two, perhaps, is the unspoken fear of a break down, be it a flat tire or a mechanical failure or an electronic crisis. When things do go wrong on a bike, I know very well that it is always more pleasant if somebody else is along with whom to share this little contretemps. And do a run for cold sodas while waiting for whatever.

However, in this current day and age of motorcycle technology breakdowns have become a very minor concern. My rear wheel seems to pick up a nail every couple of years, but the tubeless tire has pretty much reduced that problem to a half-hour inconvenience.

In truth it is the me-ism that prompts my lone-wolfish ways. I don't mind being alone; I rather like my own company. I often do rough camping, pitching a tent in some remote clearing in a national forest, pulling a cork on a bottle of wine, slicing some salami and cheese and tomato to put in a stout heel of bread—I really don't need any ". . . thou beside me singing . . ." in order to enjoy the wilderness. That, by the way, is a mis-quoted line from the 12th century Persian poet, Omar Khayyam.

Don't get me wrong: I love The Wife a great deal. When my parents were celebrating their 55th wedding anniversary, Sue asked her father-in-law what made for such a long and happy marriage. "Don't be around each other too much," he said. Good advice, at least for the likes of us.

Also Sue and I abide by the "No news is good news" rule, which means there is no need to call. If anything terrible happens, the authorities will get in touch with the next of kin. I sometimes travel with people who have to, must, speak with a Significant Other at least once a day. Having to make that daily call is, for me, an entirely unnecessary burden.

And then there is the Unexpected Company that I mentioned earlier; one of the discreet pleasures of solo travel is that I meet so many more people along the way. Two guys traveling together stop, they talk to each other. One guy stops . . . some local might well start chatting with me, asking about my motorcycle, telling me about his town, inviting me to put my tent down on his east 40 and come by the house for supper. "She's making fried chicken tonight; we eat at six."

Traveling alone gives me lots of lovely flexibility. If I want to do a 900-mile day, fine. If I want to stop at 3 p.m., fine. If I decide that morning that I don't want to go via St. Louis, but want to cross the Mississippi River at Hannibal instead, no discussion.

I often do travel with a friend or two or three, going camping for a couple of nights, all is well. And traveling with The Wife is always fun; sometimes she is on her own bike, sometimes she is a passenger. But at least 80 percent of my travel is alone.

My longest solo trip was more than two years in length, from '73 to '75, when I rode around the world. Sometimes I did have company, either on another bike or as a passenger, but in the main I was alone. And whether I was in Australia, Asia, or Africa, one of the most commonly asked questions was: "Don't you get lonely?"

"No," I would reply; "look, I'm talking with you, aren't I?" And that is the pleasant truth of traveling alone, whether it is in North America or anywhere on this globe . . . I am more likely to meet those interesting people.

So if you are riding through the Boston Mountains in Arkansas and you see a well-packed bike parked in the shade beside the road, and a balding, bearded fellow soaking in a stream, that might be me. Stop and say hello.

Daylight to Darkness

April 2003

I've been on the road for a week, and my rough calculations indicate that I'll be about 250 miles from the stable when the sun starts to set. Which means I will probably tuck into a motel in Barstow, California, and then cross the Mojave Desert early in the morning, with the sun at my back.

However, life is moving at a brisker pace than anticipated, and I am already leaving Las Vegas in mid-afternoon, the traffic rolling along the Interstate at an immodest 85 mph. At Baker, California, the big Bun Boy thermometer is reading 93 degrees on this fall day, the clock on my dash saying 4:31. It is too early to quit by the time I get to Barstow, though the sun is getting low on the horizon and the headwind is at full throttle.

Riding into a setting sun is flat no fun at all. I've got a full-face helmet on, and that solar orb is ready to burn my peepers. Yes, your eyes can be sunburned. At this point many riders would run a strip of gaffer's tape across the top of the faceshield, and try to get some relief thataway.

However, I've got a gadget which beats that six ways to Sunday. It is a rectangle of light, flexible black plastic, about 9 x 1.5 inches, which attaches to the top of the faceshield by three suction cups, keeping the strip out from the shield a little more than half an inch. It works really, really well.

Unfortunately I cannot tell you where I got this thing, as I've had it for more than 15 years, and there is no name or trademark anywhere on it. I think it was one of those marvelous little garage inventions, which the inventor sent to all magazine editors sometime in the mid-1980s, and then the notion died a'borning. It is exceedingly difficult to make any profit off an inexpensive item with a limited market, and in the end we riders are the losers.

I put that simple visor on my helmet, and I am set to tackle the Mojave Desert—where the wind is blowing west to east at a good 40 mph. Fortunately I have a fully faired bike, otherwise the 70 miles of Route 58 from Barstow to Mojave, town of, would be unbearable. At least to my wussish self. Several bikes are happily going along in the opposite direction, with the wind and sun at the riders' backs.

Gas up at Mojave, and the sun is just slipping down behind the Tehachapi Mountains—and home is only 180 miles. I can do it.

Crossing Tehachapi Summit in the dusky light, I see the final red sunnish glimmers as I descend the west side. By the time I get to I-5, it is full-on dark, with a new moon shining in the clear sky.

Most of the night-riding I do is in short hops, coming home from a dinner at a friend's house, that sort of thing. And most of it takes place on bigger roads used by a good deal of traffic, with constant headlights both behind and in front, brightly lit signage off to the sides, no real sense of darkness.

I could take the Interstate and Route 46 over to my home, but that is a pretty boring, heavily trafficked ride. I'll stick to Route 58. I clean my faceshield and clear glasses as well as I can, knowing that every little nick and scratch is going to refract light from any oncoming cars and complicate my vision. I know that I will meet a little traffic on my way to McKittrick, and there is sometimes that small moment in passing an oncoming vehicle when it seems I cannot see anything, be it a coyote crossing the road or a bag of trash fallen out of a pickup. That temporary blindness, which may last only a split second, always disconcerts me.

McKittrick is quiet, nothing but a few yellowish street-lights burning and a couple of pickups parked in front of the Penny Bar. From here it is 75 miles to my door, rather curvaceous miles, I should add, which run over hills and through ranching country. I've been along this road more than a hundred times, but this is the first time at night. Having teethed on six-volt motorcycles with weak headlights I really do appreciate the 12-volt sealed beam unit on my ST.

I learn a lot. Out of McKittrick the little-trafficked road starts a 20-mile climb to the Temblor Summit; the pavement is good, the yellow lines a bit faded. And then at the summit I pass into San Luis Obispo county—and I had no idea that CalTrans could do such a brilliant job of illuminating a rural road. It appears that anytime SLO county has any extra state-highway money, it gets to work on Route 58.

Twisting down the west slope of the Temblors the newly paved road is all fresh double-yellow, with two rows of Botts dots, one row on each side of the reflective yellow paint. On the edges of the two-lane asphalt are reflective white stripes, and beyond that, just off the shoulder, are light metal stakes with either white, or triple-red, reflectors on the tops.

The white stakes materialize as I come into a curve, and lead me around the bend. The red ones, with three small circles, seem to indicate potential hazards if one pulls off the road too much, like an entrance to a culvert going under the road.

At a modest pace the road is very easy to read, and I meet only one car in those mountain miles, and its headlights are properly adjusted. Country drivers seem to pay more attention to proper alignment than do city drivers, who never really get much opportunity to see how good, or bad, their lights are, as they are always in a procession of traffic.

My ST1100 has a knob on the dash to set the beam right where I want it, and the light is good. Although a pair of secondary lights angling out at maybe ten degrees would be nice, because wheeling through sharp curves I'm finding I want a little more peripheral vision. But I shouldn't complain.

When the double yellow becomes single yellow and a dotted line, Mr. Botts' little invention gives me a heads up, as on one side of the road center the dots will not reflect my oncoming light, on the other side they will. I have never really admired this engineering subtlety before, but it gives me a whole new sense of security when riding at night.

The ride becomes really fun, the black road unrolling before me, the stripes and dots and reflector posts keeping me well informed of where I should be going, which way to lean. I meet less than a dozen cars on that 75-mile stretch, and all are courteous, if occasionally too curious as to what this pediddle (single headlight) really is—a big truck with one headlight out, or a motorcycle.

Home! How very nice. I am much happier being here than in a Barstow motel.

Road Credits

July 2003

My favorite day of the year is not Xmas, not my birthday, not Halloween, but Ride To Work day, an event promoted not by the US Congress, but by the Aerostich company, which makes motorcycle riding gear. Every year I hope that there will be several million fewer cars on the roads that day. I can list all the advantages of riding your motorcycle to the office or the factory, from changing your dreary commute to a pleasure trip, being able to park close to the entrance, bonding with your bike, dazzling your co-workers with the beauty of your machine, and, best of all, leaving your colleagues behind in the traffic jam when you all head for home.

I think the Ride To Work concept is brilliant, sort of the motorcycle-riding commuter's counterpoint to July 4th. On the 4th we get the day off and go ride the back roads, but on RTW day we go to work but look forward to the commute on the front roads . . . if you get my drift. Why more motorcyclists don't ride to work every day that the weather allows beats the stuffing out of me.

The entire population of these United States of America should support Ride To Work, as it benefits the nation as a whole. Let me explain why.

The other day I was sitting behind the steering wheel of The Wife's pickup, driving up the Cuesta Grade on US 101 at about two o'clock on a Tuesday afternoon, with my Suzuki DR650 strapped down in the back. Nothing wrong with the picture; I had dropped the bike off for a service a couple of days before and had just picked it up . . . along with a couple of cases of merlot from the local discount wine shop. Trucks are useful.

Tuesday was a work day, and the grade was moderately busy, two lanes going uphill, two going down, with lots of cars and trucks. And two motorcycles: one had just passed me splitting lanes, and another was coming towards me. I put less than a thousand miles a year on Sue's truck, more than 30,000 on various motorcycles. The 3.9-liter V-6 Dodge Dakota averages about 18 mpg in the real world, whereas my overall average mileage for all the bikes I ride is probably around 40 mpg.

At the moment I knew where I was going . . . back to my office at home to work. I had no idea what everybody else was doing on the road. Why weren't they in factories or air-conditioned cubicles or building houses somewhere? I turned on the radio and some talk-show host was carrying on about cutting back on driving so we could cut back on oil imports. Then a caller came in with a notion about increasing taxes on gas-guzzlers—SUVs already pay a lot more in taxes just paying for the gas they consume. A woman said she thought the DMV should base its annual registration on the rated gasoline consumption of a vehicle—which might make a lot of buyers think twice.

The next caller had an interesting angle: gas prices should become progressive. A driver would start the year with a ration booklet having stamps for 1,000 gallons, say at a buck a gallon, and if he went beyond that he would have to pay a higher amount for the next booklet, say two bucks. I wondered how Detroit and the oil industry would like that; I could see a storm-cloud of lobbying on the horizon.

I came over the top of the grade and headed up the Salinas River valley, the traffic moving at a steady 80 mph—everyone going somewhere. But that rationing idea got me thinking. It would have to be called by another name, since the word "rationing" has a somewhat negative connotation, something which happens only in wartime.

A couple of days later Joe came over for a cup of coffee. He's an engineer and appears to be doing a competent job in keeping our local nuclear power-plant generating, and he has an architect wife, two kids, three dogs, and a cat. I brought up the subject of "road credits." His is a high-mileage family, and he calculated that the mini-van is driven about 20,000 miles a year, his pickup about 15,000, and his aged Jaguar sedan about 10,000. Plus he and wife Becky both have motorcycles, but since they are in the soccer-parenting phase of life, and father/son bonding is currently achieved by flying gliders, the bikes rarely see the road.

So Joe's family is knocking back 45,000 miles a year, at a guesstimate of 15 mpg. That is 3000 gallons of refined petroleum product, the price of which seems to be going up every day. What if the federal government, trying to cut back on the deficit, decided to put a national tax of a dollar on every gallon? Joe and Becky would be out three grand. Or, using that coupon method, they get a thousand cheap gallons, the next thousand costs double, the third thousand double again.

As a corollary I do believe we should tax vehicles according to their weight. Gasoline isn't the only petroleum byproduct we deal with. How about asphalt, and the cost of road repair? I promise you, a thousand motorcycles with an average laden weight of 800 pounds, for a total of 800,000 pounds, do a heckuva lot less damage to the roadways than ten 80,000-pound trucks. Bikes can run day and night along US 101 and never dent the tarmac, while the thousands of big rigs moving through the Salinas Valley every 24 hours mean that the authorities are going to have to plan for fixing, even rebuilding, the road at regular intervals.

We motorcyclists consume a lot less gas than the average sedan or pickup, and our light weight means we have virtually no effect on the roadways or bridges. And we can put four bikes in a parking slot intended for one car.

Maybe the DMV should think about having zero registration fees for motorcycles and actually promote their use. What a daring thought! Motorcycles are, unless grotesquely modified with excessively loud exhausts, environmentally friendly, as they use less petroleum byproduct, and less space, than a car. Ride yours to work and tell your riding buddies to do the same.

Would it not be nice to see Ride To Work day sponsored by our Congress? Write to your reps in Washington, and pay a visit to www.ridetowork.org.

Travel Writing 101

October 2003

You take a trip somewhere, you have a great time, you want to tell the world, at least somebody, about it. Some tripsters are marvelous raconteurs, who can keep a roomful of listeners riveted to a tale of crossing Texas on I-10; others, unfortunately, lack that ability and will put a bunch of hyper-active kids to sleep while talking about dodging grizzlies up in the Yukon. One of the realities of traveling is that after you get home, other than having a few photos, the experience seems to fade. Almost like a dream.

One way to keep the traveling experience alive as long as possible is to sit down with a sheet of foolscap and a quill pen, and your penknife to keep your pen's point sharp, or at the keyboard of a computer, and try to turn your adventure into words. Sometimes the right words come easily, more often they don't.

I've pretty much made a small career out of writing about where I've been. I love to travel, and love it even more when I'm on a motorcycle. I also enjoy the process of writing about it

On my shelves are many more travel books than motorcycle books—one good reason being that there are a lot more of the former than the latter. And the genre precedes the invention of motorcycles by a lot of years. A recent best-seller has been *Undaunted Courage,* Stephen Ambrose's describing the Lewis & Clark Expedition of two centuries ago, America's first trans-continental travel story; the Ambrose version is a lot more readable than the original journals. Pick up a copy of Adlard Welby's *A Visit To North America* and you can see what a trip with horses and carriage from Hoboken, New Jersey, to Harmony, Illinois, was like back in 1819/20. Only trouble is in finding the book, as it was published in 1821, and last reprinted in 1905. Today we are more likely to buy a paperback copy of Bill Bryson's *I'm a Stranger Here Myself,* a jocular, and very perceptive, look by an American traveling about these United States.

The focus of travel writing can be divided into two major groups, the familiar and the unfamiliar. In the first, you the writer are telling the reader about a place you know extremely well, like Barbara Barber's *Sunday Rides on Two Wheels.* Barber's home is in southern Wisconsin and she has written about what she knows best; this is not a literary exercise, this is information. If you live in Kansas City, everything within a hundred miles is your backyard. You could write a nice piece about riding up along the Missouri River to St. Joe. Or maybe describe small-town life as you pass through Coal and Tightwad and Racket heading down to Lake of the Ozarks.

Writing about what you know best is a good way to begin. I live close to California's Big Sur Highway, which I have ridden a hundred times, and a hundred other motorcyclists have written about traveling those hundred miles of road from Cambria to Carmel. For me to write an article about the Big Sur, I need to make it different from all the rest, give it a fresh look, make the reader want to come out and ride it himself. Maybe slant it to the years of the Great Depression, when completing the road was a way to keep men employed, and how the clouds of hard times can have a silver lining.

The other kind of travel books are by writers who have only been to that place they are writing about once. Many travelers think they have to write about something new, something different—whereas they really only see a sliver of life when they go to parts unknown. Admittedly, that thin slice can be enthralling, fascinating, as it was when Ted Simon had finished his trip around the world, writing about it in *Jupiter's Travels.* Now, 30 years later, he is following his first path a second time, and I imagine we will soon be happy to read another excellent book on that sliver.

For many American motorcyclists, a trip to a new place is better than returning to Sturgis each August. Every summer hundreds of Lower 48 motorcyclists head to Alaska, and every fall editors at the motorcycle magazines are flooded with stories of winging up the Alaska Highway, and the day by day life of such a trip. Most of these accounts make suitable family reading, and could be included in the annual Xmas letter, but to appeal to 100,000 readers, the writing has to be exceptional.

A while back some wordsmithing pundit, who apparently was neither well-read nor a deep thinker, wrote a long piece on the art of travel-writing, and maintained that only an adventurous traveler could possibly write about his experiences, that mere tourists were not qualified. Bunkum! One of the best travel books ever written was *Innocents Abroad,* by Mark Twain, about a package tour he took around the Mediterranean in the summer of 1867.

Several years ago I was with a Lotus Tours group riding across Tibet on a glorified dirt track, somewhat grandly called the Friendship Highway, going from Lhasa to Kathmandu, in Nepal, and wrote about it for an E-zine (www.vividlight.com/articles/114.HTM). It was one of the easiest pieces to write I have ever done. First, Tibet was all so new and eye-opening to me, that any place or person I described seemed so very different from what I, or my readers, knew. Second, the actual ride was pretty adventurous, as we were dealing with 800 miles of bad road, crossing muddy mountain passes at over 17,000 feet.

But it was only that sliver of Tibet I saw. Shortly after I was there a cousin went to Tibet, but with a half-dozen botanists taking a trip into some remote valleys, looking for new plants. His views were quite different from mine, as he had seen more of the old Tibet, I had seen mostly the new. My readers got only my view.

Traveling is an intensely personal experience. Forty years after my first long trip, motorcycling around Europe with a high-school friend on a pair of 250 singles, I wrote about it, relying on an old map and faulty memory. When my friend read the little memoir, he felt mine was a rather different trip than the one he remembered.

We all have our stories; every one of us has enough material tucked away in the old brain for an interesting autobiography, not that we will, or even should, necessarily get around to writing it. However, if you do take a trip that you want to remember and think others would like to hear about, try writing about it. It may be a grand success, garnering Pulitzer prizes and all, or it may never get published. But no matter what, 30 years from now, when you open a drawer and find that manuscript, you will relive that little adventure all over again.

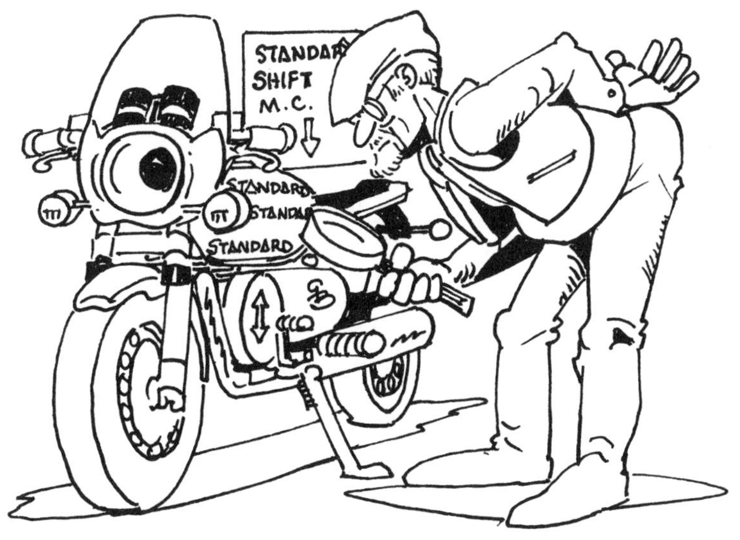

Keeping up Standards

January 2004

A while back I stopped off in Cleveland, Ohio, to see a friend, Bruce Linsday, a man partial to riding vintage bikes. I had met him on a trip to the old Soviet Union in 1988, when he had shipped his '38 EL over for the occasion. He and another fellow were at his shop, both with elderly tank-shifters, and a third hand-shifting, foot-clutching Harley WL was also parked. That was going to be my ride for the afternoon. As well as Bruce's little test of my competence.

Having squandered my savings on a much-used '51 Indian Chief when I graduated from high school in 1958, I was familar with rocker clutches, and believe I acquitted myself with relative honor. An automotive parallel might be when someone, having learned to drive on an automatic transmission, finds himself in the driver's seat of a manual.

Which brings me to the fact that I am sort of sorry that we forced all the bike manufacturers to standardize the foot-shift patterns—left side, down for first. What a shame! Back in the 1960s Harley Big Twins had left-side foot shifting (a tank-shifter was available), the Sportsters shifted on the right. Same company, two bikes, three gear levers—the rider learned his particular way. Brit bikes of yore shifted on the right, until 1975 when the DOT forced everybody over to the left. The last new right-foot shifter I was on was an Indian-built Royal Enfield Bullet, in India; to get the Bullets into this country they have had to construct some complicated linkage to cross the pattern over to the other side.

On one hand I can appreciate the bureau- and safety-crats trying to make life both safer and easier for the consumer, but I fear that if we give these well-meaning non-entities any task, they will probably ruin the whole concept. The European Union is running up against that; according to EU safety standards, acrobats in a circus have to wear hard hats. Let us not forget that in the Reagan years the DOT spent tens of thousands of dollars developing a "safer" motorcycle that used the rear wheel to steer—that was money wasted.

As far as shifting gears on a motorcycle, I think each model could be labeled "Standard," with left-foot shifting, down for first, or "Non-Standard," which would mean the rider would have to think about things. Not a bad idea.

Last August I was visiting friends in Santa Fe and my hostess came back from a trip into town, saying that this was the busiest weekend of the year due to some Indian crafts festival. Six times she had heard people tootling horns, six times, whereas on a normal day one never heard a horn within the limits of that mellow city. A couple of hours later she was giving me a guided tour, sitting on the back seat of my Harley, and on some quiet, bucolic, traffickless back street, lined with lovely adobe walls, she said to turn left at the next intersection. I blew my horn. "What was that for?" she asked. Sorry! It was inadvertent. I meant to hit the turn signal, but my mind was lollygagging and my thumb had done its "standard" move, which on a Harley meant hitting the horn button.

Save for the Harleys and some BMW models, all bikes have pretty much a "standard" turn-signal switch up there by the left thumb. Since I ride all makes and models of motorcycles, do I think that the USDOT should mandate the design of turn-signal controls for motorcycles? No. If BMW buffs feel that the simian approach to signaling a turn is the way to go, more power to them.

I'm not against standardization, mind you, and in some instances I think it would be a good thing. For one, I would have standardized shower controls. Many are the motel showers that I have gotten into where I can't figure out how to turn the water on, and if I manage that, how to control the temperature. Scalding hot or ice cold. I favor two individual faucets, one with a big blue C, the other with a big red H.

The keyboard on which I am typing these mortal words is a bit of standardization dating back 130 years. The old-fashioned typewriter was a rather crude device back in the 1860s, where one tapped a key and the key activated a long arm with a letter on the end that would smack into an inked ribbon which would then be pressed against a piece of paper. The biggest problem was that when the typist got humming, the long arms could get snarled. In 1873 a bright soul figured out a keyboard in which the most used letters were separated by the lesser used, greatly diminishing the possibility of an entanglement, and the first six letters were QWERTY.

Although word processing (as I am doing at this moment) does not suffer the mechanical complications of typewriting, that QWERTY board was so standard that it moved right over to the computer age. Here is a curiosity: I can work that QWERTY set-up pretty fast, but my brain has no idea where the letters are—only my fingers. If you ask me to tell you where all the letters from A to Z are on the QWERTY board, I probably could not do it. But I can type the alphabet lickety split.

The keyboard of an Italian typewriter is different, so QWERTY is an English-language standard. English used to mean Whitworth tool sizes. European equals metric. American equals SAE (Society of Automotive Engineers). Forty years ago if someone had a BMW R60, a Triumph T120, and a XLCH Sportster in his garage, he had three separate toolboxes. Whitworth is gone, but the US persists in fighting off the metric standard. Most American-brand vehicles, including Harley-Davidson, are a combination of US and metric. Standardization is efficient, and this all started back 150 years ago thanks to a factory that made rifles with interchangeable parts.

It is convenient that spark-plug hole size and threading became pretty standardized many years ago. Six-volt electrical systems morphed into 12 volts, with fuses and batteries easy to find. A nut vibrates off my bike, I can (usually) find a replacement in the local auto parts store.

Standards are good, especially in weights and measures. When we buy a pound of coffee beans, we know how much we are getting. If the map says it is 200 miles to the next town, and I've just filled my five-gallon tank, I figure I can make it. But just remember that a standard 2x4 piece of lumber is really only 1.5 x 3.5 inches.

We should not try to standardize beauty; we all have different notions of how things should look. I like the Ducati Multi-Strada from an aesthetic, as well as rider's, point of view. Nor should we overdo the standardization of function; I think if Indian built a true limited-edition retro-bike, with a tank-shift, it would sell out in a flash.

Here is a toast to the non-standard stuff in our world, whether it is two hamburger patties with half a bun in the middle, a Bundaberg ginger beer in a Lucas refrigerator, or right-side shifters, up for first.

Adventurous Touring

February 2004

A few months back I wrote a travel piece about riding from Canada to Mexico—along dirt roads. That prompted a great deal of positive response, which pleased me immensely. Because I believe that a whole, big section of our continent exists out there that has been virtually untapped by the motorcycling segment of our population.

That is the part of North America which is accessible only along bad roads. A good road, by our standards, has smooth pavement, with occasional amenities such as gas stations and motels. A bad road offers minimal services and goes from broken, pot-holed, crumbling pavement to no pavement. On numerous occasions I have found that gravel or dirt is quite preferable to the cracked and cratered asphalt that exists. These bad roads are where I find my own little adventures.

Many are the times I have been on a street bike and an inviting unpaved byway appears. I remember well blundering into Chaco Canyon, New Mexico, on a BMW R69S, creeping along 20 miles of corrugated dirt road, beating that poor beast near to an early death. With care and diligence we made the trip, and a commendable trip it was, with a campsite all by my lonesome under the stars, and Anasazi ghosts in my dreams. I'd do it again in a flash—but I would choose a different bike. Maybe BMW's F650GS.

A hundred years ago there were perhaps two million miles of road in this country, used by wagons and stagecoaches, all of it dirt except for some brick-paved streets in towns and cities. Getting stuck on the muddy, rutted roads was a commonplace problem. Early motorcyclists were often better off than the car people, as a lightweight motorbike could be ridden or pushed around a big mudhole, while a car could get stuck and have to be towed out by a team of horses. For a fee, of course. A fellow named George Wyman, riding his "motor bicycle" across Iowa in 1903, wrote that he found some sections "more swamp than road."

Thirty years later the miles of road criss-crossing the nation had grown by a million, but less than a quarter of that was paved. Today we have four million miles of local, county, state and federal byways and highways, and, according to the U.S. Dept. of Transportation, only two-thirds of that is paved. A third of our roads are dirt? That figure surprises a lot of people, but those are mostly city folk who have little appreciation for the the fact that much of our fertile breadbasket is criss-crossed by unpaved "farm" roads. Dirt roads also give access to our mountains and forests and deserts.

Burble along the Kansas portions of I-70 or I-35, and few passers-through will be aware that most roads in that state are dirt. An enterprising rider could cross from Colorado to Missouri without hardly ever putting a wheel on pavement. I do understand that some diligent souls are compiling a cross-country road-route, east to west, that is 95 percent or more on dirt.

Which brings me around to my cherished belief that the next gentle sea-change in our motorized two-wheeler market will be in the direction of those often odd-looking machines we refer to as dual-purpose. These are not off-road bikes, but street-worthy motorcycles that happily run along a good road, but can handle bad pavement and dirt roads with equal aplomb. These models, singles, twins, or triples, come either with saddlebags as standard, or as an OEM option, or as an aftermarket purchase, which means that travel is expected. The smaller singles are often used as solo rides, the bigger machines, like BMW's boxer GS and Triumph's Tiger, can easily carry two-up for ten thousand miles. Honda's delightful 600cc TransAlp, which was sold here only in 1989 and '90, still sells well in Europe; we'll see how the new 650 V-Strom goes.

The latest example is Ducati's new Multi-Strada. Europe seems to have embraced the dual-sport notion quite happily, eagerly buying these two-wheeled equivalents of an SUV. Aprilia, BMW, Triumph, and KTM (fix that saddle!) have big bikes which are way easy to ride over gnarly roads, be they twisty, bumpy pavement or dirt.

Are we Americans going to take to this the way the Europeans do, abandon our rolling sofas and cutting-edge sport bikes for these dual-purpose machines? Will the next big surge be in the direction of go-just-about-anywhere adventure bikes?

The cruiser market has been going gang-busters for the last 15 years, and while it will still be important, I think it has peaked. Big scooters? Will we finally come to appreciate that commuting by car is too cumbersome, whether we're tied up in traffic jams or looking for a parking space? Maybe when gas starts pushing $3 a gallon, economy will have real meaning, but I just read a take from the Bureau of Labor Statistics saying that motorcycling as a means of commuting has dropped since the mid-1980s; that is depressing.

Serious sport bikes? They will always be a part of the market, have been for many years, like today's Ducati 999 and Yamaha's 180-horsepower R1—cool to be seen on, great fun to ride (for short distances), but not too suitable for a run up the Dempster Highway.

Full-comfort touring bikes? These have been around ever since Harley began selling the faired and bagged Electra Glide some 35 years ago, followed by BMW's RT, and then the slew of Japanese bikes beginning with the Gold Wing Interstate. We are a nation of travelers, and these single-track 'Bagoes are loved by many who like to stick to the high ways *(sic)*. The genre has expanded to include sport-touring and cruiser-touring, but all these pretty much demand a decent road.

Next time I'm out in Death Valley, looking at the turn-off to Titus Canyon, thinking of those 25 miles of dirt road stretching across the Amaragosa Desert to Leadfield Summit and then down into the Grapevine Mountains, I hope I'll be on a dualie, not some low-slung cruiser or high-powered sport-bike.

Profit Margins

March 2004

A group of us were out for a Sunday romp and at lunch a fellow I know slightly, a newish rider, asked me about getting a replacement tire for his bike. Like I'm an expert on the differences between Avons, Bridgestones, Continentals, Dunlops, et cetera? I told him that all the top-name brands are good, that they all probably make a tire that will fit his rim, and that I really was not qualified to make any recommendation. Maybe he could decide based on the aesthetics of the tread pattern; we all had a laugh.

A couple of days later I got a call from him, and he started right off grousing that a local franchise dealership, Mo's Motorcycle Emporium, had what he wanted, with a $140 tag. Running up an Internet mail-order shop, he could get it for 90 bucks. Plus S&H. Where, he asks, does this dealer get off making all that money on a tire?

Well, gather around, friendly readers, and listen to MBA 101, your basic course in Motorcycle Business Administration. Lesson 1: A motorcycle dealership operates like any other capitalist enterprise, money laundering excepted: If it doesn't make a profit, it is out of business.

A dealer has a lot of overhead, beginning with the cost of his building; he is either paying rent, or the monthly mortgage. Plus electricity, water, and the guy who picks up the discarded, worn-out tires every three months. He probably has eight, ten, or more employees, which means salaries, health insurance, workers comp—all that goes along with the questionable privilege of allowing him to order people about. He has 30 bikes on display, which means flooring costs. He has spare parts, and the OEMs do not give those out for free. Plus he stocks accessories and clothing . . . chrome widgets, riding suits, gloves, helmets.

As I sit here, my only dependents being a couple of cats (The Wife is not in the least bit dependent on me) laying on the table whose shed fur gets in the ports of this machine, I am powerful glad I do not run a business. But I am glad that I do have shops in the locality who can put on a new tire, adjust valves, do the kind of work that I either do not want to do, or am not qualified to do. Mostly the latter.

To keep such an operation going, the dealer has to make a certain margin of profit, and selling new bikes is only a minor part of the bottom line. If the dealer pays the OEM X amount of dollars for a bike, he can hope to make 15 percent with the MSRP—as the Manufacturer's Suggested Retail Price is referred to. Which helps to pay the salary of the salesman and the janitorial service that keeps the showroom spic and span.

The profit on a new bike does vary, according to how well that model is selling, or how the market is doing in general. Hot model, hot market, profit is up; weak and weak, the dealer may be happy to move it out the door at cost so he does not have to pay flooring.

Off to one side is the parts and accessories counter. When you need a new clutch cable for your Typhoon 1000, it is very nice to have a dealer close by. With any luck the counterman looks up the part number, disappears for a minute, and comes back, cable in hand. How much will it cost? The OEM has a set dealer-price for the part, and the mark-up on spares varies a lot, averaging maybe around 40 percent . . . which may sound excessive to an unbusinesslike customer, but that is what it costs to keep a retail shop going. Some dealers have been known to abuse their position in society and charge a bit more. If you have two Typhoon dealers in the area, call them both, see if the price varies; nothing wrong with second opinions.

A customer appreciates a dealer with a big inventory of parts, so that when he needs that cable, the dealer has it in stock. Just as you like him to have the right size and color of jacket when you are in the mood to buy one. But inventory is costly. Your supermarket manager says he only makes two percent profit on his stock, but his entire inventory turns over every 72 hours. A motorcycle dealer feels himself fortunate if he can move his motorcycles, parts, and accessories in three or four months. And he really hates to clutter up 20 feet of shelving with parts for the Tornado 750, which never sold well and was discontinued last year.

Out in back is where the messy business of servicing and repairing bikes takes place. The service manager has got his microfiche screen, and there might be a window to allow you to see the mechanics working. You don't want to fiddle with the 16 shim-adjusted valves on your Typhoon, so every 15,000 miles you bring it in and pay one of these guys $70 an hour. Seventy bucks!? Wow! But I promise you, these wrenches are not taking home $70 an hour for a 40 hour week. The beginners may be making an hourly wage, the fast guys are working flat rate and could be billing 50 hours; the rest goes into the gross profit of the shop, which is a far cry from the net, as in the aforementioned overhead. For all that old oil, dead batteries, there's a surcharge for disposing of these environmentally hazardous items.

A dozen years ago, up in my neck of the woods, a local bike enthusiast retired from the phone company, and he and his wife put their savings into a small shop selling aftermarket Harley parts, and doing a little fixing in the back. "The dealers are charging too much; we can do it for less," he said. Two years later the place had vanished; they hadn't crunched the numbers right, and had been cutting too many deals with their ever-growing number of close friends. If the necessary profit is not there, the shop is history.

At Mo's a little corridor with a sign reading EMPLOYEES ONLY leads down to a small windowless room where Gladys, a very nice woman who used to teach calculus in high school, keeps the books for the dealership. She had better be good, because the city, state, and feds are interested in the outcome. As is Mo, who has a wife, two kids, a dog, a car payment, and a mortgage on a house two miles from the dealership. Gladys has to make sure that bills are paid, salary checks are issued, taxes and insurance are dealt with, and that there is enough money in petty cash to buy a large can of Sanborn's French Roast for the showroom coffee pot.

Don't begrudge your dealer a fair profit margin. Unless you want to mount that mail-order tire yourself.

Back from the Dead

April 2004

Why do so many business people try to re-do what was done in the past, rather than starting afresh? Hollywood is one of the main culprits, as Cinema City seems bound and determined to rehash some good movies of years gone by with remakes, none of which are ever even half as good as the original.

A new *King Kong* may be in production as you read this, and there will probably be a remake of *The Wild One* before long, with Johnny Depp playing the Brando role, Steven Segal the Lee Marvin character.

Of more interest, to me at least, are the attempts to revive defunct motorcycle marques, brands that were well-known in their day, and whose post-mortem fame, or infamy, various entrepreneurs have tried to exploit. In my mind, this is a bit like digging up a coffin and trying to bring a corpse back to life.

In the last few years two expensive attempts were made to re-energize dead American brands, Excelsior and Indian; they have both failed. The more notable marque is the Indian, which effectively ceased production in 1953. For a few years following the official funeral, British-built Royal Enfields had Indian badges on the gas tanks, then in the 1960s entrepreneurial Americans, among them Floyd Clymer, tried their hands at keeping the brand going, either with reproductions, re-badging, and even a half-new motorcycle, as in Clymer's Indian-engined, German-framed Scout. In the 1970s and 1980s a slew of little Italian and Taiwanese imports appeared, with *Indian* writ prominently on the sheet metal, followed by some serious scam artists, bringing ignominy to the historic war-bonneted logo.

Then, in a most American way, the whole matter ended up in the courts in the 1990s, and following a decision, the new Indian Motorcycle Company was born, producing Harley clones. I wished it well, although its selling points seemed to be the scripted name and skirted fenders rather than any technological innovations. The so-called "proprietary" Chief engine that was touted in 2002 was merely a Harley-style bottom end with new cylinder heads . . . which did not work very well. After selling about 13,000 bikes, the company declared bankruptcy in October of 2003; it is now in Chapter 7, I believe, which means it is dead. At least for the moment; if there is a revival in the future I would recommend calling the first model the Phoenix.

The other Lazarus-bike that did not work was the attempt by the Hanlon brothers to revive the Excelsior-Henderson name; they raised $90 million for this exercise, built their first revenue-producing bike in January, 1999, filed Chapter 11 less than a year later. The fiscal implosion was mainly due to three factors: the Hanlons spent the investors' money unwisely; they did not build a very good motorcycle; and the brand had been broken (i.e. out of business) for so long (since 1931) that there were very few people who could remember Excelsiors, much less want one.

Brit brands have also been subjected to revival techniques. One of the latest is the Vincent—right down to the very old-fashioned badge that reads THE VINCENT HRD CO. LTD. STEVENAGE HERTS. No new Vincent motorcycle has emerged from the Stevenage works since 1955, although several European builders are putting together contemporary versions out of reproduced parts. I'm all in favor of making spare parts, as it allows enthusiasts to flog their bikes as they should be, and if anything breaks, it can be replaced. As the years go on, the Vincent name seems to acquire more myth, more legend, and more value, until the price for an original Black Shadow approaches the fictional.

Now an American, Bernard Li, claims he has the rights to the fabled name, at least in North America, and believes that if he slaps it on a gas-tank, it will sell a new Vincent Black Lightning—albeit one that is powered by a Honda engine. If it is a great bike, I can see buying one . . . but its greatness will be the determining factor, not the name. Why not call it the Bernard Li American Motorcycle, and sell it as the BLAM? Li's absence from the most recent Vincent Owners' Club International Rally was commented upon, but his presence was not missed.

Then there is Oregonian Kenny Dreer and the Norton Saga. He has a small measure of fame as a consummate expert in restoring old Not-Runs, the last English one being produced in 1976, but now has ventured into the mine-covered field of selling new Nortons that look like the old. He is building a modern parallel-twin engine and sophisticated chassis which looks rather Norton Commando-ish, and he hopes this will appeal to those who like a combination of nostalgia and modernity. He may survive, as he sensibly sees his market as limited, and intends on keeping production limited as well.

Triumph, it should be noted, is not a revival but a continuation, and CEO John Bloor has his own view of the future. He is building thoroughly up-to-date machines while giving them names that have historical significance. Plus he has a helluva lot of his own money to invest in his own company, which is always useful.

Another curiosity is the Laverda, a noble, if relatively short-lived brand that began making small utilitarian bikes back in 1949, gaining fame with 750cc parallel twins and 1000cc in-line triples in the 1970s and early 1980s; the last new model was the 1000 SFC of 1985. The Moto Laverda company went into receivership in 1987, and since then several efforts have been made to bring the marque back to life. The name is now owned by Aprilia, which is trying to resurrect the brand with a new 1000 SFC—which has an Aprilia V-twin engine rather than an in-line three. Whether some 21st century buyers will be attracted by the name alone remains to be seen.

The names of half a dozen other dead Italians, from Gilera to Rumi, occasionally surface, and then sink again. Would the prospective buyer prefer to spend his money on a phantasm, or a new Ducati?

On the other hand, a new motorcycle company that is building sound machines is Victory, which has the financial backing of the well-respected, and profitable, Polaris firm. Sales got off to a slow start for this Wisconsin company when the line was introduced in 1999, but with the latest cruiseresque product, the bikes are looking better and going faster. I rather like the heroic-sounding name, Victory, like the successful Triumph.

With all this revivaling going on, before long I can see some defunct Japanese brands reappearing. Anybody for a Zebra 600? Or a Moon Dog 1200? If Hollywood asked me to re-shoot *Easy Rider,* I'd get Chris Rock to play the Fonda part, Jim Carrie as Hopper.

Heading for the Stable

May 2004

Maps, I always need maps. Which is the primary reason why I pay my dues to Triple A every year; the organization has good maps, free to members. The other afternoon I had been down in our county seat, San Luis Obispo, doing a few errands, and ended up on the south edge of town at the AAA office, which is right by the US 101 freeway. Very convenient.

I picked up my maps, put them in the tankbag, started the engine . . . and very nearly turned left to get back on the freeway. Home was 17 super-slab miles away, and I could be back in time for the five o'clock news and a nice cup of tea. "What am I doing this for?" I asked myself. "A drone up the highway just to hear that the world is not a perfect place? When I could take the back way and have a lot more fun?" I turned right.

Home is a powerful magnet. "Home is where, when you have to go there, they have to take you in," wrote Robert Frost. However, sometimes we should turn on that de-magnetizing gizmo we all seem to have. A few weeks ago I was way up in northern California, doing whatever it is I do, and finished the project a day earlier than planned. "Oh, goody," I thought, "I can be back in the comfort of my own home tomorrow night." I called Sue to tell her not to shoot if a motorcycle came down the drive after dark. She responded, "You're not supposed to be back for two more days. I'm doing some work in the bedroom, and it won't be finished for a day and a half. Go amuse yourself."

Which I did, happily, finding new roads and avoiding the freeways. What had I been thinking? Hundreds of miles of unexplored road were all around me, nobody was expecting me anywhere, and I had been headed for the stable?

A lot of years ago a woman I was dating said she wanted to go horseback riding, and we went out to a ranch in the country, rented a couple of docile nags, and trotted off. Barely trotted, as the horses were more inclined to walk; they had been on this loop trail a thousand times, and were not about to exert themselves.

Until we got to the apex of the loop, and my personal steed knew that the stall and hay, and probably oats, were waiting for her and broke into a brisk trot, then a canter, and, with a little urging, a gallop. I lost sight of my companion, but figured her horse would know where to go. The fast ride was good fun, and we slowed to a cool-off walk as the stable came into view. Still no sign of friend. I waited, then nag and I retraced our route, soon to find my companion on foot, leading her horse by the reins. When her steed picked up speed, she had fallen off; the horse, well-trained, had stopped, but she had not wished to remount.

I could say that was the beginning of the end of that particular relationship. But the point of the little story is the eagerness with which we can view going home.

In one of Sue's home-improvement magazines I saw an ad for Andersen windows that read: "Funny how 'I can't wait to get there' always turns into 'I can't wait to get home'." That may be a token of appreciation for how nice a home can, and should, be, but if not kept under rein, it can detract from the traveling experience.

I well remember talking to a fellow on an organized motorcycle tour I was taking, and he confided that he had a problem. This was his third tour in five years, and each time he looked forward greatly to the adventure, bought new gear, loved the anticipation, but was troubled by the fact that on the first day of each tour his focus shifted 180 degrees and he began to think about getting home. The trip became a personal countdown, worrying about the diminishing amount of clean clothes, imagining things that might be going wrong at work, asking himself why he was spending all this money to be in Europe when he really wanted to be sleeping in his own bed. But six months after he got home, he would begin planning his next trip.

The beginning of any worthwhile journey is like riding into a sun-filled day, full of promise and wonder. All you want to do is to aim towards the horizon, with a host of superb roads and interesting adventures ahead. The accomplished traveler never wants to get to his destination, just to keep on moving. But a vision of the stable can intrude.

Thirty years ago, when I began a three-year trip around the world, one of the reasons that I could love every day was that I had no home to go home to. What few possessions I owned were stashed in my parents' garage, which meant I could keep that far-seeing vision of the never-ending road. Maybe I would find my own Shangri-la, or a little thatched hut on a lovely beach. Or the perfect winding mountain road with a nice hotel at the top, where I would spend a comfortable night so I could ride that road again, and again, before moving on.

Now I have a home, and a very nice one, which I love dearly. It has changed my view. I may go off by myself for two, three, four weeks at a time, finding those new roads, seeing new sights, having new adventures, but the pleasure of home is always there.

Back to the Triple A office . . . It was 31 miles going home the longer way, via Turri Road and over Devil's Gap on Highway 41. I missed the news, but on second thought, I hadn't really missed anything, and I'd had a very fine ride instead.

Home is good, but you should always take the most interesting road to get there.

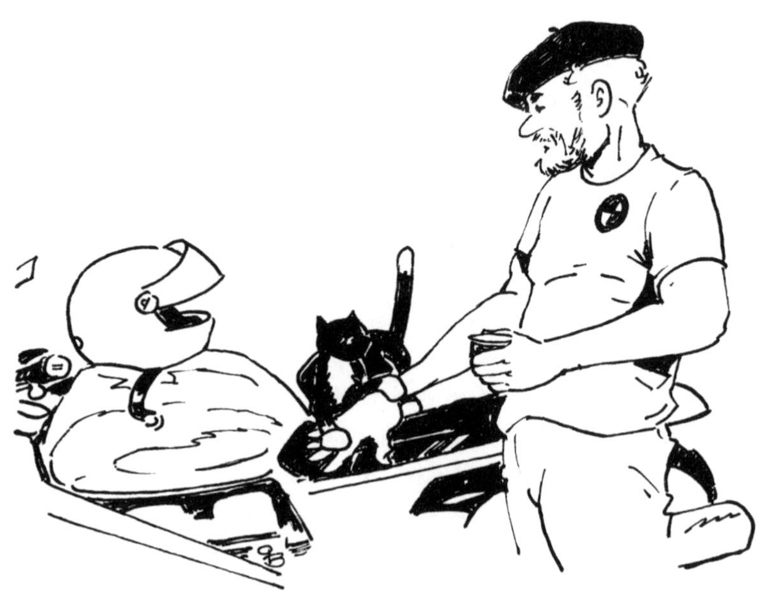

Learning Curves

June 2004

> *Some learned soul, perhaps Al Einstein, once said that space is curved, and if one could look far enough, one would see the back of one's own head; the curves we're dealing with here are a little more pronounced.*

Is there a rider amongst us who does not appreciate a bend in the road, a curve, a chance to lean that motorcycle over, just a little? Or maybe more than a little. It doesn't matter what you are riding, a low-slung cruiser that scrapes a muffler at 25 degrees, or a sport bike that still has clearance at 45 degrees.

Around my small part of the world we have lots of curvy roads, mostly with little traffic because motorists generally like straight highways. Car drivers are not into that subtle, and sometimes not-so-subtle, sensation of the lean; centrifugal forces just throw them from one side of the car to the other. When a motorcyclist corners, all he might feel is a slight gravitational push as the suspension compresses. And the satisfaction of a curve well-carved.

Yesterday I had a shop put a set of Avon Azaros on the ST1100, and to scrub them in I took the 40-mile way home, via Las Pilitas Road. That's a nice rural road, running some seven miles through wooded hills, the occasional open field, only a few families living along there. The authorities have recently been kind enough to resurface the whole stretch, and the asphalt is narrow enough not to warrant a center line.

I turned off the straightish Pozo Road onto Las Pilitas, and that very feeling of the bike angling over caused a warm feeling in my body. We, the bike and I, headed up a little ridge, left, right, left, right, left, right, never staying perpendicular for more than a second. Crest the ridge, and we did the same going down to the Salinas River.

I have taken all manner of machines over the road, from Harley Softails to dual-purpose singles and seriously sporty twins, triples, and fours. The style of the ride, as well as the rider, determines the angle of the lean. The rotational nature of a motorcycle makes the lean such a pleasure, always using power to the rear wheel; it is more banking than steering. Maybe I maintain a steady throttle in a bend, more often I'm accelerating, as I like to slow before the curve, then power through. Not too much gas, just enough to make the bike want to finish the curve by standing up straight.

This is all very easy, very mellow. I'm not scraping pegs, let alone knees, just following the grainy black surface of the fresh asphalt. I am not even really aware of what it is I am doing, the lean seems to be coming all by itself. When a novice rider is learning the basics, he or she hears about countersteering—push left, go left. After ten thousand miles on the road, the rider may never consciously think about that "countersteer" word again; he just does it.

It is like tying a tie; ask me to explain in words how to do it, I couldn't. But put a tie around my neck, and in a flash I'll show you a presentable Windsor knot. Just as I cannot really explain about cornering.

We arrived at the old girder bridge crossing the Salinas River, a single-lane relic of decades past; I hope it stays forever. *Las Pilitas* roughly translates to "the waterholes," and local lore has it that even in the driest years water could be found along here by digging a little in the river bottom.

One of our cats came from here. A few years ago Sue and I rode out one sunny day, two-up, for a picnic. Parking the motorcycle by the bridge, we climbed a fence, spread out a blanket, and had lunch and a nap. Returning to the bike we were putting on our jackets and helmets when a tiny ball of black and white fur came tearing out of the tall grass headed straight for us. Obviously abandoned by some heartless beast, this kitten did not care if we were aliens from outer space or not, she just wanted salvation, running straight into Sue's arms and snuggling inside the jacket for the half-hour ride home.

A few hundred yards east of the river a short concrete bridge crosses over Las Pilitas Creek, leading to a slightly gentler road, still lots of left and rights, less up and down. While I love that constant side to side movement, I am also constantly wary. The wheel of a pickup truck may have thrown some dirt into the inside of a corner. If it is just a dusting, I keep on at my speed, steady throttle, knowing that even if my tires do slip a little on the loose stuff, they will grab the pavement again before anything untoward happens. If there is a lot of gravel, and I can see far enough ahead, I might go wide. Or brake hard and tip-toe through.

The stability of a motorcycle under power is quite astounding; The biggest no-no is to back off on the throttle when confronted with a patch of gravel in a curve. Keep a steady hand and ride it through, letting your tires do their job. The front wheel does the steering, the rear provides that gyroscopic precession that keeps you and the bike upright. Most of us are not even aware of the inputs we put into the handlebars, but they are always there.

Las Pilitas is pretty much a two-gear kind of road. If the yellow warning sign reads 15 or 20, I'm down to second; otherwise I'm merrily rolling along in third. Once one finds the rhythm of the road, any road, the traveling is easy. Very little thought has to go into the handlebars; it is just a natural movement.

Trees, fences, a couple of horses, a few cattle, a barn, the occasional house, all provide an in-depth background better than any video game. The road, the lean, the pleasure of feeling my body move closer to the ground; for me it is an extremely visceral sensation.

This is not risk-taking, this is merely enjoying what it is that a motorcycle does. A rider and horse jump a fence, a glider pilot finds a thermal, a snow-boarder catches big air over a mogul, a surfer gets the ninth wave, a golfer lands his ball on the green in one shot—I derive that feeling of satisfaction in every corner.

Arriving back home, I killed the engine and got off the bike, the Pilitas cat jumped up on the saddle. She doesn't care about going around curves, her satisfaction comes from knowing I'm back—with some cans of tuna fish.

Got Bread?

July 2004

I love motorcycles, but food is also of great interest to me. Maybe too much interest, as I look down at the scales in the bathroom. Or try to zip up that very handsome Thurlow deerskin jacket that I got back in 1981; it is more than a bit snug these days, with Sue saying it makes me look rather like a sausage.

But a motorcyclist must eat, must keep up his strength. We don't want any rider feeling faint from hunger as he rolls down the highways of America. But that does not mean we have to stop at a Sizzler for lunch and consume a large steak with baked potato slathered in butter and sour cream. Or a triple cheeseburger and fries at McBurger. A meal can be a lot simpler.

When I'm traveling, I always have part of a loaf of bread stashed somewhere on the bike. Bread is the staff of life, and I am usually very happy with a couple of slices and something in between. If the bread is really good, maybe I don't even need much in-between.

Bread packs easily on a bike, and doesn't go bad. Just stale. Although I think that some sliced loaves have enough chemicals in them that they never dry up. Bread can get squashed, but squashing never hurt the taste.

We are becoming a pretty bread-savvy nation, and most grocery stores have greatly expanded their bread selection over the last 15 years. My local supermarket boasts a faux-bakery; the dough is brought in all prepared and the "baker" has only to put the trays in the oven, and Presto!, hot loaves of French-style bread. At 99 cents, that is a fair price. What we don't eat with supper will go for making sandwiches on the morrow.

A very good bakery, Hush Harbor, has started up in my town, which turns out all sorts of excellent pastries and breads, charging $3.00 or more a loaf. They are very much worth the extra expense. Nowadays when pulling into Smalltown, USA, I'll ask the local at the gas station if there is a bakery around. Often there is one, with a plump fellow in a large white hat just pulling a rack of sheepherder loaves out of the oven. No, don't bother slicing it, I like tearing pieces off.

Good bread can almost be a meal in itself. A couple of hundred years ago a fortunate family would have gathered around a table with a big round loaf in the middle, and maybe a little pot of hare stew for dipping; that's where the "breaking bread" concept came from. Breaking bread was the basis of most meals.

Last August I was in Milwaukee, rubbing handlebar tips with a quarter-million Harley riders. That city is famous for motorcycles, and beer, and also for bratwurst. I had more than a dozen brats while I was there, but though the wurst were good, the bread they came with was really dull. Commercial hot-dog rolls are notably tasteless, while a brat is enhanced by a good crusty bun. I developed a taste for brats when I was in the army in Bavaria, and to this day I believe the world's best brats are served at the central railway station in Munich, a city also noted for motorcycles and beer. However, that is because the sausages are served with crunchy sesame rolls. And the right mustard.

When I'm on the road I generally stop at a grocery/deli at lunch-time, and have the counterman put together a sandwich which I can later eat under the shade of a tree down the way. Most delis have expanded their bread offering in recent years; along with the standard white, wheat, or rye, you can choose sourdough or pumpernickel or hard rolls. As well as some tasty meats and cheeses.

Others delis are more traditional. When I am near Fly, Tennessee, I go up the road a couple of miles to take a break at Robert's Country Store in Bethel. It is a nice, old-fashioned store, with wood floors, shelves crammed with foodstuffs and hardware, and in the back a white cooler case. Look in the big viewing window in front, and there is ham and bologna and souse and cheddar and Swiss. I order up a souse sandwich, on white, with the fixings; nothing wrong with white bread.

Every year I try to have my traditional annual Spam lunch—usually alone and in the privacy of some remote corner of Death Valley, as most of my friends would not understand. I like Spam; perhaps not every day, but once a year is fine. My father liked Spam, having acquired the taste during World War II. My mother did not like Spam; my wife does not like Spam. But give me a can of Spam, and a loaf of sliced bread, something Wonder-ish, and I will have a cheerful meal up on top of Hunter Mountain, or down in Echo Canyon.

Those pearly whites of mine will cut through that half-baked flour and compressed meat bits, and I will savor the taste. Good stuff, adequately nourishing, though a bit lacking in roughage. Okay, so I'll have a Cobb salad for supper.

I do feel that food should be remembered. No, that does not mean I can tell you what I had for breakfast on the 10th of July, 2003, but that for three or four hours after eating, you should be happily smacking your lips. Which is my problem with "Fast Food;" when on the road I sometimes stop at a quickie joint because it is fast and cheap, but the memory is about exciting as was the aftermath of eating a can of ham and lima beans in the old C-ration days.

Sue, my wife, was raised on a farm, and understands food. And baking bread; she can turn out a loaf of Irish soda bread from scratch in less than an hour. Steaks? I ask her if she wants to go out to eat and she says she'd rather I go out and buy a really good piece of beef, which she'll put on the charcoal grill. Done to a turn and accompanied by hot soda bread and a good salad.

But back to me, motoring through some national forest. I've got a small tent and a sleeping bag, half a loaf of day-old sourdough bread, some cheese, and a tomato. Did I mention the bottle of wine? The sun will set within the hour, and I see a sign for a campground. It's a mile up a dirt road, and no other person in sight. I set up the tent, build a fire in the pit, toast the bread, melt the cheese a little, slice the tomato—the evening is good. As is my appetite.

Life is short; no point wasting it on boring food.

Riding with the Enemy

October 2004

When I get out on an open country byway, all by myself, negligible traffic, I feel liberated, freed from the constraints of normal, everyday life. In the springtime, riding south on Bitterwater Road, hillsides green, I can see the pavement rolling out miles ahead, climbing low hills, negotiating the minor curves and turns of the valley, not a vehicle in sight, and I fear no man. Just the occasional steer wandering across the road on this open range.

Put me on Interstate 80 near Hammond, Illinois, during a dark, rainy rush-hour evening, and I understand the true meaning of fear. A motorcyclist is like some fragile gazelle caught up in a herd of elephants thundering off to some pachydermal destination, oblivious to this small creature trapped in their midst. That is the big problem with the multi-wheel guys and gals, whether they are driving cars, SUVs, RVs, box trucks or semis—they tend to be oblivious. They share that herd mentality, focusing on the taillights in front, forgetting to change lanes in anticipation of their exit, generally not even noting anything as minuscule as the headlight on a 500-pound motorcycle.

The chances of the Average American Motorist (AAM) becoming more aware of motorcycles during his daily commute is, as Jimmy the Greek might have figured it, way worse than ten to one: longish odds. The number of registered drivers in this country is well over the 200 million mark, while the number of motorcycle-conscious drivers, including motorcyclists, their extended familes, and friends and strangers attuned to two wheels, is probably less than 20 million.

What do those non-conscious 180+ million think and feel about motorcyclists? Unfortunately, most of them do not think about anything much at all, and when a motorcycle passes by on the road they barely register the fact—unless the pipes are obnoxiously loud and the driver feels that law enforcement agencies should crack down on these noise polluters. In our own defense we must consider these drivers as elephants, concerned with little else but keeping half an eye on the road and the brake-lights while adjusting the CD player, talking on the phone, and making notes on a pad. These are not malicious creatures, just dumb enough to be a potential hazard, a benign sort of enemy.

Only a very small percentage of Americans have actually had hands-on experience with motorcycles. In some rural states at the age of 14 a kid can get a permit to legally drive himself to school in the old pickup. At age 16 many young drivers have the right to get behind the wheel of Mom's Viper, should Mom be silly enough to offer the keys. By 18 these prospective AAMs have learned all they will ever know about driving, which is usually not a great deal. I talk with these people frequently, maybe in the post office parking lot, or at a freeway rest stop, and ask them their views on motorcycles. The great majority say that they look at us in a fog of ignorance, not understanding why we are out there battling the elements when we could be in air-conditioned, or heated, comfort.

The two most common complaints are that aforementioned excessive noise, and large groups of riders. Loud pipes do not save lives, but they do make enemies. While the problems created by 30 or more motorcyclists moving along at a measured pace in close formation, which may be a bit slower than the AAM cares to go, are immense.

Speed, to my surprise, is a much less objectionable issue, at least on the open road. Most AAMs do understand that one of the pleasures of riding must be in the ability to go fast, and only fault the riders if they do some seriously stupid overtaking maneuvers. In urban situations it is rather different, as when a motorcycle is sneaking down the gutter while a Lincoln Town Car is preparing to make a right turn—having forgotten to put on his signals. The Lincoln driver is intent on avoiding pedestrians, and the sudden arrival of a motorcycle alongside his right front fender can be quite unnerving, which can create hostility.

Visibility is a major problem, as the AAM, in his usual semi-comatose state, is just not trained to see an object like a motorcycle. Not even a fully dressed-out Electra Glide with five lights on the front. The experts say that is because such an apparition is outside of a driver's "normal" viewing expectation, and thus is blithely ignored. "What flying saucer? I didn't see anything." Lack of muffling does not help, as the exhaust points the wrong way, but a loud horn can serve to alert a somnolent person behind a steering wheel.

In my admittedly unofficial polling method there seems to be very little genuine anti-motorcyclist sentiment amongst the AAMs. Hyper-aggressive drivers, the road-ragers, are mad at everyone, not just us. Maybe if your wife just rode off with a Gold Winger you develop an attitude, or your husband spent the kids' college fund on a Ducati 999R. But these are way, way in the minority.

Infrequently I have met with genuine hostility on the road, several times from truckers who did not seem to want me to pass. The great, great majority of professional teamsters are good drivers with a healthy respect for the world of vehicles around them, and they are a pleasure to deal with. Several times I have had roadside troubles, and truckers have spent time helping me out.

There are the exceptions, like the dolt that a friend and I came across the other week. We were on a narrow back road, one and a half lanes max, perfect for motorcycles, and after sweeping around a curve I came up on and quickly passed an empty dump truck rattling along at a much slower speed. I don't think the driver was even aware of my presence until I was past. I motored on, looking in my rearview for Larry. No Larry. Miles down the road, at a three-way split I stopped. And waited. Along came the truck, right down the middle of the road, preventing Larry from overtaking. He turned into an old mining complex just before the intersection, and I was tempted to follow and ask him what prompted this anti-social behavior. I did not, thinking of tire irons and handguns, and figuring his mean-spiritedness would turn into cancer soon enough.

We have to share the road with the elephants. Our survival, so to speak, depends on our awareness. Of the twit cutting across four lanes to make the exit. Of the on-coming, left-turning driver who should be declared legally blind. Of the soccer mom, late to pick up the kids, shooting out of a driveway without looking. Of the tourist on the scenic road who is trying to steer and take photos at the same time. Of the ditz at the wheel dialing a number to explain why he is late for a meeting, but that he is hurrying to get there.

These, and others, are the enemy. And in this case, the best defense is to ride defensively.

Falling in Love

March 2005

Rather dull folk have sometimes accused me of being obsessed by motorcycles, addicted to them; I prefer to think that I am purely and simply in love with motorcycling. Though I promise those who worry about the definition of matrimony that I will never try to marry any of these objects of my devotion.

In my personal view of this particular universe, as I understand it, we get one chance at the terrestrial life . . . which means we had better make the most of it. I believe I have, and for me an important part of my life is riding a motorcycle. I love riding a motorcycle, any motorcycle, and a life should be as full of love as possible. This is not to be confused with the love of family and friends, but is rather the transcendental love we can have for places, or objects, or activities.

It has not been an easy task coming to terms with the fact that not everyone loves to ride a motorcycle. Many of my friends and acquaintances have absolutely no desire to throw a leg over a bike and head off to the nearest horizon. Strange, perhaps, but true. In their "free" time they would rather go and whack a harmless little white ball across acres of lovely green grass, a notion that has always escaped me. Or strap a surfboard to the luggage rack on top of thecar's roof and drive for hours to find a wave to ride. I remember well the time I was 600 miles down in Baja, pulling into the San Juanico campground at Scorpion Bay, where I met four surf guys who had left San Diego the day before in an old van, just because they had heard that a big swell was heading across the Pacific and would be at Scorpion in 48 hours; that is love of surfing. Tennis, tiddlywinks, base jumping, each to his or her own choice.

The average life-span of the average American is roughly 75 years. Or 900 months. Or 3900 Sundays. However you want to figure it. The first 18 years are pretty cluttered up with the drudgery of school, interfering parents, lack of money, that sort of thing. Then the world starts to open up. And we have choices to make. And how do we make our choices? Perhaps this is where that Biblical talk about "free will" comes in, which I think is quite applicable to motorcycling. What prompts a person, like me, to take up motorcycling as a teenager, and then pursue the passion relentlessly for the rest of my life?

Darned if I know. Perhaps somebody looking to write a doctoral thesis will do a DNA sampling of a thousand motorcyclists, a thousand non-motorcyclists, and see if there is any quantifiable difference. My only entirely unbiased thought is: I doubt it. Having met thousands of motorcyclists over the years, I could not describe any unifying characteristic, other than the love of motorcycles. I don't think that motorcyclists are into serious risk-taking, because there are a lot riskier ways to spend your off hours—like alligator wrestling or flying ultra-lites.

Having a tolerance for a low level of risk is fine, but 99.9% of us are far more interested in riding tomorrow than crashing today.

I am fully aware that there is more to a life than motorcycling. I have to sleep, I have to eat, I have to earn a living, mow the grass, feed the cats, take care of familial responsibilities. But we all have, or at least most of us have, some of that free time, in which we can do what we want. Maybe it is pruning the rosebushes, or reading a Dan Brown thriller, or planning a trip to the Antarctic. Or getting on the bike and heading out for a half-hour ride.

On a practical level I love riding because traffic is much less of a botheration, parking is greatly simplified, and I get good gas mileage. On a more visceral level, I love the power, love the handling, love the lean angles. On a quasi-ethereal note, I love being out in the open, love the smells of the countryside, love the unobstructed view.

I try to be sensitive to non-motorcyclists, but admit that I have no understanding of, for example, the people who rise long before dawn to drive down to Morro Bay, get on a fishing boat, motor out to sea along with 30 others, most of whom will become seasick during the day, tangle lines all morning, and come back with a few mackerel that, on cost per pound, would have been considerably cheaper to buy at a supermarket. But they love it; they must, otherwise why would they suffer so?

Which is probably what the driver in the Volvo is thinking as I motor past him during a major rainstorm. He is warm and snug, and the garage-door opener will make sure he doesn't suffer even one drop of rain. Whereas I am exhilarated, loving this low-key battle with the elements.

We all know that motorcycling itself is a many-faceted avocation. I am essentially into road riding, traveling, going places, be it the post office or the Dolomites. But within our clan the differences are major. The Iron Butt battalion is about as removed from the Orange County Chopper regiment as earth is from Cassiopeia. I sometimes ride long distances in a short time, but only to get some place. I can appreciate, to a minor degree, the guy who spends fifty grand on a custom bike which is absolute eye candy, but a misery to ride more than a hundred miles; he is into two-wheeled showmanship, in which the bike is the show, not the rider. As opposed to the super-bike racer whose talents are the show, as all those fully faired bikes look very much the same at 150 mph.

I love watching trials riders whose idea of a good time is to aim for an obstacle and then go over it, rather than avoid it, as I would. I have grudging admiration for those riders of MV Agusta F4s and CBR1000RRs who whizz along the public roads at semi-sonic speeds while not having the governor's cell phone number at hand. Or the old-bike buffs who putter along on ancient machinery.

Having ridden a fair number of antique (pre-World War II) motorcycles, I wonder if I would have been as passionate as I am had I come along a generation or two earlier than I did, forced to deal with atmospheric valves, bad dirt roads, minimal brakes, all that. Having teethed on equipment made in the 1950s, I did not expect much from the brakes of a Moto Guzzi Falcone, nor the reliability of a much-thrashed British vertical twin, nor the handling of a Harley Duo-Glide. My first bike, a 1954 NSU 250 Max, was quite exceptional for its time, having a single-cylinder SOHC engine and mono-shock rear suspension, but if I still had it and tried to chase a 250 Ninja through a corner, I would very soon come to appreciate its limitations. But that is what was available at the time, and I expect that had I grown up with machines like an Indian Power-Plus or a Norton 16H I would have taken them to heart as well.

It is much easier to fall in love with twenty-first century motorcycles, which do everything so very well. This makes me wonder what a fellow born 30 years hence will think of an "antique" K1200LT or a V-Strom 650 when he gets to be a rider. However, I bet when he throws a leg over his 250cc Shazam in 2050 he will probably experience the same initial emotions as I did when I first got on my NSU—"Boy, I love this!"

MAP (Manually Activated Positioning) vs. GPS (Global Positioning System)

April 2005

There is a big difference between knowing where you are going, and understanding which is the best route to get there. If you are in a hurry, you want efficiency. If you are traveling, out to see the country, the world, you want scenic, you want interesting; you want the byway, not the highway.

The basis of traveling, whether it's getting to your old army buddy's house in a strange city or going from Cairo to Cape Town, is knowing both where you are and where you are going. Let's say your buddy lives, in Silver Spring, Maryland, and you're at the I-95 welcome center near Jessup. The place has lots of maps, lots of info, and with a high-lighter pen the woman behind the counter shows you how to continue down the I-95, west on I-495, south on US 29, left on State Highway 391, and then a right on Greenbrier Drive.

Even I, with my addled brain and lack of neural coordination, can remember four directions, as I take one last look before folding up the three-foot by four-foot map into its four-inch by nine-inch traveling configuration.

Or, as a result of superb advances in electronics and micro-processing, I could do the non-visual positioning, punching in the "here" and "there" on my GPS unit. And with all the latest hi-tech stuff I do not worry about having to squint at a tiny screen at 70 mph on a startlingly sunny day, because now a charming little voice in my helmet can give me directions as I go. "You stupid person, you just passed the turn onto 391. Now, dummy, you want the second left, onto Woodside Parkway."

I like the whole GPS concept, and look on it as a growing child. The biggest problem is the software, the digital mapping, that is essential. Just like paper maps, you need the right map for the right place to get the GPS to function. North America is pretty well covered, as is Australia and Western Europe. Eastern Europe, stretching out to the Ural Mountains, is covered in a rough manner, but certainly has a way to go, especially if you are looking for the fast road to Yetkul. Africa? Asia? South America? Rather basic digital maps, at best. I imagine Iraq is pretty well plotted these days, but I'm not really planning on a trip there to see the tower of Babel just yet; the first map actually may have been made in nearby Babylon, drawn in 2500 B.C.

Beside me is a "manually operated" map of the entire United States, and in that little LEGEND box it says that the scale is 1:5,702,000, which means that it is a pretty useless map for navigating. It shows the bigger highways, and that is about it. There is also a map of California's San Luis Obispo county, where I live, which gives me a different scale, with one map-inch equaling about 4.75 miles; using a little rough math, that puts the overall scale at about 1:300,000.

That, in my thinking, is a good, usable map. It shows all the roads, paved and dirt, and allows the viewer to pick and choose his route. You go down to your local cartography emporium, or your mega-bookstore, and look at the maps on display, and you will find that nearly all of them have a scale printed on the cover. 1:1,000,000 is okay for generalizing, 1:300,000 is really useful. I was in the Dolomites last summer, that Alpine sub-range in northeast Italy, and bought a 1:150,000 map, which was really too detailed for maximum effectiveness. For whatever reasons, most American maps do not promote the general scale, pushing the "so many miles per inch" approach; I wish they would list the 1:WHATEVER scale on the cover, so I would know immediately what I am dealing with.

Which brings me back to the GPS. When traveling I am perfectly happy snuggling up with a map at night, plotting where the next day might take me. Imagine I'm at a motel in Hot Springs, Arkansas, and on a late June evening I am sitting out under a tree with my AAA map. The legend does tell me the scale is precisely 1:899,712, or "one inch equals approximately 14.20 miles," which is pretty much the norm for most U.S. state maps.

What a large paper map allows me to do is to look over the terrain I'm going to cover the next day, and make some choices. Let me see, I want to head northwest, up towards the Grand Lake O' the Cherokees. I can take 7 north to Hollis, west on 314 to Onyx (nice name), north on 27 to Danville, west on 10 to Havana, up the east side of Magazine Mountain on 309, et cetera. I know nothing about these roads, but according to the map I will be following rivers, going through national forests, climbing mountains.

Can I do that with a GPS? No. I can certainly program this route into the gadget, and take all the guesswork out of the trip, but when it comes to initially plotting the route the paper map is probably more important than any digital map.

Back 40 years ago when I was young, and in the U.S. Army in Germany, a couple of Brits from their Special Air Service came to our unit to give us some basic instruction in desert navigation. At that time you used a watch, a compass and the stars, as well as any map you could get your hands on. A year later, out of the army, I did drive across the Sahara Desert, using a Michelin map to guide me, but stayed on the main *pistes* (tracks), rather than cutting across the way soldiers would do in order to sneak behind enemy lines. Today I would definitely carry a GPS, though I doubt there is precise software, as tracks come and go with sandstorms and shifting dunes. When I came to a fork in the *piste,* with a GPS I could find out precisely where I was and then make a decision.

I was reading a book by a fellow who was motorcycling around South America a couple of years ago, and at one point he wanted to cross the Bolivian Altiplano to get to Chile. He had all the most sophisticated GPS equipment—which was of no real use because there was no suitable software. Nor was there any good paper map; take a wrong turn at any of the scores of unmarked intersections and he could end up a hundred miles down a dead-end road. As a result for four days he had to follow a Land Cruiser driven by a local.

Given a choice, I will always opt for a MAP. Though a GPS unit with a pleasant voice would be nice when battling traffic in Chicago. Over the next 20 years I think that the two will learn how to happily co-exist.

A Beautiful Day

June 2005

The day begins the way it does for most motorcyclists: in bed. The sun comes up over the Chicago Ridge before seven o'clock; Sue and I tend to be early risers which is why the bedroom faces east. I can see a little fog in the valley below, which will soon burn off. Spring is in the air and on the ground; as well as in between, with the trees budding. It would be a nice day for a ride somewhere.

I pull on sweats and slippers and venture forth. The thermostat is at its nighttime setting of 60, and the thermometer reads 61; I up it three

degrees and the furnace clicks into action. As well as the cats, coming out of their warm cubbies in anticipation of some flaked tuna in sauce. Hold it, you cats; first the coffee. Ground French roast in the filter, water in the reservoir, turn the machine on, open cat-food can, equal amounts in five bowls.

With the first cuppa in hand, I go out to get the paper; the outside thermometer reads 38 degrees. Walking up the misty 200 yards to the road I say "Good morning" to our herd of deer, and to the flock of turkeys. The Sunday paper is suitably thick—mostly with ads.

Refilled cup in hand, I settle into an easy chair with the paper, and soon a cat on lap. An hour passes, the funnies have been read, and last night's dishes need to be washed. Whoever cooks does not clean up, and Sue had made a noble shepherd's pie. Before plunging hands into soapy water I turn on the TV to watch "Meet the Press," where various people explain to the moderator how they can bring peace and prosperity to the world.

Looking out the window over the sink I see the fog has vanished, and a few puffy clouds dot the Wedgewood-blue sky; the grassy slope running east from the house is an Irish green, with yellow daffodils and white narcissus giving range to the colors.

Nine o'clock, the phone rings. "Let's go for a ride," says John.

"Good idea," say I; "How about King City? Mexican lunch."

"Fine. Meet at ten thirty, Templeton park? It'll have warmed up by then."

Done. We call the usual half dozen suspects. Two have sorry excuses, but six of us show at the park, gas tanks full, one each BMW, Ducati, Honda, Kawasaki, Suzuki, Triumph.

"What a great day! Thanks for calling," is the general salutation. Most rides need some sort of catalyst to get going, and John had provided it. A beautiful day for a ride; 50 degrees and climbing. We freeway 15 miles up to San Miguel, cross the Salinas River, and take Indian Valley Road. It's a small road, serving a dozen ranches over the next 40 miles; most of it single-lane asphalt; there is no traffic. On this early spring day it is a byway of beauty as it parallels Big Sandy Creek. Most of this is cattle country, but a few fields have been turned, long brown furrows crossing the valley, seeds just sprouting.

The valley ends and the road climbs up and over the Cholame Hills, then drops, rather precipitously, into the San Andreas Rift; no quake today. The hills are so damned green it looks like a Disney production, with the narrow strip of blacktop, now called Peach Tree Road, curving along the sides, two, three, four bends visible at one time. We're riding fairly fast, though never exceeding our own personal limits. Off to our left is San Lorenzo Creek, hidden deep inside the sheer dirt walls it has cut in eons past. Who needs to go to Patagonia or the Alps when we have this?

A ranch must be moving some cows, as half a dozen pickups with horse-trailers are parked by a large barn. We cross over CA 198 and continue up Peach Tree Valley, almost a mile wide, with lots of contented hamburgers on the hoof. At a small intersection called Lonoak the wall of a farm's out-building still has the faded word GASOLINE visible, though gas has probably not been sold there for 50 years or more. A sign points left, reading KING CITY 15; in ten miles we are crossing over the Gabilan Range and heading straight and flat and slightly downhill across the Salinas Valley to that town. Huge fields are sown with lettuce and tomatoes, with large processing plants in the distance. We've covered about 85 miles.

Back in the 1880s one Charlie King bought 13,000 acres hereabouts, and the local community inherited his name. It is a major agricultural center these years, and the ag business requires a lot of workers; most of these are now of Mexican origin—which means that there is good Mexican food in town. Like at El Lugarcito Michoacan on Broadway; mariscos, tacos, enchiladas, burritos—order at the window and within five minutes the waitress brings the plates out to our patio table in the sun. Good food, good weather, good roads, good friends—it's a beautiful day indeed.

For the ride home we cross over to the west side of the Salinas River, where we will still be on back roads, although slightly more trafficked. Maybe one car every five minutes instead of every 15. To get out of the fertile valley we take Jolon Road towards Quinado Canyon, passing grapes, grapes, and more grapes; we are either going to become a wine-drinking nation, or a lot of farmers are going to go bust.

Once a main stage route, avoiding the flood prone Salinas Valley, the Jolon Road now supplies access to Fort Hunter Liggett, and recreation for many motorcyclists. We see a number coming our way, first a covey of sport bikers, left hands tilting up from the handlebar in salutation, then a small flock of cruiser types, with cheerful waves from both riders and passengers. It is the sort of day where everybody feels that it is good to be alive and on the road again. The lightly wooded land has fat cattle grazing beneath the trees, barely acknowledging our presence. An occasional calf, bored, looking for action, makes a big commotion about our passing by running away from the fence line; his peers ignore him, and us.

We turn onto Interlake Road, which lies between two large reservoirs, the San Antonio and the Nacimiento, storing water from two of the main tributaries of the Salinas River. The pavement is excellent, as this secluded back-road never sees a heavy truck. Flowers are beginning to appear in the meadows, blue lupines, red and orange poppies, purple irises. We are soaking up the sun and the wind, admiring the horses, the sheep, the goats, even the occasional llamas. And the ground squirrels forever playing chicken with the motorcycle wheels.

The Nacimiento Reservoir appears full, with excess water flowing over the spillway; the six-year drought appears to have broken. We slip around the back roads via Adelaida, onto Vineyard Drive, along to the Mastantuono winery, about two miles west of Templeton, where we stop under an old oak tree. All agree it has been a beautiful day, a great ride, and we go our separate ways.

Confessions of a Motorcycling Life

October 2005

I've been doing what I do for a heck of a long time. I first learned to ride a motorcycle back in the fall of 1955, after a friend, Dick Tatlock, bought an old Harley 125, the kind with the rubber-band front suspension. This showed a certain amount of trust on Dick's part, as five years before I had crashed his new bicycle. He was the first kid on the block to get a bike with a Sturmey-Archer three-speed and caliper brakes, and I had applied a little too much pressure on the front brake.

Anyway, there I was bashing along the trails and paths beside the Mill River, learning how to shift, clutch, brake. The next year I got my license and bought my own bike, a used NSU 250. In the summer of '57 we took our first long trip together, about 2500 miles; Dick had sold his "dollar and a quarter" and bought a BMW 250. He still rides, I still ride, our wives ride. I love to ride; a day without some saddle-time is a poor day indeed.

I'm at a party, somebody asks, "What do you do for a living?" Reasonable question, providing a framework for building a good conversation. We all have to work, unless we get our money the old-fashioned way, by inheriting it.

"I ride motorcycles," I say. And write about them, but that's secondary. If the asker has any interest in motorcycles, positive or negative, we're off on a roll. If his eyes begin to roll upwards in their sockets, I politely say, "Nice to have met you," and wander off to bore someone else.

When a piece of paper asks me to list my profession, I am tempted to put down "Motorcyclist." But I usually wimp out and write "Journalist." Unless it is at the border of some paranoid country which fears the free press, in which case I rely on "Educator." In truth, the journalism is merely an adjunct to the motorcycling. I write because I get paid for my efforts; I ride motorcycles whether or not I get paid.

Had my benighted college offered a degree in "motorcycle journalism," I undoubtedly would have led a very different life. But I disliked writing back then, the wearisome papers on the dissolution of values as portrayed in William Faulkner's opus, or Herbert Spencer's theory of the unknowable. As it was, though I was reading motorcycle magazines during my college days it never crossed my mind that I could earn a living from motorcycling, whether by writing, racing, or anything else.

In high school I belonged to an AMA club, the Aces Up, headquartered in Stan Djuba's garage in Amherst, Massachusetts, which had three or four Harley 125s as a racing stable. Those were the days of scrambles, enduros, and hare'n'hounds, cheerful events that took place in farmers' fields on weekends. At one point Stan thought he could make a racer of me; several times we hauled a 125 over to a quarter-mile oval dirt track, with a jump, and I would try my best to tear around and around on one of the little "pea-poppers," as the Harleys were known. However, Stan's final analysis was, "Clem, you'd be okay if you didn't fall down so much." No budding Chris Carr here, so making my career as a racer was out.

Being a mechanic, twisting wrenches, might have been another option, but I came from a family that considered a wheelbarrow to be sophisticated machinery. Adjusting the chain on a bicycle was a major operation. If anything ever needed to be done on a motorcycle, I would call on friend Sandy Sheehan to come help—or rather, do the job while I watched and fetched him glasses of lemonade. Sandy left off riding motorcycles when his car got rear-ended and did his back a mischief, but he is still into fixing things, though now they tend to be old and valuable blue-grass musical instruments, at his shop in Cambridge, Mass. When he's not hosting blue-grass radio shows.

Owning a motorcycle shop? Sorry, but my mother's side of the family has all the business genes, and none of those got passed onto me. I would probably unintentionally bankrupt any entrepreneurial enterprise within 24 months.

No, I was a rider, and that was as far as my expertise could take me. I rode a lot, most of it in North America and Europe, a little bit in Asia after I convinced the US Embassy to provide me with a Vespa 150 when I was working in Saigon. I paid for my motorcycles and my travel by being a soldier, a teacher, a diplomat. Until that fateful day when I was 33, bored with what I was doing, and decided to take a trip along the Hippie Highway, from Istanbul to Kathmandu. I quit the job, sold my car, stashed my few possessions in the rafters of my parents' garage, and took off.

Eventually it stretched out to a trip around the world. I had a camera and snapped pictures occasionally, kept notes on where I had stayed, whom I had met, but not being a writer by trade I never thought of doing a book. The only thing I wrote were postcards.

At some point I was faced with an absolute lack of money, no job prospects, and a huge gap in my résumé. Maybe I could write *The Next Great American Novel,* sell the movie rights, and retire in wealth and splendor to a life of riding motorcycles. I decided to become a writer of fiction, with the GI Bill paying for a Master of Fine Arts program. Following which I was doing the aspiring-writer thing, driving a cab and papering my walls with rejection slips. Nobody seemed to want my short stories, and my first (and probably last) novel was best left unpublished.

I was also doing articles about riding in odd spots around the world. I wrote a story about motorcycling to Afghanistan, which was a pleasant place in 1973, and received a check for $100. Wow! These stories were easy to write; with a map, my few notes and photos, I could tap out a couple of thousand words on Australia, or Zimbabwe, or Guatemala, as though I were behind the handlebars of a motorcycle, reviewing my trip.

I still persisted with the fiction of writing fiction, until a motorcycle magazine editor called me up one April day in 1980 and asked if I would like to be paid to ride motorcycles. "We don't pay much, but you'll have all the motorcycles you want to ride."

"Let me think about this," I replied. Two seconds went by. "Okay, give me a week to clear up my affairs here in Boston, and a week to ride out to California. Be there two weeks from next Monday." Done deal!

And that is how easy it was. The writing got easier as I progressed from my beat-up manual typewriter, an Olivetti 22, to an IBM Selectric, and later to a computer. A great time-saver, is word-processing, as I am a three-draft kind of writer, and not having to roll fresh paper into the carriage for each successive draft saves me much grief. The writing, though, is still a sideline; my main line of business is riding, purely riding. It does not matter if the bike has 250 or 2000cc, whether it is hot or cold, wet or dry, jungle or desert, I am happiest when I'm on a motorcycle, going somewhere.

Dirty work, but somebody's got to do it.

The Hell of Travel

February 2006

You're a thousand miles from home, and at least 20 miles from the nearest town, it's raining cats and dogs, it's six o'clock on a Saturday evening, and some errant bit of jagged metal has just ripped an unpluggable hole in your tubeless rear tire. And you can't get a connection with your cell phone. Wouldn't you rather be sitting at your own dining-room table, warm and secure, cutting into a nice piece of grilled salmon? You bet you would.

However, sometimes we forsake the comforts of home for the unknown perils of the open road. Why anybody with the sense that God gave a mouse would do such a bizarre thing is open to an endless debate. Blazing hot deserts, freezing cold mountain passes, strange diseases, disgusting food, bugs in the bed, pettifogging bureaucrats—the whole range of possible unpleasantnesses awaits the traveler.

Why do we travel? Nobody has ever come up with a really good reason to leave a snug house and a refrigerator full of food and venture out into the relative unknown. I'm not talking about emigration, about looking for a better way of life, as many of our ancestors have done, but taking off for a week, a month, a year, just to go "see the world." That was an old U.S. Navy enlistment slogan, tempting the Kansas farm boys to enlist and have adventures in ports of call all over the globe.

I would judge that 98 percent of *Rider* readers go traveling on their motorcycles. The American classic is the sea-to-shining-sea trip, which can take a week on Interstate 80, or a month on the back roads. You can call up your AMA travel service and have them plot your route and book your rooms. Or you can go with the bravery of a credit card, and hope for the best . . . trusting you do not arrive in Walsenburg, Colorado, during the annual rodeo, when every motel within 50 miles is booked solid. Which is why when I am traveling solo, I usually have a sleeping bag bungied on somewhere; I have needed it.

I like to travel in an unrestricted way, because I never really know where I'll end up of an evening. Last fall I was taking some back roads along California's Sierra Nevada range, going south from Yosemite to Lake Isabella, and I figured I'd be at Kernville, on the lake, by nightfall. But side-trips consumed extra time, and come dusk I was up on the Western Divide Highway in the Giant Sequoia National Monument, 50 twisty miles away from my destination. Fortunately, the Ponderosa Lodge, sitting at 7200 feet, had a room left, because a long, deer-dodging ride in the dark does not make me cheerful.

Travel can be of long duration, or reasonably short. I'm not talking about the 500-mile weekend, with a night at a favorite watering hole in the middle, but going off to places you have never been before. Like how many St. Louis motorcyclists have yet to travel through the Arkansas Ozarks, riding all those delicious little back roads? Or Manhattanites taking a week to meander their way up the Connecticut River to the Canadian border on the blue highways?

Ever read *Blue Highways,* by William Least Heat Moon? Great travel book, by a fellow who spent a year or more traveling the little-traveled roads in America in an old van. *Blue Highways* was to the 1980s what John Steinbeck's *Travels with Charlie* was to the 1960s, when Steinbeck and his dog Charlie roamed about this country in a pickup with a camper on the back. Nobody yet has written an equivalently successful book while riding a motorcycle, but that will come, I am sure.

Inter-continental traveling has its own rewards, and suffering. Back in the early 1930s a Connecticut Yankee named Robert Edison Fulton picked up a Douglas motorcycle in England and headed east through the Balkans, Turkey, Iran, et cetera, finally ending up in Japan, then California, and riding back home. A great book came out of the trip, *One Man Caravan,* telling of the good, and bad, times. I spent a couple of years riding a BMW around the world in the mid-1970s, just because the world was there. I crossed the aptly named Desert of Death in Afghanistan, and wandered through the ancient ruins of Zimbabwe under a full moon, both activities rather more difficult to accomplish today. Maybe my traveling gene was influenced by a great, great, grand-dad, one Bartolomeo Galletti, who took a steam-powered trip, by ship and train, around the world in the 1870s. He wrote a book called, uninspiredly, *Il Giro del Mondo* (The Trip Around the World); he was rather mystified by the Mormons he met in Utah, but did admire their work ethic.

In this day and age travel is a great deal simpler, except for the vagaries of politics and plenitude of land-mines. If you don't want to do it yourself, you can pay good money and have a motorcycle tour company pick you up at the Istanbul airport, provide you with a bike and a guide, plus a chase to carry your bags, and go have a splendid time in Turkey. Though you might have to get up at too early an hour and rush breakfast in order to meet the day's schedule.

Travel is not for everybody. Which is good, because I do want enough people to stay at home and keep the gasoline pumps working, the restaurants staffed. Myself, I love to travel, because I simply want to see what is around the curve, over the mountain, beyond the horizon . . . it's my curiosity gene.

As the old saying goes about curiosity killing the cat, I firmly believe that satisfaction brought it back.

Travel by motorcycle is tough. A motorcyclist is open to the elements, and everything has to be packed just so. The automobilist merely takes his overnight bag, slams the car door shut, and checks into the motel; with us it is a more complicated procedure. So why do we do it, put up with this discomfort and inconvenience? I don't know. Is it to smell the fresh-mown hay alongside a country byway? To have small boys look at you with envy? To ride a little-used road and have unimaginably beautiful vistas open up in front of you?

Back to matters at hand. You're standing by the flat-tired bike when the rain stops, and a pickup towing an empty low-boy trailer pulls over. You explain the situation. No problem, says the driver, who even has some tie-downs stashed behind the seat. A stout board serves as a ramp, and soon you are off. "My cousin Jim has a motorcycle shop," your host says, "and he probably has a tire that'll fit. This'll give him a good excuse not to go to church tomorrow. There's a motel just a hundred yards up from the shop, and a nice restaurant next door. You'll be fine, and back on the road before noon."

A brilliant rainbow fills the sky in the evening light. You're really glad you're not at home watching the news.

Foreign Travel

April 2006

What's foreign? Timbuktu? Kathmandu? Saskatoon? Heck, when I went up to northwest Minnesota to meet my fiancee's family that was plenty foreign to me, with strange accents and food I had never eaten, like czarnina (blood soup) and lutefisk (cod preserved in salt and lye). But I'm thinking even more foreign than that, perhaps Greece, or Bolivia. It is the season to go traveling, and while most of us will be happy touring around these United States, a good many are going to cross international borders.

Looking at the United Nations roster, there are 191 countries accredited to that institution. And a couple which aren't, like Taiwan and the Vatican City. Big ones, like Russia, with 3.5 million square miles, little ones, like the Republic of San Marino, with a manageable 24 square miles. We'll leave all that politicking and squabbling to others, but the point is that there are a lot of nice places in the world to go ride motorcycles.

I'm all in favor of international travel, and I've been in more than half of those countries, mostly on a motorcycle. The more places I've been, the more people I've talked with, the more I understand how the world works, and what a complicated place it is. Especially when it involves going from one sovereign nation to another.

Which means having a passport. Less than ten percent of Americans have a passport, but with the current unrest in the world that little document is becoming increasingly necessary. It used to be that a driver's license or a birth certificate was all you needed to go visit Canada or Mexico, but that is changing. Which means that even to ride to Alaska is going to require having a passport. If you want to go visit the birthplace of your Irish great-grandmother, nee Brannigan, in County Cork, better have that identifying document in your pocket.

Easy to get, though; your local post office can give you the paperwork to fill out, or download from the computer at www.travel.state.gov. Fill in the forms, get a certified copy of your birth certificate, have a photo taken, write a check for $97, and stop by your local "designated passport application facility" to let them see that you and the photo do match up. There are about 7000 of these "facilities" in the country, and in my town the most convenient is the post office. If you actually were born in Middletown U.S.A. on 10/30/60, and have not been convicted of a heinous crime, you will get this little blue book, roughly 3.5 x 5 inches with PASSPORT writ large on the cover, along with the seal of the United States of America, back in the mail.

Many of us who want to go ride the New Zealand Alps or the European Alps will probably sign up for an "organized motorcycle tour" with Beach or Bosenberg, and all we will need is the passport in one hand, helmet in the other. This is a very nice way to go traveling, with the OMT staff taking care of all the logistics. Sometimes the client has to do a little personal work, like get a visa. Edelweiss was doing a tour in Brazil a couple of years back and notified the American clients that they needed to get a visa for that country. A few strokes of the computer's keys and I had Brazil's visa form and instructions in front of me. A hundred bucks! I called my nearest Brazilian consulate and made noises about the visa's costing too much. I was told that $100 is the price the US charges Brazilians for a visa, and Brazil was just evening the reckoning field.

Speaking of consulates, many people do not understand the difference between a consulate and an embassy. An embassy represents the

United States in its relationship with a country, say Italy, and deals with political and economic concerns involving the two. A consulate, on the other hand, deals with individuals, and issues visas. In Italy we have an embassy and a consulate in Rome, the capital, and five other consulates in cities around the country. It is the consular officers who concern themselves with the citizens, whether it is an Italian seeking a visa to go visit the U.S., or an American who finds himself in trouble in Italy. If you do something stupid and end up in a Naples jail, a consular type will come visit and suggest a few lawyers who might help; it is not the consul's job to get you out of jail, as that is up to you. If you run out of money, the consul will not front you a grand to get home; that is your responsibility.

I was a U.S. consul in Naples at one time in my life, and got to know a mechanic who was good at fixing motorcycles—like my BMW. One evening he invited me to his local bar, where we discussed the problems that good, honest, hard-working Italians had in securing tourist visas to the U.S. One of the fellows at the table reached into his pocket and pulled out five passports—all fake, all good fakes, any one available for a couple of hundred dollars. Thirty years along, passports, especially American passports, have become more sophisticated, with swipe-card codes built in.

If you have the opportunity and inclination, foreign travel on a motorcycle is great fun—and while traveling with friends is always good, traveling alone has its own considerable rewards. Pull up in front of the Kasbah Kafe in Morocco with half a dozen other riders, and you chat amongst yourselves. Pull up by yourself, and the locals will come to you, asking sensible questions like, "Aren't you lonely?" or "How do you afford to do this?" Responses: "No, I'm not lonely; I'm talking with you, aren't I?" or "I have very little money, which is why I'm on this miserable motorcycle rather than in an air-conditioned car."

Let's say you have this overwhelming desire to ride to Panama; you have your passport in order, with all necessary visas stamped in, proof of ownership for the motorcycle, a "How To Speak Spanish" handbook, and you are off. Having the right paperwork is one thing, dealing with the customs officials is quite another. Presume that all these low-level government employees are underpaid, and they see an American on a large motorcycle on vacation. This is when the "bite" can come in, a little shakedown. However, if you slip the guy ten bucks, the next motorcyclist will probably be held up for twenty. I have crossed probably a thousand borders in my travels, and never paid a bribe; being polite helps, and if that fails, I can be pleasantly obnoxious. Years ago I was going from Tunisia to Algeria and a customs clerk, angling for a little baksheesh, said he could not clear me until his superior came back, and that would be three or four days. After pitching my tent right in front of the office, I got my passport stamped and was on my way.

If your paperwork is not in order, then you might have a problem best resolved by contributing to the local home for unwed mothers. Or you could sign up with one of MotoDiscovery's Rio Grande to Panama tours, and let them worry about things. But either way, you are going to need that passport.

Expand your horizons, expand your mind; anyone with a bit of time and money can throw a leg over a bike and go see most any place he wants to. It might be a fellow from Manhattan headed off by himself to Mexico's Yucatan, or a woman signing up with Ayres Adventures for a tour of South Africa. New places and new people mean new ideas, and that is what traveling is all about.

Managing Risk

June 2006

It is not easy to acquire the skills that make one a very safe motorcyclist. The basics of learning to ride are relatively simple. If the motorcyclist-aspirant can ride a bicycle and drive a stick-shift car, he or she should be well on the way to a long and happy and safe career as a motorcyclist. And the more miles he rides, the better rider he should be. That is the "experience factor," where we learn to deal with unexpected sand in the corner, the leg-biting dog rushing out from behind a bush on a wet day, the on-coming left-turning Buick. Experience is essential to safety.

However, bringing that experience to the fore is the problem. How many of us have been looky-looing at the scene of an accident and nearly created a second accident? Or become overly focused on a traffic problem ahead, failing to appreciate that the real problem is the oblivious soccer dad in the mini-van, with cell phone and coffee cup, coming up from behind? Somehow we have to balance our awarenesses.

But we all suffer lapses. After many years of riding, and more miles than I care to add up, I still fall prey to stupid moments. The other day I went to an urban trailer park to drop a book off at a friend's place. We had a cup of coffee, a chat, and then I got on the Harley to leave. The trailers were all pretty much cheek by jowl, the park was on reasonably flat ground, and what wasn't covered by trailers was asphalted. I clicked into gear and puttered off, thinking distractedly about several other errands that needed to be done, and as I went around a 90-degree corner the bike went into a shallow concrete drainage ditch that crossed the asphalt. I was not expecting this, and as the bike's front wheel went down and up I inadvertently twisted the throttle, and that torquey monster had me accelerating toward a trailer 20 feet away. This was all a surprise, all due to inattention on my part, and I might have frozen for a moment to wonder just what was happening. Fortunately I had the meager wits about me to whack the throttle closed and get matters under control.

No big deal, you say. From my point of view it could have been a big deal had I hit the curb, smacked into the trailer, and broken a leg. It was one of those little events, almost inconsequential, which gave me a small shiver down my spine. The point I am trying to make here is that I was not paying attention, because I was going slow, and there was no traffic, but had I been focused on what I was doing I would have noted that ditch and been prepared. It did not matter how much I knew, it mattered that I was inattentive. I wondered how a neophyte rider might have done, or perhaps an elderly gent on a Gold Wing who might have delayed reflexes.

Motorcycling, as we know, can be a risky business. When the driver has four wheels beneath him and four airbags around him, a foolish move can result in no injuries and a bonanza for the insurance company. Try the same move on two wheels, and the end result can be vastly different.

Like going down a country road and seeing a flock of geese, or a single egret, take off from a pond into the sky. I turn my head to watch, and maybe watch a little too long, the bike drifting a little too close to the edge of the pavement. It is unnerving how quickly things can go awry.

While traveling on a heavyweight bike a while back I was making a very tight, full-lock U-turn in order to set the bike up for a photo, and, being unused to the gearbox, just as I was about to power on and straighten up the bike, I found myself in neutral. The bike began to tilt alarmingly, and we all know how that generally goes: Crash! Fortunately I am a big bloke and could slam my foot down on the ground and manage to get the bike upright. But I should have made sure I was in gear before beginning the turn.

I just finished reading a book by a woman (*Riding in the Shadows of Saints*, by Jana Richman) who was riding alone from Nauvoo, Illinois, to Salt Lake City. As a crow flies this is some 1200 miles, and she was also making many little side-trips as she followed the old Mormon Trail. She was on a BMW R100RT, which is a pretty big bike for an average-sized woman, even when experienced, with all the problems that come with a lightweight person handling a weighty machine. She talks freely about her fears concerning riding, like not wanting to make U-turns, concerned about the drop between the pavement and the shoulder on a country road, and worried about parking when there is a slope. And what to do if she has to pick the damned thing up. Let alone looking in the rearview mirror on a rainy day and finding some idiot trucker with his grill three feet off her license plate. Legitimate worries, real-life risks. And she managed them well. When racing a motorcycle one has to be 100 percent on, which does not really provide the opportunity to enjoy the scenery. A non-competetive alternative is a ride around town, not quite as demanding as a race track, but it is best to be on the *qui vive,* since you are dealing with stop signs and traffic lights, erratic motorists and delivery trucks, potholes and jay-walkers. Statisticians say that most accidents occur within 20 miles of home, which is natural since we spend most of our time around where we live.

However, it is when we are on the byways of this continent that we learn to achieve the best balance between road wariness and scenic admiration. The sensible thing to do when riding over Wyoming's Beartooth Pass is to stop, or at least slow way down. But if there is traffic on the road, you need to pull off. And if the local road crew has just put down the 18th layer of asphalt and it is a good quarter of a foot down to the dirt shoulder, that can be trepidatious. I've bounced down into dirt pull-outs so I could stop for a look-see, and wondered how I was going to get back on the road, the pavement being so abrupt.

Then there is the parking issue, which is not really risky, just possibly embarrassing. If the street is heading downhill into the curb, turn that bike around and back in. Unless you have reverse gear. When the Gold Wing first came out with reverse gear I was rolling a test bike through

Arizona, and stopped at Prescott's historic Hassayampa Inn for a sarsaparilla. The street I parked on was sideways steep, and I cheerfully nosed the 1500 down to the curb; it would require three men and a boy to push it back out. A bus-load of Europeans were sitting at tables on the terrace, and many were undoubtedly motorcycle savvy, wondering, "How on earth is he going to get that huge machine out of there?"

I had my refreshment, strolled back out, heads turning to see how I was going to perform this miracle, put that big baby in reverse—and loved the reaction.

We lessen our risks, be they to body or ego, by thinking about what we do—and thinking all the time. Unknown curve in the road coming up? Could be a decreasing radius turn. Act accordingly.

Management Rule #1: When in doubt, slow down. Or, if that Kenworth is right on your butt, speed up.

The Kindness of Strangers

September 2006

One dark night in the fall of 1958 I was rolling along Massachusetts Route 2 on my '51 Indian Chief and, Blink!, my headlight disappeared. No, I don't mean the headlight fell off, just the light it emitted vanished. I pulled over and stopped. Engine worked, lights did not. As an 18-year-old college freshman about the only two things I knew about motorcycles were how to patch an inner tube and how to adjust a chain. I had no tools, no flashlight, no nothing, and two-lane Route 2 was not exactly a busy place on a Sunday evening.

A fellow came along in a sedan and asked if I had troubles. Yes, I do, I said, but probably they are not going to get fixed tonight. There's a motel a couple of miles down the road, he said, and offered to lead the way for me. We got to the neon sign, my savior wished me good luck, and off he went. I walked into the motel office, a student with just a couple of bucks in his pocket; these were those halcyon days before plastic money, and gas cost about 25 cents a gallon.

My parents lived in Northampton, about a hundred miles from Boston, where I was going to school. The Indian and I would make the trip about twice a month—not for the parents' sake, but because my girlfriend was there. This day I had gotten a late start for the return trip.

The old boy behind the counter listened to my story, looked at my student I.D. card, put a rotary dial phone up on the counter and told me to call my parents. Papa answered, I explained the situation, handed the phone to the motelier, who, after a moment, said, "A check will do fine, Mr. Salvadori," and gave him the price and the address. I had a bed for the night, and was away at dawn in order to make my first class on that Monday.

Try that today and see how far you get, whether it is at the Motel 6 or the Sheraton. I work hard at keeping my motorcycles in good shape, so they do not break down. And I also have a couple of credit cards in the old wallet to keep the financial wolf away from the motel door and the $3 a gallon pump price. However, in truth I never worry too much about roadside problems. I don't even own a cell phone, so when I came drifting to the side of the road due to foolishness on my part, or some mechanical failure, I figure that the milk of human kindness will come to my aid.

A bit ago I had a fuel-injected test bike, and one afternoon Sue said she wanted to go for a short ride on her bike, did I want to come along. Off we went, and I noted that my mount's low-fuel warning light came on as soon as we left town, and gas stations. Ah, I thought, there is probably at least a gallon in there, good for 40 miles. It turned out to be less than a gallon, with the engine quitting some 30 miles later as we were returning to town. It was ranchland out there, few houses, but I coasted to a stop about a quarter-mile from a driveway. I took Sue's bike and went up to the house, where the owner did indeed have a container full of gas, and he brought it out to the bike in his pickup. Very kind of him.

Back in 1970 I had a Vespa 150 as my official, government-issued transportation; I was working in Saigon, which was a traffic nightmare, and declined a Ford sedan in favor of the scooter. One Sunday I decided to go visit a friend who worked in a provincial capital some 20 miles north. The girlfriend, an American who worked for *The Washington Post,* and I took a leisurely ride out to Phu Cuong, had lunch, a look around town, and headed back mid-afternoon. It was a minorly important road, with occasional scatterings of small houses here and there, benign during the day, but I would not exactly care to be out at night. We came into a little hamlet, with a buffalo-cart going across the road, and I had to shift down to first; the clutch cable broke. Trying to operate that handlebar gear-change without a clutch was not going to work, but the village was pretty much asleep, all the shop-fronts closed. My passenger was not impressed by the situation.

Children soon came and formed the inevitable circle around us, and then an elder, with a wispy white beard appeared. With my extremely minimal Vietnamese I made the appropriate salutations, and then found that we both spoke French. After listening to my plaint he sent one of the kids off, telling me to push the scooter a hundred yards along, in front of a shuttered store where several cannibalized scooters sat rusticating in the weeds. Five minutes later the shop owner appeared, opened up, took out his soldering equipment, and fixed the problem. My elderly friend wished us well and allowed that it was just as well we were leaving before darkness fell.

I find that people all around the world are essentially the same, friendly and helpful. It's the bad-asses who get the headlines, but they are in the great minority. As the old newspaper joke goes, a hundred cats climb up a hundred trees, and 99 climb down; they're not the news.

In 1966 I was running along Texas Route 59 on a new Triumph TR6, headed to Mexico, when I heard a big bang and the engine stopped. I pulled over, and even my innocent eye could understand the problem, as a broken connecting rod was sticking out the hole it had punched in the crankcase. Again, this was a Sunday afternoon and there was little traffic, and I was a few miles north of Victoria. A family-filled car stopped, the driver had some rope in the trunk, and he towed me into town. We left the bike in front of the closed dealership (only a real fool would want to steal it), and then he took me to a nearby storage yard where he kept a travel-trailer that I was welcome to use. Good Texas hospitality.

Or Iran in 1973. I was traveling two-up on a BMW R75/5, and on a lonely mountain curve the rear-end went all squirrelly. I kept the shiny side up, got over to the side of the road, and had an inspection. The differential had obviously overheated and was ruined, the rear wheel moving sideways along the axle a couple of inches, with the inner race of a bearing actually welded to the axle; I couldn't even get the wheel off. This bike was not going anywhere, until a stake truck appeared and stopped. No common language existed between me and the driver, but he understood the problem. Fortunately the bike rolled, in a wobbly fashion, and he had a plank, so we managed to get the bike up on the bed;

he turned the truck around and drove us to a railroad station. Eventually a train bound for Tehran came along, and the bike was pushed on. All was well five days later.

Many of us limit our travels because we do worry about things going wrong; we shouldn't, especially in the U.S. In this day and age we have cell phones and towing plans that pretty much cover every possibility, but even when those might not work, we can pretty much rely on the kindness and good will of passers-by to help us out.

Great Day in the Morning

January 2007

Some days are better than others, some rides are better than others. If the right mood, the right weather, the right traffic (lack of) all converge at the same time, a good ride can become a great ride.

Last summer I awoke one Saturday morning shortly before 6 o'clock . . . not unusual as I am pretty much of a dawn riser. The magazine, sponsoring a little editorial outing, had rented a bungalow in Carmel Valley, California, and the bedrooms were full of snoring souls, while I had enjoyed the sofa-bed out in the living room. Though the work commitments were done, I intended to schmooze with the boys for a while, but as I put the coffee pot on a little voice whispered in my ear, "Forget all that stuff; let's ride!"

By 6:15 the bike was packed and we were coasting out of the parking area so as not to wake the sleepers. Heading up the valley towards Carmel, I was crossing over the Carmel River on Highway 1 less than 15 minutes later, past the Carmelite monastery hidden in the woods to my left, up Huckleberry Hill, and the highway sign at the top indicating that the next 74 miles will be very twisty and turny indeed.

Most of us have "favorite" roads, a stretch of byway ten miles, a hundred miles, long which we may have ridden ten times, a hundred times, but always look forward to riding again. One of mine happens to be the Big Sur Highway, the hundred miles between Carmel in the north, Cambria in the south.

I first rode this strip of pavement in 1967, when I took advantage of the GI Bill and went to graduate school in Monterey, just over the hill, literally, from Carmel. I had a Triumph TR6R and every couple of weeks I would head down south along the coast. Depending on time, money, inclination I might go to Nepenthe, a rustic hangout hanging out over the ocean. Or make a loop via the Nacimiento-Fergusson Road, Fort Hunter Liggett, and the Carmel Valley Road. Occasionally I went all the way to Ragged Point, which was just a wide-spot in the road back then—now it has an expensive motel, good restaurant, along with the wide-spot snack bar and pricey gasoline.

In truth, not much has changed in 40 years, thanks to the Monterey county having passing a bill in 1961 to preserve the Big Sur. Although the prices have gone up.

In the summer the Big Sur coast is often socked in by a chilly sea fog, but this early morning is miraculously clear. Crossing over Malpaso Creek I am now officially in Big Sur . . . or *El Sur Grande* as the Spanish called it 200 years ago from their headquarters in Monterey. The road here is straightish, dipping, weaving, a bridge every couple of miles, most built back in the 1930s when constructing the Big Sur highway was a WPA project.

We cross over Bixby Creek on the 1932 bridge made briefly famous by a sixties TV character named Bronson, showing America what freedom really was from the seat of a Sportster. Now the ride, the road, gets really fun, with a great swoop curving along the flank of Sierra Hill, running up to Hurricane Point, and, yes, on a stormy day this is not the place to be. Then the road flows down into a long, half-mile 180-degree arc, curving over Little Sur River.

A rise, a hilltop, down past the coastal meadows and the Point Sur lighthouse, into the tall trees along the Big Sur River. This is the tourist-based community of Big Sur, and in these past 25 miles I have passed all of two cars, sleepy drivers commuting to work at a hotel or restaurant. I throttle back in the shadowed woods, past Big Sur state park, in case of any early risers; it is not yet seven o'clock.

Up the long hill and then drop down into an leisurely S-curve, Nepenthe on the right; not open at this early hour. Dozens of streams coming off the Santa Lucia Range have created dozens of little canyons, and the highway loops in and out, following the rugged contours. I swoop down past Partington Point, then past another state park, and the road again straightens a little, running through a wooded stretch. About 90 percent of Big Sur is owned by us, the people, but a few hundred small holdings are left, one being the Esalen resort that flashes by, a New Age nirvana when I first went there in 1967 to hear Joan Baez sing, now priced out of my range.

I'm into a rhythm, snicking up and down through the gears, keeping the revs in a torquey range, rarely using the brakes since I know the road well enough to anticipate the curves. Some day I will count the corners in the Big Sur, but not today. A sharpish bend leads into Lucia, where the $30 motel of my youth is now $200, and the gas pumps got pulled by EPA mandate a few years back. However, the same two-lane road curves around the same bluffs, tucks into the same ravines to cross over the same little creeks, and the same bits need to be reconstructed every couple of years. I slow after passing the little Lucia store, knowing there is perennial repaving on the road shortly ahead, a stretch of dusty dirt. The whole trick to a "favorite" road is that it is one the rider is familiar with, one with no unpleasant surprises.

Over the bridge above Limekiln State Park, past the campground at Kirk Creek, then the Nacimiento-Fergusson Road, then some leisurely turns, and the slight descent into Pacific Valley. Here is an open stretch along the coast, and I can run the engine up to redline in third and fourth . . . blowing out that carbon as the old boys used to say. Exhilarating! The road is still shaded by the Santa Lucia mountains, but the sunlight is glinting off the dark blue water.

The pavement glides into some woods that shield the campers at Plaskett Creek, then back out on the coast, zip by the food/bed/gas establishment at Gorda, and the road soon acquires a new vision. Here in these next few miles the highway builders were forced to do a surfside road, as the mountains rose from the ocean so steeply that no road could be built higher up. Constant repairs are made along this stretch, being subject to storm damages, but I know where the pavement gets bumpy.

Leave the rocky beach, a few dozen more curves, and into Salmon Creek Canyon, a delightful rush inland for a couple of hundred yards to a low creek crossing, a waterfall in the background, then up to the posted 20-mph corner, a reminder that Big Sur highway signage should be taken seriously. We go from Monterey county to San Luis Obispo, and a long twisty run down to Ragged Point. Even there, nobody is stirring.

The road wiggles from the mountainside down to San Carpoforo Creek, and we leave the mountains behind, coastal plains ahead, the road built for speed. The Piedras Blancas lighthouse goes by, and soon Hearst's fancy castle can be seen to my left. It is not yet eight o'clock, the world is just waking.

Cambria is stirring, the coffee properly hot at the Redwood Café. Great ride!

Full Moon Rising

February 2007

The other evening I turned this machine in front of which I am sitting to START—which happens to mean OFF in computerese—and went down the stairs to feed the cats and myself. Sue was away in Minnesota visiting her Dad, which meant that I was in charge of such things. The five felines were easy, with a can of whitefish and tuna creating minor gastronomical excitement.

I walked into the kitchen to pour myself a glass of wine and contemplate my gustatorial options—and looking through the open door directly east saw a full moon rising, a harvest moon. Absolutely stunning! I went to sit on the back steps and admire this vision. Our house is on the west slope of a small river valley and looks across to the low hills on the far side, some five miles away, and the moon was this perfect orb seemingly balanced on this ridge. Took me back to 1969 when Neil Armstrong stepped on the surface; I watched that whole thing from lift-off to splash-down because I was stuck in bed recuperating from a bad case of hepatitis, A type, which I had contracted in South America. A pretty exciting time . . . the moon landing, that is, not the hepatitis.

I have no great desire to go to the moon—I admire those astronauts but I do not do well enclosed in small spaces, which is a requirement of getting there. I'll stick to terra firma, thank you very much, and enjoy my wanderings on this planet.

By this time the moon had separated itself from the earth and was floating in the evening sky. Beyond that ridge over which the lunar vision was rising is Black Mountain, and beyond that the Temblor Range, and then the Sierra Nevada mountains, and Nevada and Utah and Colorado and the Rocky Mountains. There is one helluva lot beyond the horizon, which is something we should never forget. I've seen a lot of it, and would like to see more, but will never see it all. I could spend years just exploring Nevada, with thousands of miles of old dirt roads, ghost towns, the lot. You don't have to go to Timbuktu to have an adventure, you can go to Ruby Valley and have an equally fine time. A lot less expensive, too.

A friend recently e-mailed me some pictures of an absolutely lovely (my word) road in Bolivia, built into the side of a vertical mountain, straight up on one side, straight down on the other—and I would really like to ride that stretch of dirt. On a nice day, of course, as dirt roads on rainy days can be more than exhilarating—especially when there is a 2000 foot drop and no guard rail. The Yungas Road, or the "Most Dangerous Road" as some non-Bolivians like to call it, runs from the capital of La Paz northeast to the town of Corioco, and has been handling truck traffic since 1935—with a largish number of fatal accidents. Not from collisions, mind you, but just falling over the edge.

Maybe I'm a bit on the strange side, but the thought of riding that road is purely pleasurable. A bit of a risk, a heck of a view.

Sitting there on the porch I thought of all the places that moon's light (yeah, yeah, it's reflected, I know) has shone upon, over the entire planet, and about how many I've seen, how many more I will see . . . and how many I won't. Motorcycles have taken me to see the moon over ancient Zimbabwe, over the ruins in New Mexico's Chaco Canyon. For me, going someplace most always involves motorcycles; I don't want to sit in a bus or a rented car, I want to ride.

I probably will never get to Siberia, because I have no great desire to battle mosquitoes the size of small birds. Nor China proper, as there are just too darned many people. I have long thought of riding up alongside the Nile River through Egypt and the Sudan, although politics may well keep me away from that. But I might well get to Tasmania, which I understand is delightful.

I won't get to see all the places I would like to. Too many places, too little time. I have just read a book called *The Last Hurrah,* by a sixtyish New Zealander who decides that he needs to have one more adventure, and convinces an even older friend, and one of his own sons, to ride a pair of aged motorcycles from Peking to Holland, over the Karakoram Highway. I imagine that most of us have never heard of the Karakoram, a road which follows one of the old Silk Routes and goes over the 15,400-foot Khunjerab Pass between Pakistan and China. The vehicular road, as opposed to the old horse-path, was finished in 1986, with much hoopla—and it is just one of those roads I have wanted to ride.

On the other hand, less than three hours from here is a dirt road running into the Sequoia National Forest, going up more than 5000 feet from the Kern River to Greenhorn Summit. I've been thinking of riding Rancheria Road for more than 20 years, but somehow don't get around to it. And here I am wanting to go to the Karakoram, ten thousand miles away. I can handle both notions.

The first book which really made an impression on me, other than *The Little Engine That Could,* was called the *Complete Book of Marvels,* about many of the wondrous places in the world, both natural and man-made. The inscription on the flyleaf shows my father gave it to me when I was nine years old. The author, Richard Halliburton, traveled in the 1930s to places like the Grand Canyon and Mt. Everest, the Golden Gate Bridge in California and Angkor Wat in Cambodia. Great places to see, especially from the saddle of a motorcycle, though I admit my trip to Angkor in 1966 was on a bicycle, pedaling from the nearby town of Siem Reap.

Mind you, I'm very happy here at home. Sue does not object to my itch to travel, though she has stipulated that if I'm gone more than three months she will come and find me. My serious traveling, my three-year 'round the world odyssey, took place before I met her, but I do much shorter trips every year. And some armchair traveling as well; nothing wrong with dreaming.

After I hit the $80 million lottery I'll jet (First Class) off to any destination I want at any time, and my arrangers will have a motorcycle waiting for me at the airport, all documentation prepared. Until then there will have to be a bit of planning and accounting.

By now several of the cats have wolfed(?!) down their dinners and have come to sit beside me, licking their paws to indicate contentment. My wine-glass is empty. Maybe I should focus better. All right, I'll do Rancheria Road. But if I had my druthers, would it be the Karakoram or that road in Bolivia? The moon will shine on both. I'm going to make supper.

About the Author

Clement Salvadori got hooked on motorcycles as a teenager and has been addicted ever since. He graduated from Harvard with a B.A. in government and served in the U.S. Army's Special Forces as a demolitions expert (a skill he still occasionally applies to motorcycles). Using the G.I. Bill he acquired a master's degree in foreign relations and became a Foreign Service officer with the U.S. Department of State.

Following several overseas assignments, Salvadori realized he enjoyed traveling more as a motorcyclist than as a diplomat, so he quit his job and proceeded to squander what savings he had on a three-year trip around the world on his BMW R 75/5. When a motorcycle publication actually paid him money for a story he had written about riding to Afganistan, he saw a whole new career opening up.

Since then he has written hundreds of articles for motorcycle magazines and is the author of *Motorcycle Journeys through California and Baja*, now in its second edition, and *Honda VF and VFR Interceptor* in the Whitehorse Press Motorcycle Collector Series.

He lives in southern California with his wife and several cats, and is willing to put up with droughts, floods, fires, and earthquakes in order to ride every day.